W9-CEY-577

Schools of the 21st Century

RENEWING AMERICAN SCHOOLS:
THE EDUCATIONAL KNOWLEDGE BASE

*Series Editors:* Henry M. Levin, *Stanford University*, and
Jeannie Oakes, *University of California–Los Angeles*

# Schools of the 21st Century

## Linking Child Care and Education

**Matia Finn-Stevenson**

Yale University

**Edward Zigler**

Yale University

Westview Press

A Member of the Perseus Books Group

*Renewing American Schools*

All rights reserved. Printed in the United States of America. No part of this publication may be reproduced or transmitted in any form or by any means, electronic or mechanical, including photocopy, recording, or any information storage and retrieval system, without permission in writing from the publisher.

Copyright © 1999 by Westview Press, A Member of the Perseus Books Group

Published in 1999 in the United States of America by Westview Press, 5500 Central Avenue, Boulder, Colorado 80301-2877, and in the United Kingdom by Westview Press, 12 Hid's Copse Road, Cumnor Hill, Oxford OX2 9JJ

Find us on the World Wide Web at www.westviewpress.com

Library of Congress Cataloging-in-Publication Data
Finn-Stevenson, Matia.
  Schools of the 21st century: linking child care and education /
by Matia Finn-Stevenson and Edward Zigler.
    p.  cm.—(Renewing American schools)
  Includes bibliographical references and index.
  ISBN 0-8133-2246-4 (hc).—ISBN 0-8133-2247-2 (pbk.)
  1. School-based child care—United States.  I. Zigler, Edward,
1930–  .  II. Title.  III. Title: Schools of the twenty-first
century.  IV. Series.
LB3436.F56  1999
371.7—dc21                                                           99-23216
                                                                         CIP

The paper used in this publication meets the requirements of the American National Standard for Permanence of Paper for Printed Library Materials Z39.48-1984.

10    9    8    7    6    5    4    3    2    1

# Contents

# Illustrations

# Preface

This book is about efforts to link child care and education, as exemplified by the Schools of the 21st Century (21C) program. 21C, conceptualized in 1987, was first implemented in Independence, Missouri, and Leadville, Colorado, in 1988 and has since expanded to 600 elementary schools in seventeen states. The program includes several components, the core of which is all-day, year-round child care for children ages 3, 4, and 5, and before- and after-school and vacation care for school-age children. The program is implemented on the basis of the needs of the community and the resources available and, as such, differs from community to community. However, all 21C schools adhere to the program's guiding principles and all share a common goal: the optimal development of children.

We have worked hand in hand with the educators who pioneered the implementation of the School of the 21st Century, sharing with them our knowledge and learning from them about the possibilities and challenges inherent in efforts to provide child care and family support services. In many of the school districts, the program has grown from implementation in one or two of the elementary schools to all schools in the district. The 21C pioneer educators not only have implemented the program in their district but also have joined the 21C National Faculty, helping other educators implement the program. They have established exemplary programs that have been nominated as 21C National Demonstration Sites, as listed on the following pages. Their commitment, vision, and hard work laid the foundation for the program, and both their continued affiliation with the National Faculty and their leadership will take the program to its next phase of growth. We are grateful to educators at the National Demonstration Sites, to the staff they represent, and to the children and families they serve.

# National Demonstration Sites, 1999–2001

## *Arkansas*

**The School of the 21st Century**
427 East Poplar Street
Paragould, AR 72450
Vicki Shelby, Director

## *Colorado*

**The Center**
315 West 6th
Leadville, CO 80461
Kathleen Carothers, Principal

## *Connecticut*

**The Rogers Magnet School**
83 Lockwood Avenue
Stamford, CT 06920
Mary Jennings, Principal

**Six to Six Interdistrict Magnet School**
601 Pearl Harbor Street
Bridgeport, CT 06610
Anne Hamilton, Director

## *Kansas*

**Phinney Elementary School**
12th and Fry
Larned, KS 67550
Tom Renshaw, Coordinator

## *Kentucky*

**Boyd County East Family Resource Center**
3348 Court Street
Catlettsburg, KY 41129
Norma Meek, FRC Coordinator

**Somerset Family Resource Youth Services Center**
305 College Street
Somerset, KY 42501
Julie Goodan, FRYSC Director

*Massachusetts*

**Harwich Elementary School**
Oak Street
Harwich, MA 02645
Stephanie Henderson, Coordinator

**Page/Hilltop School**
117 Washington Street
Ayer, MA 01432
Lori Harries, Coordinator

*Missouri*

**Independence Public Schools**
1231 South Windsor
Independence, MO 64055
Patricia Schumacher, Assistant Superintendent and 21C Director

*Matia Finn-Stevenson*
*Edward Zigler*

# Acknowledgments

Our work on the School of the 21st Century was supported by Kraft Foods, the Carnegie Corporation of New York, and the Ford Foundation. We thank these foundations for their encouragement and support since the inception of the program. In particular, we would like to acknowledge several individuals for their faith and commitment: Michael Mudd, Senior Vice President, Kraft Foods; Maxine Farrell, formerly Director of Contributions, Kraft Foods; Michael Levine, Deputy Chair and Senior Program Officer, Education Division, Carnegie Corporation of New York; and Shelby Miller, formerly Program Officer, Ford Foundation. We also acknowledge the support of Ruby Takanishi, President, Foundation for Child Development; and Luba Lynch, Executive Director and Vickie Frelow, Program Officer of the A. L. Mailman Family Foundation.

*M. F.-S. and E. Z.*

# Acronyms

| | |
|---|---|
| 21C | Schools of the 21st Century |
| AFDC | Aid to Families with Dependent Children |
| ASQ | Assessing School-Age Quality |
| CDA | Child Development Associate |
| CDF | Children's Defense Fund |
| CED | Committee for Economic Development |
| CoZi | Comer/Zigler school development model |
| ESEA | Elementary and Secondary Education Act |
| FIT | Families in Training |
| KERA | Kentucky Education Reform Act |
| LEAs | local education agencies |
| NAEYC | National Association for the Education of Young Children |
| NBCDI | National Black Child Development Institute |
| NCCIP | National Center for Clinical Infant Programs |
| NEA | National Education Association |
| NICHD | National Institute of Child Health and Human Development |
| PAT | Parents as Teachers |
| PTA | Parent Teachers Association |
| TANF | Temporary Assistance to Needy Families |
| TDI | Temporary Disability Insurance |
| WIC | Supplemental Food Program for Women, Infants, and Children |

# 1 The Realities of Family Life

$P$AST DECADES HAVE WITNESSED a growing and persistent dissatisfaction with American education. Since the National Commission on Excellence in Education published *A Nation at Risk* in 1983, numerous education-reform initiatives have been implemented. Despite this concern and the changes in some of the nation's schools, improvements in student achievement have not been realized, and there continues to be widespread frustration with the American system of education (Berlau 1998; National Education Summit 1996; CED 1994). The Committee for Economic Development (1994) has suggested a possible link between education and national productivity, so there are fears that the United States is losing its ability to compete with other nations.

The problems associated with American education are noted in studies that point to high drop-out rates and a significant number of students who graduate from high school lacking the basic skills necessary to perform adequately in the work place. Although low-income and ethnic minority children are at an especially high risk for educational failure, the problem extends to other children as well. The U.S. Department of Education (1990) analyzed educational testing data compiled over the past two decades and surveyed more than 9 million children in the fourth, eighth, and twelfth grades. Its findings indicate that student achievement levels are lower now than they were in the 1970s and 1980s, despite the fact that today's society demands more skilled workers. Several other studies indicate that in the United States the average achievement level of students is low, not only in relation to that of previous generations but also—perhaps even more disturbing to some—in relation to the achievement levels of children in other countries (Berlau 1998; Stevenson 1983; Stevenson et al. 1985).

These findings are cause for concern. Children who fail to acquire basic skills will be unable to negotiate life successfully as adults. Unprepared for the world of work, such children face limited opportunities and are at risk for spending much of their adult lives dependent on public assistance (Brooks-Gunn and Duncan 1997). This cycle of failure begins early. A review of the research suggests that children who fail to master basic skills by fourth grade are more likely than those who do master such skills to develop a host of problems later on, including dropping out of school, abusing substances, and becoming pregnant while still in their teens (William T. Grant Foundation 1988; Carnegie Corporation of New York 1996). Beyond the individual loss associated with a failed educational system, the nation's future in technology, science, and industry is at risk; without an adequately educated workforce, how can the United States maintain a leadership role among advanced technological societies and compete economically with other nations?

These and other concerns over American children's school performance have led to numerous recommendations, such as revamping the curriculum, raising standards, introducing technology in all schools, increasing teacher salaries and accountability, and changing school climate, structure, and governance. In and of themselves, such changes are insufficient. It is our contention that if we are to improve educational outcomes and ensure that all children have an opportunity to succeed academically, we must not only make fundamental changes in the way we teach children but also: (1) broaden our understanding of how children learn and what influences their capacity to learn; (2) provide support services to optimize the growth and development of children and their ability to profit from instruction; and (3) begin to provide such support at the birth of the child. Additionally, whereas calls for the provision of support services have traditionally been made on behalf of children in poverty, we believe that all children and families are in need of support. This focus on the provision of universal, as opposed to categorical, programs is evident in several European countries, where support services are available to all families regardless of their income level and additional support is given to those who are more in need because of poverty or disability.

In this book we describe the School of the 21st Century (21C), a child care and family support program that we developed and helped implement in many schools around the country. Although there are other similar programs that use the school for the provision or coordination of nonacademic support services, 21C is unique in its universal approach and in the provision of support services to all children regardless of their family income. Before describing the School of the 21st Century, we need to discuss the changes in family life that, in effect, resulted in the need for 21C and for other similar programs.

## Changes in Family Life

We call for schools to provide support services because children today are growing up in circumstances that sometimes damage their ability to succeed in school. These circumstances are not necessarily an outcome of the school experience but, rather, are associated with difficulties in family life. American society has undergone vast economic and social changes in the past forty years. These changes include transformations in the structure of the family and in the roles and responsibilities of men and women, all of which contribute to the stress experienced by both adults and children.

## Isolation and Fragmentation of the Family

Numerous studies have underscored the vulnerabilities of families and the difficulties that many parents have raising their children. All families, regardless of their incomes, experience a loss of leisure time, feelings of harassment and hurriedness, and a lack of time to spend with children (Hewlett 1992; Hewlett and West 1998). Coleman (1987) describes these conditions in terms of a decrease in *social capital*, which he defines as the presence of a number of adults in the family to provide support in time of need. This decrease has been brought about in part by the fact that in many families both parents are working (a fact discussed later in the chapter). Also, the past few decades have witnessed the increased isolation and fragmentation of the family. Young families move frequently in search of employment, so they no longer have convenient access to long-time neighbors or close friends, who, for previous generations, provided a support system that mediated against stress (Packard 1983).

The fragmentation and isolation of the family are perhaps most evident in statistics that point to the increase in the number of single-parent families. Currently, one out of every four children in the United States lives in a single-parent household (CDF 1998). Among African Americans, that ratio increases to one out of every two children. It is projected that more than half of all babies born in the latter part of the 1990s will spend some time in a single-parent family (Hernandez 1993).

Although single-parent families differ, they are generally characterized by female heads of household, the presence of children under age 6, and poverty (National Center for Children in Poverty 1996). In many cases, single-parent households are the result of children being born to unmarried mothers. These children and their parents encounter various unique stresses. For example, such families are sometimes headed by a teen parent who may lack not only the financial resources but also the emotional resources to handle parenting. Although effective programs have been developed to help these young parents (Seitz and Apfel 1999; Olds et al. 1998), many of them postpone or forgo their education and become dependent on public assistance. Their children are more likely than children of older parents to suffer health and behavioral problems and to perform poorly in school (Furstenberg, Hughes, and Brooks-Gunn 1992). Some of the children, at a later age, become teen parents themselves (Brooks-Gunn and Chase-Lansdale 1995).

Some single-parent households are the result of divorce. The rate of divorce, especially among families with children, rose dramatically between 1965 and 1979. Since 1979, the rate has declined and seems to have leveled off (Furstenberg 1994). Nevertheless, about 40 percent of children will experience the divorce of their parents (Behrman and Quinn 1994). Needless to say, such a high percentage indicates that divorce is an issue affecting people of all socioeconomic levels. In 75 to 80 percent of the cases, the children will live in a single-parent household for a time and will later experience the remarriage of one or both of their parents, so they will have to live in a blended family and adjust to living with new relatives.

Although divorce does alleviate many of the difficulties associated with living in a dysfunctional family, changes in marital arrangements create new stressful situations for children, especially immediately after the divorce, and only some children are able to cope and eventually adjust to their new family life (Hetherington 1989). Many children sustain developmental disruptions as a result of their parents' divorce. Although these children may seem to be adjusting, they show delayed negative effects several years after the divorce and/or remarriage of one or both of their parents (Maccoby and Mnookin 1992; Wallerstein and Corbin 1996).

The long-term effects of divorce and remarriage appear to be related to a number of factors, including the child's developmental status, sex, temperament, and the quality of the home environment after the marital change. An important factor is the availability of support systems to the parents and the children. Children, in particular, cope with their changed circumstances better if they have access to a friend, relative, or teacher who can "lend an ear" and help sort out their feelings (Hetherington 1989; Wallerstein and Corbin 1996).

The number of stressful situations the child encounters also influences his or her ability to cope with divorce and remarriage. Rutter (1980) points out that when children experience any one risk factor—marital discord, physical abuse, instability in the family environment, or poverty, among other stressful conditions—they are not likely to suffer serious consequences. However, children do suffer consequences when they experience multiple stresses, when, for example, they experience divorce, poverty, and parental neglect all at the same time. And the effects of such risk factors on developmental outcome are not merely additive but multiplicative; Sameroff et al. (1987) note that developmental outcomes are affected by the interplay between the child and the environmental context over time, and that one state impacts on the next in a continuous, dynamic process. In a few families, divorce is relatively stress-free, with both parents making an effort to ensure that the children receive the emotional support and additional nurturance they may need to see them through the crisis in their young lives. But for many families, divorce is associated with several stressful conditions, including prolonged custody fights, life in a single-parent household, and economic uncertainty. Any or all of these stressful conditions can last several years and affect the child at different developmental stages. Over time, these multiple stressors create problems for children and inhibit their ability to cope with and adjust to their new circumstances.

Children whose parents suffer emotional and psychological difficulties as a result of divorce are especially likely to experience multiple stressors in addition to the divorce. In such situations, the parents' distress is sometimes so acute that they fail to attend to the needs of their children and to recognize their children's painful experiences with the divorce (Kurdek and Blisk 1983). Teachers may be among the first to notice the difficulties children have with divorce and remarriage, since such difficulties are often manifest in a decline in school performance, a failure to socialize with other children, an increased absence from school, and unprecedented behavior problems.

## The Plight of the Middle Class

As we indicated earlier, we are concerned about developmental outcomes for all children, regardless of their family income level. Although policy and program attention is usually focused on poor families, middle-class families are experiencing stressful conditions as well. The isolation and fragmentation of the family and the frequency of divorce—as well as issues such as maternal employment and the lack of good quality child care, which we will discuss later—affect all families, including those who are considered middle class. Traditionally, much of the research that has focused on the family has looked at the conditions and experiences of children in poverty, so there is a wealth of information on this population but not as much on other children. It is well worth considering the effects of poverty, but it is also vital to underscore the plight of the middle class.

One of the greatest challenges facing middle-class families is the maintenance of their economic status. Since the 1980s, earnings have declined (Economic Policy Council 1986; Reischauer 1987; Betson and Michael 1997), and this decline has contributed, in part, to the need for both parents in a family to work full time just to make ends meet. Uchitelle (1994) notes further that some families have to rely on three sources of income, and so one of the parents takes on a second job. In addition to the stresses of declining income and the need for both parents to work while also raising children, middle-class families experience other burdens: They have to pay taxes; they incur work-related expenses such as child care; and they are not eligible for subsidies or programs that many poor families receive. Furthermore, middle-class families use a large percentage of their earnings for health-related expenses (Betson and Michael 1997), since many such families do not have health insurance or have to pay excessive amounts of money for such insurance when their employers do not share in the cost. Indeed, economic hardships are of such magnitude among middle-class families that if the poverty level threshold was measured differently—that is, if income was measured after taxes and work-related expenses had been deducted—many more families with children would be considered poor. As Betson and Michael (1997, 32) note, "the official poverty measure does not accurately reflect the relative economic well-being of families."

## Children in Poverty

Even according to the current measure of poverty, many children in the United States are growing up poor. The poverty rate has decreased in recent years, but the decline in the poverty rate has eluded families with children; one out of every five children under age 6 lives in poverty (CDF 1998). Indeed, children under age 6 are more likely to be poor than any other age group, and children ages 6 to 17 are the next group most likely to be poor (Corcoran and Chaundry 1997).

It is also important to note a new trend, which significantly changes conventional assumptions about poverty. Cook and Brown (1994) note not only that the overall child poverty rate has increased during the past twenty years but also that the largest growth in this rate—76 percent—occurred in the suburbs, which were once considered most immune from the poverty crisis. Hernandez (1997) makes a similar point about rural families in America, noting that whereas in 1988 poverty rates in rural areas were the same as those in central cities, by 1991 rural rates were higher. The exact cause of this drastic demographic shift in poverty is unknown. It could stem in part from an economy that has become so unstable and unpredictable that people who once considered themselves comfortable, or at least safely above the poverty line, have unexpectedly slipped below it.

Several factors are associated with the escalation of poverty among children, including the increase in single-parent households, discussed earlier. Other factors include budget cutbacks in social services and the decline in real family income.

The decline in family income and the increase in the number of families with children in poverty affect adults as well as children. However, for children the consequences of being poor are especially serious and include assaults on their physical and mental health. McLoyd and her colleagues (McLoyd 1990; McLoyd et al. 1994) and McLeod and Shanahan (1993) found that the chronically stressful life events experienced by poor families result in the inability of parents to raise their children. Others have found that poor children are exposed to multiple risk factors, which are associated with behavioral and mental health disorders and delinquency (Yoshikawa 1995; Brooks-Gunn and Duncan 1997); Sameroff et al. (1987) found that a child's IQ is a function of the number of risk factors associated with poverty.

**Poor Health.**   In a review of the health conditions of children in the United States, Klerman (1991) notes that children's health is of general concern. In particular, children in poverty experience many more types of health problems, as well as a higher mortality rate, than do children who are not poor (Bridgeman and Phillips 1998). Health conditions disproportionately affecting poor children include HIV infection, asthma, dental problems, measles, lead poisoning, health-related problems associated with child abuse and neglect, and unintentional injuries (CDF 1998). Additionally, low birth weight, which is potentially associated with developmental delays and an inability to do well in school, is more prevalent among poor infants, as are learning disabilities.

Acknowledging that the reasons for the higher rates of health problems among the poor are complex, Klerman (1991) notes that poor families have little time and no money to spend on health-promoting activities and that their lack of adequate housing and transportation further exacerbates the problem. Poor families also face obstacles in obtaining health services. However, Klerman found that, independent of access to health services, several demographic and psychological factors are associated with poor health, including a less-than–high school education, birth outside of marriage, single-parent household, teen parenthood, and stress and depression.

**Hunger.**   A problem related to poor health is the lack of nutritious food or, in many cases, of food of any sort. A report published by the Center on Hunger, Poverty, and Nutrition Policy (1995) at Tufts University states that there are 6 million children in the United States who regularly begin their school day with no food. As noted in Box 1.1, 4 million children under age 12 are hungry for some part of each month. Although school breakfast and lunch, among other food programs—for example, the Summer Food Program and the Supplemental Food Program for Women, Infants, and Children (WIC)—exist to help poor children, such programs are not accessible to all eligible children because school districts are not required to participate in these federally funded programs. It is estimated, for example, that less than half the school districts in the country offer school breakfast (Brown, Gershoff, and Cook 1992).

Research on children and nutrition points to the importance of addressing children's hunger. Meyers and his colleagues (1989) found that children who participate in school breakfast programs have significantly higher achievement-test scores than those who are eligible but do not have access to such programs; children who participate in these programs also have much lower school absence and tardiness rates. Reviews of the research (Brown, Gershoff, and Cook 1992) show a conclusive link between nutrition and cognitive development. Even moderate under-nutrition of a relatively short duration (the type most frequently found among children in the

BOX 1.1   Key Facts About U.S. Children*

In 1997, there were approximately 70 million children in the United States, according to the U.S. Census Bureau.

## Child poverty

1.5 percent of all children under age 18 are poor.
11.1 percent of White children are poor.
39.9 percent of Black children are poor.
40.3 percent of Hispanic children are poor.
19.5 percent of Asian/Pacific Islander children are poor.
22.7 percent of children under age 6 are poor.
49.3 percent of children in mother-only families are poor.

Of all poor children:

62.5 percent are White.
31.2 percent are Black.
68.8 percent are in working families.

## Families

68.7 percent of children live in two-parent families.
27.0 percent of children live in one-parent families.
4.3 percent of children do not live with a parent.

## Child care

An estimated 13 million children under age 6 with working parents are in child care.
62 percent of women with children under age 6 are in the labor force, as are 77 percent of women with children ages 6 to 17.
Nearly 5 million children ages 5 to 14 are home alone after school each week.
Only approximately two out of five 3- and 4-year-olds eligible for Head Start's comprehensive services were served in 1997.

## Infant mortality rates

29,583 babies died in 1995—a rate of 7.6 for every 1,000 live births. The infant mortality rate for Black babies (15.1 for every 1,000 live births) is decreasing but remains more than twice that for White babies (6.3 for every 1,000 live births).

## Low birth weight

7.3 percent of babies were born at low birth weight (weighing less than 5 lbs., 8 oz.) in 1995.

## Prenatal care

In 1995, 4.2 percent of babies were born to mothers who did not receive prenatal care or did not receive it until their last trimester.

## Insurance

11.3 million children through age 18 (about 15.1 percent) had no form of health insurance throughout 1996.

Nine out of ten uninsured children have parents who work, and six out of ten have parents who work full time during the entire year.

## Immunization

23 percent of children between 19 and 35 months of age are not fully vaccinated against dangerous but preventable diseases.

## Gun violence

5,254 American children and teens from birth to age 19 died from gunfire in 1995.

## Hunger

4 million children under age 12 go hungry for some part of each month, according to the Food Research and Action Center.

13.2 million children received food stamps in fiscal year 1997.

14.7 million children received free or reduced-cost school lunches in 1997. Only a portion of these children received subsidized school breakfasts, and even fewer received summer meals.

7.2 million infants, children, and pregnant women received WIC (Supplemental Food Program for Women, Infants, and Children) benefits in fiscal year 1997.

## Education

14.2 percent of 19- to 24-year-olds in 1996 had not completed high school.

In 1996, only 28.1 percent of White 25- to 29-year-olds had completed four years of college; only 14.6 percent of Blacks and 10.0 percent of Hispanics in this age group had completed college.

## Teen parents

512,115 babies were born to teenage mothers in 1995, a rate of 56.8 births for every 1,000 15- to 19-year-old girls.

## Abuse and neglect

3.1 million children were reported abused or neglected in 1996; nearly one million cases were confirmed.

An estimated 1,046 children die from abuse and neglect each year.

An estimated 502,000 children were in foster care in 1996.

*Primary source:* Children's Defense Fund, 1998.

United States) can influence children's behavior as well as their ability to concentrate and perform complex mental tasks.

Hunger and other conditions related to poverty are not isolated phenomena. Rather, they occur simultaneously with such environmental insults as inadequate or nonexistent housing. These factors and others interact to impede the child's development. Hence, whereas at one time mental dysfunction and low educational achievement, among other problems, were assumed to be inherent negative traits of poor children, we now realize that these stem from environmental stresses, as well as from the feelings of powerlessness and frustration often associated with poverty (Albee and Gullotta 1997; Albee 1986).

## Maternal Employment

Poverty affects a large segment of the population of children, especially children under age 6. When multiple factors—poverty, single-parent families, and race—are taken into account, it is estimated that 40 percent of all children are at risk (CED 1991). However, non-poor children are also at risk since many of them experience stresses associated with societal and family life changes. We have already discussed some such changes (e.g., divorce) that affect children regardless of their family income. Another change that has had far-reaching effects on the way children are growing up today is the entry of a large number of women into the labor force.

This development, related in part to the economic hardships faced by many families—as well as to other societal changes—is especially apparent among women who have children. Whereas in 1973 30 percent of mothers with children under age 6 were working, as were 50 percent of mothers with school-age children, by 1997 65 percent of mothers with children under age 6 and 77 percent of mothers with school-age children were working (CDF 1998). Among mothers with infants the change has been even more dramatic. In 1977, less than 30 percent of women with infants a year old or younger were working. In 1991, 53 percent of mothers with infants a year old or younger were working (U.S. Department of Labor 1997), and in 1998 55 percent of mothers returned to full-time work within weeks of the birth of the baby (CDF 1998). This phenomena is especially prevalent among college-educated women.

Some years ago researchers focused on the question of whether maternal employment was associated with any negative consequences for children. They found that other factors, such as the mother's overall satisfaction with her life, are more crucial than whether she is employed out of the home (Hoffman 1986, 1989). Another important factor was the stress associated with maternal employment. In many dual-worker families, both the parents and the children experience inordinate amounts of stress. The

---

BOX 1.2   Schools' Response to Hunger

Larry Brown, keynote speaker at the National Academy, the annual conference of the Schools of the 21st Century, challenged educators to address
one of the problems facing a growing number of children: hunger. Brown
(1998) noted that educators need not wait for national policies or state
grants; they can help children by having nonperishable foods such as boxed
cereals, crackers, and milk in long-life containers available in the hallways or
the back of the class, so children who are hungry can help themselves.

---

stress stems in part from the fact that although women have assumed new
roles in the workplace, they have not abdicated their traditional responsibilities as homemakers. This situation has resulted in role conflict and guilt
among mothers in particular (Hoffman 1989; Moen and Dempster 1987),
as well as in changes in lifestyle that permeate the entire family. Friedman
(1987) found that close to 40 percent of employed parents, both men and
women, indicate that they frequently experience severe conflict, guilt, and
stress. These changes in the family mean not only that children spend less
time with their parents but also that they are affected by their parents' attempts to juggle work, child rearing, and household responsibilities.

## Parental Leave

The changes associated with women's participation in the workforce are
numerous and affect the family, as well as other institutions. These changes
require the enactment of policies to support families, such as a policy that
allows for a leave of absence from work to care for a newborn baby.

We know from research conducted over the past several decades, as well
as from the more recent explosion of information on the capabilities of
newborn and very young infants (e.g., Shore 1997; Carnegie Corporation
of New York 1994), that the first few months of life represent a critical period for the development of attachment between the parents and infant.
Attachment develops within the context of a secure parent-child relationship, as parents nurture the baby, who thrives and is encouraged to become
increasingly autonomous (Ainsworth et al. 1978; Stern 1988; Cicchetti and
Cummings 1990). However, the first few months after the birth of the baby
also represent a stressful period, which necessitates the adjustment of all
family members to the newborn (Belsky 1981; Brazelton 1985). Reviewing
the research on infant development within the context of the new realities
of family life, which require that mothers work out of the home, a Blue
Ribbon Committee on Infant Care Leave recommended that parents be
given the option of taking a leave of absence from work for the first six
months after the birth of the baby, with the first three months being a paid

leave, at 75 percent of the parent's salary (Zigler and Frank 1988; Zigler, Hopper, and Hall 1993). This recommendation was made in the interest of infants' development, as well as in the interest of the mental health and well-being of parents. However, for many years there was political resistance to the idea of a parental leave policy. Although several states (Finn-Stevenson and Trzcinski 1989), and eventually the U.S. Congress, passed legislation mandating that businesses provide unpaid family leave, the legislation is limited. The federal legislation, for example, affects businesses with fifty or more employees. However, approximately 50 percent of the workforce works in small businesses with less than fifty employees, which means that most families have no opportunity to benefit from a leave policy. Furthermore, the legislation provides for only twelve weeks of *unpaid* leave, thus single parents and those parents who depend on two incomes to survive cannot take advantage of the leave and have to make some arrangement for child care (Hofferth and Chaplin 1994).

## Child Care

Given the lack of good, affordable child care, parents face an unprecedented set of problems. The lack of child care is one of the most widely recognized social problems today. Virtually everyone—working parents, chief executives of major national corporations, and policymakers at every level of government—is either experiencing difficulties finding child care or discussing ways to address the problem.

The attention the child care issue is receiving is not surprising, given the increase in the number of infants and children who need such services. However, this attention belies the fact that the issue has been a major social problem for over two decades. At the 1970 White House Conference on Children, the need for child care services was noted as the first of several priorities the nation must address. In 1971, Congress passed the Child Development Act, which would have enabled the nation to begin to build a system of child care services. However, President Nixon vetoed the bill (Nelson 1982; Zigler and Lang 1991), so the problem was exacerbated and has reached crisis proportions today.

Although the crisis is national in scope, child care continues to be regarded as an individual family problem that parents must address themselves (Gormley 1995; Cohen 1996). For example, although more businesses now offer child care or help with child care arrangements by making provisions for flextime and part-time work, the percentage of companies actually involved in these programs is still extremely small (Kagan and Cohen 1997).

Although the Family Support Act of 1988, which was in part an attempt to train welfare-dependent mothers of young children for work outside the home, included provisions concerning child care, a lack of suffi-

BOX 1.3   Changing Expectations of Welfare:
The Impact on Children

Since the mid-1930s, the Aid to Families with Dependent Children (AFDC) program guaranteed public assistance for poor mothers and children. In the mid-1990s, AFDC benefits were paid to over 5 million families, affecting close to 10 million children. However, in the past two to three decades policymakers and the American public in general have become increasingly frustrated with welfare, and attempts by the federal government to address the issue have resulted in several legislative actions. In the 1970s, the Work Incentive Program provided job training, and in some cases work, to a small percentage of welfare recipients whose children were of school age (Blank and Blum 1997). In 1988, Congress passed the Family Support Act, which mandated that mothers on welfare with children age 3 or older must be employed, in school, or in job training. The Family Support Act provided the mothers with financial assistance for child care and mandated child care assistance for a one-year transition period for mothers who leave welfare and get jobs. In 1996 Congress passed the Personal Responsibility and Work Opportunity Reconciliation Act. This law ended the federal guarantee of assistance to all eligible families by shifting the responsibility for assistance to state government. The 1996 welfare law gives states discretion in choosing which families to assist and how to respond to families who cannot find work (Venner 1997). Provisions of the law include: (1) the federal government provides a lump sum block grant to each state for Temporary Assistance to Needy Families (TANF); (2) families can receive assistance for up to five years over a lifetime; and (3) states will receive full federal funding only if, by 2002, half of the adults receiving assistance work at least thirty hours a week (Greenberg and Savner 1996).

Because of the welfare reform legislation more mothers of infants and young children are working or in training, which makes the need for affordable child care an increasingly more urgent issue. Child care subsidies are available for parents; however, the subsidies are inadequate (Kisker and Ross 1997), and the low quality of child care has created a concern that children's development will be compromised. Besides the fact that affordable, quality care is hard to find, families may need care for children during odd hours, and they are likely to live in poor neighborhoods, making quality child care even harder to find. Kisker and Ross (1997) note further that although child care subsidies help some parents, the demand far outstrips the supply, contributing significantly to the crisis regarding affordable child care.

cient funds for these provisions raises concerns about the quality of care the children receive while their mothers are in training. In a review of how states use the child care funds in the Family Support Act, researchers found that only six states have attempted to expand families' access to quality care. Most states allow parents to purchase child care from providers who are not meeting even basic health and safety regulations or the minimal standards associated with fire safety and the storage of toxic substances (CDF 1994).

In an attempt to finally address the issue, Congress passed the Child Care and Development Block Grant in 1990. Among other provisions, the law provides subsidies to low-income parents to help them meet the cost of child care. Under the law, a portion of the funds (5 percent) must also be used to improve quality and to provide early childhood education and school-age child care services (Cohen 1996). The Child Care and Development Block Grant has made a difference in the lives of many children. However, it does not meet the needs of all those eligible for subsidies (Venner 1997; Adams and Poersch 1997; Blank 1994). Even in the five states that spent the most on child care, only a fraction of eligible families received assistance (CDF 1994; Kisker and Ross 1997). The legislation also fails to address a critical issue, namely, the short supply of good, affordable child care. As such, the legislation represents, at best, only a partial solution to the child care problem. More recent legislative activities related to the child care issue include an attempt to use a portion of the funds from the settlement with the tobacco industry for child care. Although this attempt was defeated, an attempt to fund school-age child care and programs for children in middle school was successful.

## The High Cost of Child Care

One of the most critical aspects of the child care problem is the high cost of care. The cost of care depends on several factors, especially quality. The cost also varies depending on the age of the child: the younger the child, the higher the cost of care. Other factors, such as variations in supply and demand in different regions of the country, also affect the price, so it is difficult to provide an accurate estimate of how much parents pay for child care. However, we do know that since 1990, steep price increases have occurred in all types of child care; parents are now paying more for child care, whether they are using child care centers, family day care homes, in-home child care (by a nanny or "sitter"), or care by relatives (Hofferth 1996).

We also know that child care takes up a significant portion of a family's budget (Hofferth 1996). For some families, the cost of care amounts to about 27 percent of monthly earnings (Kagan and Cohen 1997). It is not surprising, therefore, that parents choose care on the basis of price, opting for the least expensive care that they can find, even if that means lower quality care. In a national sample of young families with mothers ranging in age from 20 to 27, Hofferth and Wissoker (1992) analyzed not only the cost of care but also the child care choices parents make. They found that price is a critical variable in child care choices and that "if [child care] providers raise their prices in order to improve quality . . . parents will go elsewhere" (95).

That parents, most of whom are struggling to make ends meet, choose child care on the basis of price rather than quality is understandable, but it raises a grave concern about the kind of care children receive. Child care is labor intensive; the majority of the costs entailed in providing care are related to staff salaries. An appropriate staff/child ratio for the age of the children is an indicator of good quality care (Phillips 1987), but it also means higher priced care, since more providers have to be hired to care for the children. Other indicators of good quality care, besides staff/child ratios, are group size (the younger the child, the smaller the group should be) and the education and training of providers (Ruopp et al. 1979; Phillips 1987). Both of these indicators affect the price of care (Helburn and Howes 1996). Another indicator of quality is staff stability, which refers to how long staff stay on the job. The longer they remain, the better it is for children, who need to develop a close relationship with their providers. However, staff salaries are so low in the child care field (Whitebook, Phillips, and Howes 1990) that providers often leave for higher paying jobs.

Because parents make cost the priority in choosing care for their children, many toddlers and preschool children are in low-quality child care facilities. This point is made in several national studies. In a study on cost, quality, and child outcomes in child care centers (Helburn 1995), researchers found that the quality of care in the majority of centers is poor to mediocre. In a study of child care facilities in five major cities (Whitebook, Phillips, and Howes 1990), researchers found that the best care is provided to children from upper-income families who can afford to pay for high-quality care. Next, good care is provided to low-income children who are in centers that are subject to occasional monitoring by the state to ensure some level of quality. Children from working-class and lower-middle-class families are often in poor quality centers, receiving substandard care that places them at risk for developmental problems.

Of particular concern is the poor quality care found in facilities serving infants. For infants, parents often choose family day care (child care provided by an individual in her own home), in part because this is the only option they have but also because some parents feel that the home-like atmosphere is better for infants and toddlers. Family child care has the potential for being a good choice for infants if the quality is good. However, with family day care, as with other forms of care, the quality is directly related to the cost, and parents often opt for the least cost (Helburn and Howes 1996), so millions of infants are not receiving good quality care. Furthermore, the majority of family child care providers operate underground, so we have no means of monitoring the kind of care infants receive (Ward, Shuster, and Finn-Stevenson 1992). The information we do have suggests that the quality of family day care homes leaves much to be desired. A study that looked at two forms of child care in the home—family day care (including regulated and non-regulated homes) and care by a relative—found that in only 9 percent of family day care and 1 percent of relative care did the children receive good quality care (Galinsky et al. 1994). And yet, together these two forms of home care serve close to 5 million children under age 6, or about half the children that age in child care. That quality care is a privilege enjoyed by only some children is, for individual families and the nation, a concern. Children spend a large portion of their day, every day, in the child care environment. If the environment is not conducive to children's development, especially during infancy and early childhood, it will have detrimental effects on their development and well-being. If children are in facilities where they have no opportunities for self-initiated play activities, if no one reads to them or provides them with books, if they just walk aimlessly about the room or watch television, they miss out on opportunities to develop the skills they need to do well in school. We discuss this issue in more detail in Chapter 3.

Besides concern over the care infants and preschoolers receive while their parents are working, there is concern that older children, from kindergarten to sixth grade, are home alone before and after school because their parents are unable to find appropriate child care. It is estimated conservatively that 5 million children between the ages of 5 and 14 are left without adult supervision before and after school and during vacations. We used to refer to these children as latchkey kids because many of them wore their house keys around their necks; today they are referred to as children in self-care.

Teachers have long contended that being left alone takes its toll on a child's academic performance and creates behavior problems and school absenteeism (National Association of Elementary School Principals 1986). Still, there are some who contend that being left alone can be a positive experience for children and can contribute to the development of independence. There are others who contend that the experience does not harm children (Rodman, Pratto, and Nelson 1985). Some studies suggest, however, that children who are home alone often feel lonely and afraid (Long and Long 1984) and that they are at risk for injuries (Garbarino and Sherman 1980). Additionally, in a wide-scale study on the topic, J. L. Richardson and his colleagues (1989) found that there is greater prevalence of delinquency and drug and alcohol abuse among children and young adolescents who are in self-care than among those who are in supervised programs before and after school; these findings hold regardless of such variables as family income and ethnic background. A review of several studies (Fight Crime/Invest in Kids 1997) notes a link between a lack of school-age child care and crime; juvenile crime occurs between 2 P.M. and 8 P.M., when school is out and some children are unsupervised because their parents are working.

# Public Response to Changes in Family Life

Single-parent households, divorce, poverty, and the lack of good quality, affordable child care are some of the new circumstances in which children grow up today. Although our discussion of these changed circumstances is by no means complete, it is clear that childhood is not the protective and trouble-free period of life Americans traditionally have envisioned it to be. Children today are burdened with stress on a daily basis, as are their parents, and they face higher expectations for independence. At the same time, they have to achieve so much more educationally, given the complex society in which we live.

## *Decline in Public Spending*

Although the majority of families are affected in some way by the societal changes we have described, social policies in the United States have not kept pace with the changes. As a result, the United States is in a state of disequilibrium, wherein social policies are not in synchrony with the realities of family life. This disequilibrium and the accompanying lack of support services are creating difficulties for both children and parents and are contributing to stress.

Other nations have undergone demographic shifts similar in magnitude to those experienced in the United States, but these nations have put in place a variety of supportive services for families. These services are available to families of all socioeconomic levels but provide additional assistance to those who are poor or disabled (Kamerman 1998). The United States has not only failed to develop policies that support all parents and children but also now limits the assistance traditionally provided to families in need. These limits have occurred in the context of a series of budget cuts in social services that began in the 1980s and continue today, as federal, state, and local governments address mounting deficits and an increase in the number of individuals needing assistance (CDF 1998). At the community level, agencies and organizations are finding that, although they would like to be creative in finding ways to respond to families with multiple needs, fiscal realities mean that they cannot do much beyond providing basic services.

## *Fragmentation and Duplication of Services*

Although families and childhood have changed, organizations and agencies continue to provide services as they have in the past. First, there is little if any support for the plight of working, middle-class families. These families are struggling to make ends meet, and they incur expenses associated with having to work and raise children at the same time. Such families get some assistance in the form of tax credits for child care expenses (discussed in Chapter 6), but they have difficulty finding good quality child care that they can afford.

Second, the way services are delivered to at-risk families has not changed to address current needs and changed circumstances. As a result, as Kirst (1991) notes, "some children receive redundant services for various over-lapping problems; others receive no help at all. Children with multiple problems are typically given a single label— . . . drop out, delinquent, teen parent . . . —that oversimplifies the nature of the trouble and obstructs . . . what needs to be done" (616).

The impact of this state of affairs on children is evident. For some, it manifests itself in violence and mental health problems, which affect an increasing number of children (Knitzer 1993; Institute of Medicine 1989). For others, it shows up in such problems as poor academic performance, dropping out of school, substance abuse, early sexual activity, and teen pregnancy.

## A New Hope: Commitment to Children and Families Among Some Educators

On a more positive note, however, there appears to be a renewed commitment to children and a recognition that we must support families in their child-rearing responsibilities. We know that through effective programs and services, we can help children and families (Schorr and Schorr 1988; Schorr 1997). Proposals are being made to ascertain what the differing needs of children and families are, depending on their community, and to work within the context of new structures that focus on the well-being of families (Cunningham 1990).

The emphasis also has shifted from remedial interventions, which often focused on the child in isolation from the family, to the recognition that in order to ensure the optimal development of children we must address the needs of the entire family, undertake a comprehensive approach that takes into account families' needs for multiple support services, and focus on the prevention of problems by providing services early in the life of the child.

The focus on the family, not only on the child but also on the parents—referred to as the two-generational approach to programs and services (Smith 1991; Layzer and St. Pierre 1996)—provides new and promising directions for the development of effective programs for children and families. Also promising is the emphasis on prevention services (Albee and Gullotta 1997), an emphasis especially evident in education. Many leaders in both the public and private sectors are recognizing that piecemeal remedial programs have not addressed low achievement and the increase in school dropout rates, among other problems. The Committee for Economic Development, an independent organization of 250 business leaders, has published a number of policy reports calling for the nation to subscribe to a broader view of human development and to look at "early childhood development, education, social services, job training, and economic development as parts of an interdependent system of human investments rather than as independent enterprises" (CED 1991, 3).

A similar view is inherent in the national readiness goal, which was signed into law in 1990 (National Education Goals Panel 1995). The readiness goal, one of eight education goals, states that by the year 2000 all children will begin school ready to learn. The law sets forth several objectives by which to reach this goal, including the objectives of:

- providing all disadvantaged and disabled children with high-quality and developmentally appropriate preschool programs that will help prepare the children for school
- recognizing every parent as the child's first teacher, and providing parents with access to the support services they may need
- ensuring that children receive the health care and nutrition necessary to start school with "healthy minds and bodies," and reducing the incidence of low-birth-weight babies through the provision of prenatal care

Several state governments also have taken a stand on the readiness issue, and many of them have provided support for early childhood programs. Whereas in the early 1980s fewer than ten states funded preschool education programs, by the end of the decade close to thirty states made provisions for funding such programs (Seligson and Marx 1988; U.S. General Accounting Office 1995).

Ensuring that each child receives preschool education is a step in the right direction. The research has shown that preschool programs of high quality can have a positive effect on children's development and help prepare disadvantaged children for school (Barnett 1995; Weikart and Schweinhart 1997). The focus on preschool education needs to be seen in a broad perspective, so it is available to all children (Carnegie Corporation of New York 1994). However, at a time when we need to address the needs of all children, regardless of income, the legislation in most states focuses on pre-kindergarten children from economically disadvantaged families or those children in low performing schools designated by the courts as in need of additional funds. Also, although families need all-day care for their preschool children, most state-funded programs serve children for only part of the day. Ripple and her colleagues (in review) note further that there is widespread variability in state-funded preschool programs among the states, resulting in a patchwork of requirements and services.

Another problem concerns when services are first provided. Often services are not provided until the preschool period, when the child is 3 or 4;

in such cases service providers miss the opportunity for early intervention. By the time of preschool, some children already may have sustained neurological damage, be developmentally delayed, have acquired self-defeating attitudes, or lack motivation (Szanton 1992). Quality preschool programs can help some of these children overcome or compensate for these and other problems through early identification and referral for appropriate intervention. However, children would benefit more if these problems were prevented in the first place; and prevention requires that we recognize school readiness as an issue that includes supporting families in their child-rearing efforts. Additionally, we should begin to provide services to children and families at birth or even during the prenatal period, not at age 3 or 4 (Winter and McDonald 1997).

We make this point on the basis of the developmental research that has accumulated over the years, some of which has been reviewed in other publications (e.g., Shore 1997; Carnegie Corporation of New York 1994; Zigler and Finn-Stevenson 1994). The research indicates that the capacity for children to learn and benefit from instruction depends largely on a number of characteristics, such as curiosity, motivation, the ability to sustain attention, and self-esteem. Boyer (1992) states this point eloquently:

> Children differ greatly in their capacity to learn. And it is not mainly a matter of "intelligence," whatever that slippery term may mean. The capacity of children to learn ... depends on a number of attributes: Are they curious? Do they believe they can affect events? Can they concentrate? Do they feel that anyone cares about them? Do they readily seek help from adults? Do they care about others? Those characteristics are the engines of learning—the qualities that propel learning.

These attributes form the foundation for the child's ability to succeed academically. They develop during the first few years of life and are influenced by circumstances before and after birth. For example, infants whose development has been compromised in some way during the prenatal period are at risk for developmental delays or handicaps and may have difficulty organizing their thinking and paying attention. We also know that whereas healthy infants are curious and eager to explore their environment in an attempt to learn and understand their world, infants from dysfunctional families, or families experiencing a great deal of stress, show little if any interest in their surroundings and lack the confidence to approach life and learning with excitement. Support services can ameliorate the negative effects of the stressful conditions that families experience (Garmezy 1985; Gore 1980) and should thus play a prominent role in any attempt to help children develop to their potential.

Although schools' responsibility for children begins traditionally at the age of 5 or 6, an increasing number of educators are recognizing that if they are to have any positive effects on children's education, they must redefine their responsibilities and, in keeping with societal and family changes, expand upon the traditional mission of the school. This redefinition of the role of schools entails the provision of services at an earlier age to ensure that children and families have the social, health, child care, and other services they need, beginning at birth and continuing through the school-age years. In the next chapter, we discuss these new roles educators have undertaken in schools around the country.

# 2 Remaking Schools to Fit Families' Needs

Beyond the suggestions inherent in the school readiness goal that we described in Chapter 1, there is no mandate to ensure that, as a nation, we address the needs of children and families and help each child realize his or her academic potential. Increasingly, however, schools are being considered as uniquely positioned to provide a number of social, health, and support services that children and their families may need. Additionally, as we noted in Chapter 1, many school districts around the country are implementing initiatives that are nonacademic and designed to improve the quality of life of children and reach out to and support parents. The focus on outreach to families and the provision of support services are sometimes aspects of a larger effort to improve or restructure the school, but the overall goal is to ensure that children and their parents know about and have access to the services they need.

The trend among schools to reach out and support children and families has precedence; for many years schools have addressed children's needs for a variety of nonacademic services such as breakfast and lunch, and many schools have had guidance counselors and school nurses on the staff. Current efforts to address nonacademic needs include an emphasis on the whole family, rather than just the child, as the recipient of support services. Additionally, the services have become, by necessity, much more comprehensive in nature. Susan Chira (1991), describing the various initiatives undertaken in schools, notes that "schools . . . are trying to bridge the gap between the society American schools were intended for and the one that exists today. The spread of poverty, drugs, single-parent families and two career couples has transformed the task of schools, swamping teachers who try to be surrogate parents, social workers and psychiatrists" (1). Dryfoos (1994) and others (see General Accounting Office 1994) also point out that many schools, out of necessity, are taking on various responsibilities not traditionally associated with schooling and are providing a full range of social and health services.

## Schools Reaching Out

*Promoting Parent Involvement and Participation*

The efforts to change schools to respond better to the needs of families have been implemented on an ad hoc basis and are included in only a fraction of the schools (Hamburg 1994). Nevertheless, these efforts are instructive of the way educators have responded to the challenge to help families in their child-rearing responsibilities. The initiatives that schools have implemented vary, but they often have one activity in common: a focus on parent involvement.

The concept of parent involvement is not new; we have known from early intervention programs such as Project Head Start, which began in the mid-1960s, that we can have positive effects on children if we assist parents in the task of child rearing and involve them in programs or services designed for children (Valentine and Stark 1979). So important is the concept of parent involvement that federal and state agencies have long required that the early intervention programs they fund devote time and resources to activities for and with parents.

Parent involvement is regarded as an essential ingredient to program success not only in early intervention programs but in schools as well. Indeed, in the enabling legislation, Goals 2000, which established national education goals, parental participation is listed as a goal: By the year 2000 "every school will promote partnerships that will increase parental involvement and participation in promoting the social, emotional, and academic growth of children" (National Education Goals Panel 1995, 13).

Recognition of the critical role parents play in the education of children can be traced to the beginning of the century (Bornstein 1995) and has been a central focus of Parent Teacher Associations. Traditionally, however, there was, in spite of this recognition, a separation between schools and families, with distinct roles assigned to these two institutions; schools were charged with teaching children academic subjects beginning at age 5 or 6, and parents were expected to take responsibility for children's moral and social development. Any interactions between parents and teachers were limited to brief conferences to discuss the child's progress in school, an occasional open house when parents could come to the school as a group, or parental involvement in fund raising or special events.

Traditional attitudes on the distinct roles of schools and families still exist to some degree, but more educators and parents are realizing that they can be more effective in educating and raising children if they work together. This change in viewpoint has been inspired by the success of the parent involvement component of early interventions, with many schools now implementing programs that either include parents or are designed specifically to encourage parents to participate in their children's schooling. Some of these initiatives focus on families at all socioeconomic levels, with educators reporting that an increasing number of parents participate in school functions. Parents are finding that when they show an interest in their children's school experience and get to know, as well as become involved with, what happens in school, both their children's attitude toward learning and their achievement improve (Rich 1985; Epstein 1992). In a review of studies on parent involvement, Walberg (1984) found that parental participation in the education of their children is predictive of success in school and that this applied to both poor and middle-class families.

With so much written about the importance of parent involvement, it is not surprising that more parents now participate in their children's education. However, many educators feel that not enough parents are involved. Several social factors—working mothers and single-parent families, for example—impede parental involvement in schools; often, parents simply have very little time to devote to school activities.

Additionally, in many schools parent involvement efforts are not universal but target low-income families whose children are at risk for educational failure. The extent that schools focus on parents varies, as does the scope of the activities schools choose in the effort to promote parent involvement. Epstein (1992) reviewed the research on the topic and developed a typology of school-family relationships that can serve as a guide for schools' plans in the area. Included in the typology are efforts ranging from schools simply providing parents with information about school-related activities, to having parents serve as volunteers, to involving parents in learning activities with children at home, to enabling parents to participate in decisionmaking and governance roles.

Underscoring the variations in the field of parent involvement in general, Powell (1989) writes that some parent involvement programs—whether developed by schools, churches, hospitals, nursery schools, or child care centers—may simply disseminate information about child development for parents to use. Other programs take a more active role and, for example, teach parents how to stimulate children's cognitive development or how to use effective discipline techniques. Powell notes further that some parent involvement and education programs take place in the school or in some other facility, whereas some such services are provided in the parents' home.

Twenty-five elementary schools in Iowa are illustrative of the variations in the attempt to involve parents. These schools, recipients of a state grant to develop innovative programs for at-risk elementary school students, undertook different activities, but they shared an overall goal: to prevent school failure among at-risk students. Each of the schools included a focus on parent involvement. Some of the schools designated a parents' room, where parents could drop in to use the telephone, read, or simply interact with other parents. Several schools provided parent education workshops on various topics, whereas in other schools, parents were hired as classroom aides (Finn-Stevenson and Gillette 1996). Many of the schools found that they must be responsive to the needs of families and that, if they are to be effective, they cannot expect all parents to come to the school. Therefore, in some of the schools home-visitation programs were instituted. Home visitation proved to be a critically important element, especially in cases where schools had a number of severely dysfunctional families or where parents were wary of teachers and other school personnel whom they viewed as authority figures. Some of the Iowa schools designated a guidance counselor, project coordinator, or a teacher for home visitations; others created the position of a home-school liaison specifically for this task.

## Acknowledging the Role of Parents as Teachers

Along with the increased awareness of the importance of parent involvement has come a surge of new research that has shown that from the moment of birth children are actively learning about their environment. This new understanding about children's learning fueled much of the growth of early childhood education programs and, more recently, has inspired schools to acknowledge parents' role as the child's first teachers.

The state of Missouri has been in the forefront in this regard, mandating its schools to provide parent education and family support services under the auspices of a program known as Parents as Teachers (PAT). PAT is designed to enhance children's development and their achievement in school by reaching out to parents, beginning at the birth of the child and continuing through age 3. Established as a pilot program in four school districts in 1981, PAT has become mandatory for each school district in Missouri under the Early Childhood Development Act, which was enacted in 1984. Since that time the program has grown substantially; it has expanded its scope of services and has been adopted in school districts in thirty-four states.

The program has been refined over the years. By law, all Missouri school districts must make the program available free of charge, but parents may choose whether or not to participate. The noncompulsory aspect of PAT is considered critical in avoiding negative attitudes about the program (Hausman 1990).

The rationale underlying PAT is that parents are the child's first and most important teachers and that schools should assist parents in giving each child a solid educational beginning. Toward this end, the target population is all families with children up to age 3. The services included in PAT are home visits by a parent educator who, guided by a specific curriculum, provides parents with information on developmental milestones and effective parenting skills. In the event that parents need social services, the home visitor refers them to appropriate agencies but refrains from providing social support, so as not to dilute the child-development focus of the home visits. Also included among the services are periodic screenings for children's vision, language, and social development, and additional parent education programs for parents whose children are found to be developmentally delayed.

In the early years of the program, the services were made available only to parents who had their first baby. Today, it is recognized that all parents, regardless of the number of children they have, need support and developmental counsel during the child's first three years of life. Ideally, such support would begin during the last trimester of pregnancy. However, schools have found it difficult to recruit parents at that time, possibly because parents are tired and busy preparing for the birth.

Since schools traditionally work with older children, the question becomes, How do they reach families with newborn babies? They do so by distributing brochures and other printed materials at hospitals, prenatal clinics, and physicians' offices, as well as at other locations young families frequent, such as the Laundromat and supermarket. Even with these information-dissemination techniques and the use of the media to market the program, recruitment is a challenge and many of the parents who most need the program do not take advantage of the services it offers.

Despite the difficulty in reaching some families and the fact that the program, due to limited state resources, serves less than 50 percent of the eligible families, PAT has been implemented successfully in schools and has yielded impressive outcomes. In one of the early evaluations of the program, it was found that children of parents participating in the program scored higher on all measures of intelligence, achievement, auditory comprehension, and verbal ability than did a comparison group whose parents did not participate in the program (Pfannenstiel, Lambson, and Yarnell 1991). The parents benefited from the program as well; those parents who participated were significantly more knowledgeable in a number of areas relevant to child rearing than those who did not. Perhaps even more important, participating parents were more likely than the nonparticipating parents in the comparison group to regard their school district as responsive to their child's needs. We should also note that once the children are in school, parents are more likely to become involved in their children's education (Winter and McDonald 1997).

Other states have adopted the PAT program within the context of other programs. For example, legislation in Connecticut enabled the creation of the School of the 21st Century/Family Resource Centers, discussed later in the chapter. These centers, which are also legislated in Kentucky under the 1990 Kentucky Education Reform Act, include the provision of home visitations to families with children ages birth to 3. This component of the

Family Resource Centers is patterned after PAT but is known in Connecticut and Kentucky as Families in Training (FIT).

## Forging Partnerships, Creating Linkages with the Community

Some schools, in an effort to address the needs of children and families, are forging alliances with community-based organizations and health and social service agencies (Dryfoos 1994). Sometimes the impetus to cooperate comes from schools, which are finding that children have difficulties learning and benefiting from instruction if they or their families have financial, health, social, or emotional problems. Sometimes the cooperation is initiated by social, health, or other agencies or organizations, which have come to realize that through the school they can better identify and reach children and families. Regardless of the source of the initiative, the rationale for working together and linking the services to the school is often the same: Families have multiple needs that no one organization can address effectively (Lopez and Hochberg 1993). The overall goal in many of these efforts is to ensure that comprehensive support is available and accessible to children and families.

**Service Integration and School-Linked Services.**   The alliances formed between schools and other organizations and between various agencies are referred to by various names, including collaboration, coordination, cooperation, service integration, and school-linked services. These terms, each of which describes distinct strategies for working together, are generally defined as systematic efforts to solve problems of service fragmentation (Kahn and Kamerman 1992; Kirst 1992).

The idea of integrating the various services families may need is not new. Kahn and Kamerman (1992) mention the notion of "united charities" prevalent in the 1920s and 1940s, as well as the War on Poverty and Great Society efforts in the 1960s, which gave rise to community action programs that involved several service integration strategies. There were also efforts in the early 1970s to reorganize and consolidate the human service agencies. Whereas these previous efforts represented ambitious initiatives to undertake massive change, current efforts are much smaller in scale and attempt to bring together some but not necessarily all services.

**Beacon Schools.**   Service integrations involving schools vary. The Beacon Schools in New York City are one example of a partnership between a school and the community. The project, begun by the city of New York in 1991, includes school-based community centers in several neighborhoods. Although most of the centers are located in schools, they are implemented not by school personnel but by a community-based or other type of organization, which works closely with the school and other organizations and agencies. The core funding, about $450,000 for each center, comes from the New York Department of Youth Services. The centers offer health and social services, family outreach, tutoring/homework help, substance abuse intervention, and other services determined by the needs of the community.

In the case of the Beacon program, the school becomes, in effect, a community center that is open the entire day, year-round. Why the use of the school? When the centers were conceptualized, it was argued that in large urban areas such as New York City, school buildings are often located in the heart of the neighborhood. These buildings are—at least in comparison to what else is available—relatively well-maintained, and they include classrooms, auditoriums, cafeterias, and gymnasiums that are fully equipped and ideal for serving small or large groups. Using the school as a community center is a challenge, since this use entails sharing space and establishing communications with the principal, teachers, and other school personnel. Scheduling the various activities and services to take place in the school building in addition to the regular academic program is also a challenge, but one that is attainable when all those concerned are working toward a common goal.

**New Beginnings.** Another example of an alliance between schools and the community is New Beginnings (Payzant 1992), a program implemented in Hamilton School in San Diego, California. New Beginnings was developed by the city and county of San Diego, the San Diego Community College District, and the San Diego Public School District. These institutions realized that they served the same families and that often duplication of services occurred or families needing help were unaware that services existed. These institutions also realized that families often have to go to several different agencies to solve multiple problems or to receive help with many pieces of a particular problem (Hickey et al. 1990; Payzant 1992).

Unlike the Beacon Schools, the majority of which use the school building to provide services, New Beginnings uses the school only as a source of referrals. Services are not delivered in the school but in a separate place referred to as the "center," which provides: (1) student registration and family assessment; and (2) a service plan and case management, as well as various health and social services for families needing intervention.

The school functions as a referral source through intensive training of teachers, who are taught problem identification and supportive techniques and are informed of the services available at the center. Ongoing communication between the school and center staff is considered essential in ascertaining whether the children and families are benefiting from the services they receive.

In recognizing that families have multiple service needs, New Beginnings is not necessarily unusual. However, the program is unique in its approach of ensuring that the various agencies providing services work together. It was established at the outset that fragmentation of funding contributes to fragmentation of service delivery. Hence, New Beginnings uses existing agencies' resources as a primary source of funding and reallocates funds and, in some cases, staff in a more flexible and efficient manner (Payzant 1992).

Besides the Beacon Schools and New Beginnings, there are other examples of schools working with organizations to ensure that children and families have access to the services they need. The emergence of numerous school-based health clinics is an example of the cooperation between health and education institutions. Additionally, the forging of alliances with community-based organizations and agencies is often included as part of larger efforts. The Iowa schools described earlier, for example, have identified the agencies in their community and the services they provide. As a matter of routine, the schools work with these agencies not only on referrals but also on follow-up to ensure that families are receiving the help they need (Finn-Stevenson 1992; Finn-Stevenson, Gillette, and Brown 1997).

Lopez and Hochberg (1993) describe the various cooperative arrangements made between different agencies and between schools and other service organizations. They note that ways of working together may include the following: referrals to and from other agencies; contracted services; case management; coordination of complementary services by related agencies to ensure efficient service delivery; co-location of services, in which several agencies and organizations deliver services at one site that is accessible to families; and service integration, in which several programs or services may merge into a single organization, as evident in New Beginnings, described above. Based on their study of several programs, Lopez and Hochberg note that any one program, by working with other agencies and sharing resources, can extend its range and that there is no single method of collaboration that is more effective than another. They advise, rather, that schools examine and adapt the various options for working cooperatively with other agencies and organizations toward a common goal.

**Community Schools.**   The initiatives described above may be described under the heading of community schools. Dryfoos (1998) defines such schools as those that integrate and deliver education with additional services needed in the community. Coltoff (1998), writing about community schools in the context of school reform, notes that although there exist various definitions for community schools, the concept of "educational achievement combined with needed human services, delivered through the school," is most important (5). Coltoff also notes that community schools are characterized by the following:

- A combination of school resources and outside community resources within the schools to provide "seamless programs"

- An active collaboration in the governing of the programs
- Year-round and extended school hours
- Strong parent involvement
- Community "ownership" of the effort

As noted previously, the community school concept is not new. In fact, the Mott Foundation played a central role in creating community schools about sixty years ago and continues to play a major role in the "reconceived" community school concept of today. The current efforts focus not so much on the use of school buildings as on the needs of students. As Maeroff (1998) notes, "The community school in its latest configuration assumes importance in terms of what it offers students that more traditional schools do not" (ix).

An example of a community school is one developed by the Children's Aid Society and implemented in several schools in New York City. With extensive funding from several foundations, the Children's Aid Society has made available in the schools various support services, including health and social services and after-school programs. The principal in the schools is involved, but the project is administered by the Children's Aid Society, and a staff member of the organization is based in each of the schools. These schools were developed as a demonstration of a community school effort, with the hope that the Children's Aid Society would assist other communities in implementing similar initiatives (Coltoff 1998).

## Early Schooling

Another example of how schools are changing in response to the needs of families is the increase in the number of schools providing services to very young children who attend early childhood education programs or, as they are often referred to, school readiness programs.

For many schools, the focus on early education began with the provision of appropriate educational services for special-needs 3- and 4-year-olds, as specified under Public Law 99-142, which was enacted in 1975, and the amendment to the law, PL 99-457, which was enacted in 1986 (Farran and Shonkoff 1994). Since then, schools have extended early childhood education programs to include preschool children from economically disadvantaged families who are at risk for educational failure.

Schools' involvement with early schooling has been fueled by several factors, but perhaps the strongest among these is the recognition that good quality preschool programs can provide children with the foundation for later academic success (Weikart and Schweinhart 1997). Even before the enactment of Goals 2000, which includes the national goal of school readiness, an increasing number of states allocated funds to enable low-income preschool children to attend nursery school (Seligson and Marx 1988;

CDF 1998). State funds for early childhood education are usually distributed directly to local education agencies (LEAs) (Neugebauer 1991). In some states, LEAs have the option of subcontracting with another organization or agency for the provision of these services, but often schools choose to provide the services directly.

Elkind (1991, 1987) refers to the education of preschoolers in public schools as a social experiment, noting that disadvantaged children who would otherwise not have an opportunity for nursery school experience are likely to benefit from good quality, developmentally appropriate programs. The belief that low-income children need early education experiences in order to have a strong foundation for later learning is not new; it is upon this premise that Project Head Start began in 1965 (Zigler and Valentine 1979). What is new, however, is that, increasingly, schools are the institution to provide these services (Ripple et al. in review).

We know that the kind of education children receive in preschool makes a difference not only in school achievement but also in changing the life trajectory of the children involved (Weikart and Schweinhart 1997; Barnett 1995). However, such benefits are related directly to the quality, intensity, and duration of the early childhood experiences children have; there is no evidence that short-term participation in such programs or participation in early childhood programs that are of low quality makes any difference (Crnic and Lamberty 1994).

Much more research is needed to ascertain how early childhood programs can enhance children's ability to profit from instruction and what other changes in the school might be needed to ensure school success (Crnic and Lamberty 1994). But even in the absence of such research, we know a great deal about the foundations for learning and the factors that enhance or inhibit a child's ability to succeed academically. On the basis of the available research, educators are advised that the benefits associated with early childhood education programs can be realized only if schools underscore the importance of quality in the provision of services. Quality service includes not only providing children with some opportunity for play and social interactions but also ensuring that teachers are able to provide individual attention to each child. This attention is made possible by the institution of appropriate group size and staff/child ratios, depending on the age of the children, and also by ensuring that the staff have training in early childhood education. We discuss the issue of quality in greater detail in the next chapter.

Weiss (1989) also points out that preschool programs, if they are to be effective, must include a focus on parents and the provision of any support services the family may need.

Other researchers point to the need not only for school readiness efforts that address preschool children but also for efforts that take into consideration readiness throughout the school-age years (Crnic and Lamberty

1994). Hence effective efforts to provide early education do not stop there; such efforts include a comprehensive range of other services and continued support of children throughout their formal schooling. Also, as we noted in the previous chapter, efforts to ensure children's readiness to profit from academic instruction must take into consideration the child's experiences during the prenatal and infancy periods.

## The School of the 21st Century

Given the current policy focus on improving educational outcome for the nation's children, the next few years are likely to witness the emergence of even more schools providing early education. The funding for such services may be available to some degree, especially for the provision of services to low-income children. However, many schools are moving away from the trend of targeting only low-income children. Indeed, many educators are finding that although poor children have certain needs, children from working-class, middle-class, and higher income families are not exempt from the stressful realities of family life in the 1990s. This point is made by Orenstein (1994), who followed several girls from diverse family backgrounds. Some were from single-parent families, others from dual-worker, poor, or affluent families. She found that regardless of race or socioeconomic class, the girls faced numerous stresses that challenged their development.

We made a similar point in the previous chapter. Stressful conditions that permeate family life are numerous and, as we noted, include poverty, divorce, and living in single-parent and dual-worker families. But perhaps the most difficult and universal of the conditions under which young families live today is the inability to find good quality, affordable child care.

The lack of good quality, affordable child care has reached crisis proportions with detrimental consequences for children, many of whom are in poor quality programs. In an effort to address the child care crisis, we developed a program known as the School of the 21st Century, which is a school-based/school-linked child care and family support program that has been implemented in 600 schools in seventeen states.

### Rationale for the Program

The implementation of the School of the 21st Century differs from school to school. Before we describe the variations, however, it is important to understand that the School of the 21st Century was developed in response to the lack of a system of child care in the United States. Instead of a child care system, the United States has a collection of child care services that differ in quality and make up a patchwork non-system. This non-system is difficult to tap into in order to work toward the necessary improvements, and it has potentially detrimental effects on many children (Vandell, Hendersen, and Wilson 1988; Whitebook, Phillips, and Howes 1990). The School of the 21st Century is designed to work toward establishing a much needed child care system not by creating entirely new structures but by joining with the already existing educational system.

## Guiding Principles

The program was conceptualized on the basis of six guiding principles:

First, in order to address the needs of all children and ensure their optimal development, a child care system must become a national priority and part of the very structure of our society, as is the case with education. Stable, reliable, good quality care—vital to children's development and well-being—must be a central element of such a national system. In using the term "good quality care," we refer to care that is developmentally appropriate, as opposed to basic supervision or mere baby-sitting, and that provides children with the opportunity for play and social interactions.

Second, good quality care should be accessible to every child regardless of ethnic or socioeconomic group. All children should have access to an integrated child care system in order to avoid a two-tier system wherein some children receive good quality care and others do not. Like education, child care can be universally available only if it is primarily a state-based system. The federal government's role is both to subsidize the care of the most needy (as it currently does with Chapter I of the Elementary and Secondary Education Act [ESEA] and with Public Laws 94-142 and 99-947) and to fund research aimed at identifying the means by which we can achieve good quality care.

Third, the child care system in this country must be based on the optimal development of children and should emphasize a whole-child approach that places equal weight on all developmental pathways: social, emotional, physical, and cognitive. For purposes of research, social scientists often regard each developmental domain separately and have in the past given more weight to cognitive development. However, it has become recognized widely that, in reality, all aspects of growth and development are interdependent, occur simultaneously, and should thus be given equal attention. This third principle not only acknowledges the child as a whole but also reflects the fact that although child care may be regarded as a service for parents, it is first and foremost an environment where children spend a significant amount of time. As such, its quality is likely to affect their growth and development.

Fourth, parents and those who care for and educate children must work together, hence the importance of parent involvement, which, as we described earlier, has been shown to be essential for optimal development of children.

The fifth principle calls for recognition and support and decent pay for child care providers, since they play a crucial role in the quality of care children receive. This principle encompasses support for provider training as well as appropriate pay upgrades. The relevance of this principle will become clear in the next chapter.

Sixth, a national child care system must be flexible and adaptable. Because every family has particular child care needs, a universal system must be able to provide a range of choices for child care. Inherent in this principle is also the recognition that there are differences between communities and that each school has unique needs and resources.

If such a child care system is to be readily accessible—in terms of cost as well as location—to all families, the most efficient way to implement it would be to tap into the already existing educational system. Our country has a trillion-dollar investment in public school buildings, which are supported by tax dollars and used only for part of the day, nine months a year. By capitalizing on this investment and incorporating a child care system into the already existing public school system, we would be able to increase the supply of child care, as well as ensure equitable, affordable, and good quality care.

## Service Components

The guiding principles outlined above are the rationale underlying the conceptualization of the School of the 21st Century, which, in fact, links child care and education. The program is a comprehensive approach to program delivery, and at its core are two child care components: (1) all-day child care for children 3, 4, and 5 years of age; and (2) before- and after-school and vacation care for children from kindergarten through sixth grade. These child care services are provided five days a week, year-round. (In one school district—Leadville, Colorado—they are provided every day of the year, since most employment in that community is related to the resort industry and parents need to work on weekends and holidays.) Hence, the School of the 21st Century extends the use of the school building, requiring schools to remain open year-round from as early as five or six in the morning until at least six in the evening.

In addition to child care, the School of the 21st Century includes health and nutrition components as well as three outreach services: (1) home visitation and parent education for families with children ages 0–3, patterned after the Parents as Teachers program described earlier; (2) information and referral to assist parents in finding any additional services they may need; and (3) outreach to and support of family day care providers in the neighborhood of the school. This latter service is included because family child care is a prevalent form of out-of-home care, especially for infants and toddlers, but it is also the least supported and monitored form of child care. Some family child care providers participate in training activities offered in the community, and they are registered by the state, but the majority lack training and operate underground (Galinsky et al. 1994; Finn-Stevenson and Ward 1990; Shuster, Finn-Stevenson, and Ward 1990). As noted in Chapter 1, a recent study of the quality of care in family child care found that only 9 percent of the facilities provided good quality care (Galinsky et al. 1994).

Schools adopting the School of the 21st Century identify family child care providers in the neighborhood of the school and invite them to participate in training workshops and other activities. The school becomes, in effect, a hub that enables family day care providers to get to know and learn from one another and from other professionals. Since child care providers are the major determinant of the quality of the care children receive (Phillips et al. 1998), reaching out and offering them both the opportunity to participate in training and social support is likely to have a beneficial effect on children in their care.

We have used the term "program" to describe the School of the 21st Century. However, as is apparent from the preceding description, the School of the 21st Century is not a program per se as much as it is a design for the delivery of a continuum of services to children and families. The School includes many of the services and approaches discussed earlier in the chapter, such as parent involvement and cooperation with other agencies and organizations, as well as a range of services children and families may need.

The services included in the School of the 21st Century are hardly new or, in and of themselves, unique; these services exist already in most communities, albeit to a limited extent. What is unique about the School of the 21st Century is that:

1. it provides an umbrella that brings these services together under the aegis of the school; and
2. the services are provided to all eligible children on a continuum from the birth of the child through age 12.

The School of the 21st Century does not mandate the provision of all service components that make up the program. Rather, it provides a blueprint for action and requires schools to develop and implement services on the basis of the needs of the community and the available resources. As a result, the School of the 21st Century programs around the country differ from one another. However, they share a common goal: the optimal development of children through the provision of child care and support services. And all the programs adhere to the guiding principles described earlier.

FIGURE 2.1   Service Components of
the School of the 21st Century

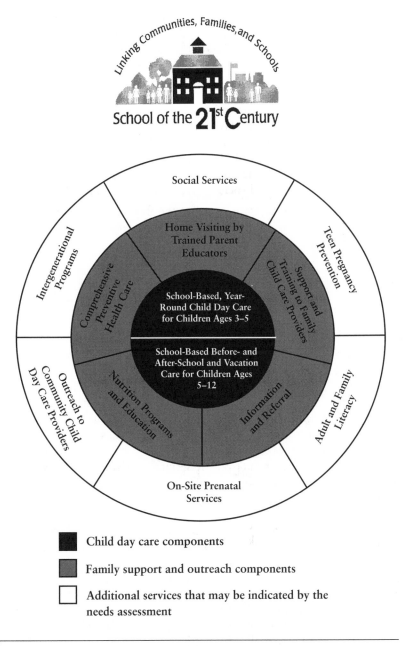

Linking Communities, Families, and Schools

School of the **21**ˢᵗ **C**entury

Social Services

Home Visiting by
Trained Parent
Educators

School-Based, Year-
Round Child Day Care
for Children Ages 3–5

School-Based Before- and
After-School and Vacation
Care for Children Ages
5–12

Intergenerational
Programs

Comprehensive
Preventive
Health Care

Teen Pregnancy
Prevention

Support and
Training to Family
Child Care Providers

Outreach to
Community Child
Day Care Providers

Nutrition Programs
and Education

Information
and Referral

Adult and Family
Literacy

On-Site Prenatal
Services

■ Child day care components

■ Family support and outreach components

□ Additional services that may be indicated by the
needs assessment

SOURCE: E. F. Zigler, M. Finn-Stevenson, and K. W. Marsland, "Child Day Care in the Schools: The School of the 21st Century." *Child Welfare* 24, no. 6 (1995): 1301–1326.

The Bush Center in Child Development and Social Policy at Yale University—under the heading of its directors, Edward Zigler and Matia Finn-Stevenson, the coauthors of this text—has guided the implementation of the program in school districts around the country. The Yale Bush Center plays a role in the School of the 21st Century program on at least five levels: (1) *conceptualization* of the idea; (2) *design* of the program; (3) provision of *technical assistance and training* to facilitate the implementation of the program; (4) *evaluation* of the program in several sites; and (5) ongoing *dissemination of information* about the program.

## Variations in Implementation

The majority of the schools provide all of the core services of the School of the 21st Century besides child care, usually phasing in the implementation over a three-to-five-year period, as opposed to implementing all services at one time. Many of the schools find that the families need additional services, such as literacy training and social services, or that the home visitation programs need to be extended to serve not only families with infants but also those with school-age children. The decision about which services to add and which services to begin with, as well as the development of an implementation plan, is based on an assessment of the needs of families, an inventory of services in the community, and an organizational audit to determine resources available within the school district and the community. In providing child care services, the intent of the School of the 21st Century is to add rather than supplant services that exist in order to ensure that all families have access to good quality affordable child care. By conducting a needs assessment, schools find out if such services are already available or if additional services are needed, and for what age group of children. In one rural school, for example, there was a need for additional school-age child care but not for preschool child care, since a good quality child care center in the community was able to address all the community's preschool needs. Rather than duplicate services, the school opted to collaborate with the existing center, and, after receiving a state Department of Education grant, the school was able to provide center staff with ongoing training opportunities.

Many of the schools find out that they need more rather than less child care than at first anticipated. In a Connecticut rural school district, the superintendent was thinking of providing a part-day school readiness program for preschoolers, noting that there may be no need for all-day child care among families living in such a rural community. However, in a needs assessment survey he found that parents did not want part-day preschool because the majority of them were working and needed all-day child care. The preschool child care in that school began by serving over fifty children and included an equal number of children on a waiting list.

In two communities, in Arkansas and Colorado, preschool and school-age child care was not sufficient to address the need; parents requested that provisions be made for infant child care as well. Caring for infants in a school setting may not be possible in all schools; hence we usually recommend that schools work with local family day care providers who offer good quality environments. However, in neither of these communities was family day care an option for parents, nor was there any other place for parents to leave their children. In both schools, changes in the building and special staffing arrangements had to be made to ensure that the program was appropriate for infants and toddlers.

The School of the 21st Century, New Beginnings, and the other initiatives described in this chapter are among several programs that call for schools to reach out to families and provide support services. These new roles for schools *are* being embraced by many educators. However, they represent a significant departure from the traditional mission of schools, and they are controversial. Before addressing the controversy, as well as the benefits, costs, and other issues associated with the schools' provision of child care and other support services, it is important to understand the need for school-based services and the connection between child care and education.

# 3  Linking Child Care and Education: The Research Base

In THE SCHOOL OF THE 21ST CENTURY we emphasize the critical connection that exists between child care and education. We believe that children's experiences at home, at a child care facility, or at another setting where they spend a significant part of their early years influence their acquisition of fundamental skills that are important for later success in school. Children may not be learning to read or write until they reach school-age. However, from the moment of birth they are learning about and attempting to understand their world. They become increasingly capable of organizing their knowledge, and they also acquire impressive social and language skills that serve as the basis for their later ability to profit from academic instruction.

Children develop these skills through play and social interactions in the context of everyday routines. A great deal of research has accumulated in the past three or four decades, enriching our understanding of how infants and young children learn and pointing to the critical importance of the early years of life. In this chapter, we will summarize some of what we have learned from this research and also will review studies on the effects of child care on children and the implications these studies have for education.

## The Role of the Environment

It is important to remember at the start that child care is an environment where many children spend the majority of their day, every day, beginning in infancy. As such, it influences the development of children.

Over the years, opposing views about the significance of environmental influences on development have been put forth in what has come to be referred to as the debate over the nature-nurture issue. Some have contended that development is wholly shaped by the genes (nature), whereas others have placed more weight on the influence of the environment (nurture). To this day there are individuals who may promote either of these extreme views. The majority of social scientists believe, however, that genetic and environmental factors interact to influence developmental outcome; a child is indeed born with genetic traits and biological conditions, but the child's experiences with parents and other adults and children are also critical.

## How Do Genes and the Environment Interact?

Scarr-Salapatek (1975) explains that development is the process by which the individual's genetic background (the genotype) is expressed in his or her observable or measurable traits (the phenotype). A given genotype, or what the child inherits, can give rise to many different phenotypes, or observable characteristics. Some genes, such as those for eye color or hair texture, are directly expressed as phenotypes and are not subject to environmental influence. However, some characteristics such as intelligence, although also partially inherited, are subject to a great deal of environmental influence. That is, the child is born with a genetic endowment, or potential, but whether or not he or she will realize this potential, and to what extent, depends on environmental circumstances and the experiences the child encounters (Plomin and Daniels 1987).

Intelligence is one trait that is highly influenced by both the genes and the environment, but there are others, such as creativity, a talent for art or music, or athletic ability. Children may be endowed with talent or special skill, but if these endowments are not nurtured they will not be expressed to their full potential. Hence, there is no guarantee that a child born with an inclination for music will excel in music; the child also needs the opportunity to learn to play musical instruments and to practice playing. Conversely, in the case of a child who has "no ear for music" no amount of music lessons or parental encouragement will result in a prodigy.

But the role of the environment is not quite as simple as the above example would indicate. One factor to consider is that children vary in the way they respond to conditions in the environment and to various life experiences. For example, although a stressful home life and poverty negatively affect some children, other children in similar circumstances are better able to cope and evidence a resilience that enables them to develop and succeed despite the odds against them (Luthar, Doernberger, and Zigler 1993; Werner and Smith 1992).

Another factor to consider is that development entails a complex transaction between environmental and genetic factors (Plomin, DeFries, and Fulker 1988; Sameroff and Chandler 1975). Consider, for example, irritability in infants. Some babies seem to be irritable from the moment of birth and are often described by their parents as "difficult." The irritability may be the result of genetic makeup or of a biological condition (for example, some premature babies tend to be irritable for a few months after birth). If the parent of a difficult baby is also irritable, or if the family is experiencing stressful life conditions, the irritability in the baby may be exacerbated, but if the parent is calm and the family is functional, the extent to which the baby's irritability will be expressed long term is reduced (Scarr and McCartney 1983). In this case the family represents the environment the child experiences, and we can see here that the environment clearly influences development. However, the genes also can influence and shape the environment; the difficult baby may be born to relatively calm parents, but constant crying and the baby's inability to sleep through the night may stress parents to the point where they are unable to cope and the family environment becomes dysfunctional.

## The Early Years

**Risk Factors.**   Environmental factors and one's experiences enhance or impede development at all stages of life. However, the early years are especially open to positive influence. These early years also are extremely vulnerable and subject to negative influences. An extensive review of the research indicates that how individuals function and how well they do in school and later in life hinges in large part on early experiences (Carnegie Corporation of New York 1994). Of significance here are environmental influences on brain development and maturation. Some studies, made possible with advances in brain scans and other powerful research tools, indicate that the child's early life experiences have a direct impact on the structure and function of the brain and affect various cognitive processes such as memory (Shore 1997). Under-nutrition, which is prevalent not only in developing countries but in the United States as well (Cook and Brown 1994), also has an impact on the developing brain. When it is experienced prenatally or during the first few months of life, the outcome is retardation in brain development and changes in the function of the brain (Thatcher et al. 1997), conditions that are often irreversible. If the child is undernourished later in childhood the consequences include an inability to perform academically and to profit from instruction (Center on Hunger, Poverty, and Nutrition Policy 1995).

There are other risk factors that can have a significant influence on the growing child: prenatal health-related problems; stress and dysfunction in the family; parents' failure to nurture the child, resulting in insecure attachments. The way parents interact with the child is also of significance; inappropriate interactions might, for example, result in low self-esteem and a lack of motivation that will affect the child's ability to do well in school.

The risk factors children experience seldom occur in isolation. Drawing on the work of Michael Rutter (1979, 1996) among others, the report of the Carnegie Corporation of New York (1994, 12) notes that

---

BOX 3.1   Brain Development in Young Children

We have known for many years that (1) human development hinges on
the interplay between nature and nurture and (2) that infants enter the world
with a vast array of perceptual and other skills and a predisposition to learning. However, breakthroughs in neuroscience have shown how environmental
experiences impact development. The new knowledge emphasizes the early
years as a time of opportunity for growth and development but also a time
when the developing brain is especially vulnerable. By the age of 3, the brains
of children are two and a half times more active than the brains of adults, and
they remain that way for the first ten years of life (Shore 1997). Healthy brain
development depends on environmental stimulation: caring for babies and
toddlers, playing with them, responding to their signals for attention: "Recent
brain research suggests that warm, responsive care is not only comforting for
an infant, it is also critical to healthy development. In fact, strong, secure
attachment to a nurturing caregiver appears to have a protective biological
function, 'immunizing' an infant to some degree against the adverse effects of
later stress or trauma" (Shore 1997, 27). It is for this reason that we stress
how important caregivers are to children's development.

---

the important point about risk factors is that they are often multiplicative, not
additive, in their effects. Consider, for example, children's risk for social and
academic difficulties. When children showed only one risk factor, their outcomes were no worse than those of children showing none. . . . But when children had two or more risks, they were four times as likely to develop social
and academic problems.

**Protective Factors.**   Just as there are environmental conditions that can
adversely influence growth and development, there are other conditions
that can help children and ensure optimal development. Some such protective factors are access to social support and supportive services when the
need arises not only for the child but also for the family as a whole. Children who experience the stresses associated with the divorce of their parents, for example, are found to be able to cope if they have a supportive
parent or another adult who can help them sort through their conflicting
feelings (Gunnar 1996; Werner and Smith 1992).

Having parents who employ positive rather than punitive child-rearing
and disciplinary techniques during childhood and adolescent years is also a
protective factor that is conducive to optimal development. In her studies,
Baumarind (1990) found that authoritative parenting, entailing both control and discipline but in a warm and loving environment, is consistently
associated with children who evidence social responsibility, independence,
and achievement orientation. Additionally, growing up with parents or
other caregivers who are dependable and nurturing in their interactions—

hugging, playing, reading, and talking with the child, and otherwise showing the child that they care—is conducive to the development of children who are happy and confident and want to learn and succeed. Infants and preschoolers whose parents interact with them in these ways are more likely to do well in elementary school (Entwisle and Alexander 1990).

Researchers also have found consistent correlation between the quality of family life and cognitive achievement, noting that parental attentiveness and the availability of playthings during preschool are strongly related to cognitive development (Bradley et al. 1989). Not only playthings are important but also the opportunity to play with them. Prior to the 1960s, developmental psychologists and educators attached little importance to play, regarding play as a frivolous activity that had little or no developmental value. Today, however, we realize that play is of crucial importance. Often referred to as the work of children, play is the medium through which children gain much of their knowledge and understanding about the world around them (Phillips 1996). It is also through play and social interactions that children acquire cognitive and language skills (Hughes 1991), and there is a correlation between play and intelligence (Singer and Singer 1979).

## Child Care as an Environment

The family is indeed the place where most of the child's learning takes place, and parents are, as we have noted previously, the child's first teachers. However, there are other sources of environmental influence on child development. Urie Bronfenbrenner (1979) underscores this point, noting the "contextual" or "ecological" influences on development and behavior. These influences include the family as well as a range of other factors emanating from the larger physical and social milieu—schools, neighborhoods, churches, economic conditions, and government policies, to name a few.

Child care, whether it is care in a center or a family day care home or by an individual nanny or a relative, is also a setting in which children are growing up and, as such, is viewed as one of several sources of influence on children's development (Hayes, Palmer, and Zaslow 1990). Just as the quality of family life influences the course of development, so does the quality of the child care environment have an impact, for better or worse, on growth and development.

This latter point is evident in a national study on cost, quality, and child outcomes in child care centers (Helburn 1995). The study examined the relationships between the cost of child care, the actual experiences of the children in the centers, and the effects of these experiences on children's development. The study noted several disturbing findings, the major one being that although child care centers vary widely, most centers are mediocre in quality and "sufficiently poor to interfere with children's emotional and intellectual development" (1). A previous study that looked at child care centers also found that child care centers, especially those serving children from working, middle-class families, are generally of low quality (White-book, Phillips, and Howes 1990). A study on the quality of care in family day care homes (Galinsky et al. 1994) found that only one in nine such settings offers quality care. As we noted in Chapter 1, the same study found that care by relatives was even worse in terms of quality.

## Child Care Research: Historical Background

In order to appreciate these most current research findings and to understand the link between child care and education, it might be helpful at this point to examine the *history* of the research on the effects of child care on children.

The research has been classified into three waves, reflecting the fact that the research has become increasingly more sophisticated, as well as realistic, over the years. No longer do we ask if children should be in child care; we accept this as a reality. Early on, in what has come to be know as the "alarm phase," researchers asked: "Should children spend significant amounts of time in child care? Is child care harmful to children? What is the difference between children raised at home and those in child care?"

This concern over children in child care stemmed in part from the research on maternal deprivation conducted by several developmentalists, among them John Bowlby (1969, 1989). Bowlby studied infants and young children raised in institutional settings such as orphanages. These children were fed and changed but had very limited contact with caregivers or other children, and they were given no toys or playthings, so they spent most of their time alone in a crib. Bowlby found that as they developed, these children were unable to relate to other children or adults and were afraid to play or explore their environment. Bowlby's findings, and those of others studying children reared under such conditions, contributed to the de-institutionalization movement of the 1950s and 1960s, wherein orphanages were replaced with foster homes. The research, which underscored the role of the mother in the child's development, led to the conclusion that mothers who leave their children in day nurseries were placing them at risk of permanent negative effects.

Also emphasizing the role of the mother in the child's development was the research on attachment. Ainsworth and her colleagues (1978), for example, noted that children who develop a secure and enduring attachment to their mother are more likely to develop optimally than those who were insecure in their attachment.

We know now that the key in the secure attachment process is the opportunity for children to develop trust and to be in a loving relationship with a primary caregiver (as opposed to the exclusive focus on the biological mother). This relationship between child and caregiver raised a concern that children in child care would develop attachments to their providers rather than their mothers, but this was found not to be the case. Nevertheless, the mother-child attachment was used by researchers to examine differences between children attending child care and those raised exclusively at home.

Because they point to some of the risk and protective factors in the environment where children are growing up, these early studies have contributed a great deal to our understanding of children's development. However, their application to children in child care is problematic for two reasons. First, the major question addressed—whether or not children should be in child care—is largely irrelevant, given that mothers in increasing numbers are working and have no choice but to place their children in some form of child care. Second, it has become evident over the years that there are variations in child care facilities that need to be taken into account.

Hence, the second wave of the research on child care focused on variations in the quality of care, with researchers asking: Do children thrive in certain types of child care more so than in others? There was also a quest to define quality care (Lamb 1998).

**Focus on Quality.** The concern over quality dates back a number of years; for example, in the 1970s federal standards were established, although not implemented, in order to ensure that states' regulation of child care centers were based on what was known about quality care (Zigler and Gordon 1982). Because quality is an elusive, value-laden term, one of the first steps was to document what factors in child care contribute to good quality care. An early study on quality was the National Child Care Study (Ruopp et al. 1979), which identified elements in child care that are predictive of positive developmental outcomes for children. The results indicated that preschoolers in child care centers that had small group sizes and trained caregivers performed better on cognitive tests, were more cooperative, had more advanced language skills, and were more persistent on tasks than children in centers not meeting these requirements.

Since that initial study, other researchers have focused on defining good quality child care and also have found that not only group size but also staff/child ratios are important indicators of quality, as is caregiver training, which was found to promote positive social and cognitive development in children (Phillips 1987; Phillips et al. 1998; Clarke-Stewart, Allhusen, and Clements 1995). In other words, caregivers were found to apply their knowledge when they interacted with children (Helburn and Howes 1996). Researchers also found that good quality programs provide developmentally appropriate experiences for the children and that in good quality centers the caregivers are warm, nurturant, and provide consistent verbal

---

### BOX 3.2    States' Role in the Provision of Quality Care

The quality of child care is important because it is "closely linked with children's social, cognitive, and language development" (Helburn and Howes 1996, 62). In defining quality, researchers have studied process quality—which refers to the experiences of children in the child care facility: Do they have playthings and the opportunity to play? Are their caregivers responding to them?—as well as structural quality. The latter refers to aspects of the child care environment that can be regulated by government: staff/child ratios, group size, caregiver training, and the amount of space per child, as well as health and safety issues. Young and her colleagues (1997) note that although state regulations represent a basic minimum, the regulations in most states fall below even that minimum. In other words, a child care facility may be licensed by a state, but that does not mean that the facility provides good quality care. Schools providing child care are often exempt from state licensing requirements. However, since these requirements are so minimal, we recommend that schools apply for state license and that they further strive to provide high-quality care by working toward voluntary accreditation by the National Association for the Education of Young Children.

---

and cognitive stimulation during daily interactions, informal play times, and planned activities. Verbal stimulation, such as reading and speaking with children and listening to them, enhanced children's language development (Howes and Smith 1995; Phillips et al. 1987; Clarke-Stewart, Allhusen, and Clements 1995). Giving the children freedom to choose when, what, and with whom to play, a style of care often referred to as child-initiated activity, was also found to be an important element of good quality. Clarke-Stewart (1982) found that children who were offered choices and encouraged to initiate activities were more competent than those who were in centers where they were told what to do.

Besides caregiver training, there are two other elements associated with staffing and related to the quality of care children receive: staff turnover and staff compensation. Children need consistency and continuity of care, and the younger they are the more important it is for them to come to know, rely on, and establish a relationship with the caregiver. Children who experience stability of care, that is, those who are cared for by the same caregiver over time, develop a sense of trust in their world and are found to perform well on measures of language, cognitive, and social development (Rubenstein and Howes 1979). They are well adjusted when they "graduate" from child care and are in first grade (Howes and Hamilton 1993). However, whether or not caregivers keep their job long enough for children to benefit is related directly to work conditions such as salaries and benefits. Generally, caregiver salaries are very low, and benefits and career advancement are non-existent, a situation that contributes to a high staff turnover, with close to 40 percent of caregivers leaving the job within six months (Helburn and Howes 1996). In centers where staff salaries are higher than average, so is the quality of care provided to the children (Helburn and Howes 1996; Whitebook, Phillips, and Howes 1990).

Parent involvement is another aspect of good quality child care. Howes (1987) found that in good quality child care programs, parents are involved in the day-to-day activities; they are welcome to observe and participate in the classroom; they serve on committees and have some say in decisionmaking. Ideally, parents and caregivers should interact often so there is continuity in the child's experiences at home and in child care. Unfortunately, many parents simply drop off or pick up their children and spend a minimal amount of time interacting with caregivers (Zigler and Turner 1982).

Although we have discussed the various aspects of good quality child care separately, these aspects of care actually cluster together. In other words, programs that have appropriate staff/child ratios, small group size, and trained providers are also likely to have stability of care (as evident in low staff turnover) and to encourage parents to participate and become involved in their children's child care experiences (Whitebook, Phillips, and Howes 1990; Howes, Phillips, and Whitebook 1992). As Phillips (1987) notes, "Good things go together in child care. . . . Quality may be best understood . . . as a blend or configuration of ingredients" (121).

## Research on the Effects of Child Care

There are different requirements for good quality care, depending on the age of the children; what is appropriate for a 4-year-old in terms of group size and staff/child ratio, for example, is inappropriate for a younger child. It is important, therefore, to look at quality in relation to the research on the effects of child care on children of different ages.

### *Effects of the Child Care Environment During Infancy*

One out of every two infants one year of age or younger is in child care and tends to be in child care for his or her entire childhood. Often, parents choose family day care for infants. If it is of good quality, the small group size and home-like atmosphere of family day care is a good choice. However, as we indicated earlier, only one in nine family day care homes were found to be of good quality.

Group size and staffing issues are of the most importance in infant care. Generally, the younger the child, the smaller the group should be. Also, infants, since they are totally dependent on their caregiver not only for routine care and feeding but also for play and stimulation, need to be able to form a close relationship with a provider over time. Hence, a 1:3 or 1:4

staff/child ratio is imperative and allows the provider to relate individually and sensitively to each of the infants under one year of age; for slightly older toddlers (ages twelve to twenty-four months) a 1:5 staff/child ratio is acceptable (Bredenkamp and Copple 1997).

Another important component of quality infant care concerns the physical space available to them. An infant care environment should be free from safety hazards and offer young children sufficient freedom and area to move about. Infants are learning to roll over, crawl, walk, and explore the surroundings, so it is important that the environment enables these developmental goals.

Staff stability and continuity of care have been found to be particularly important quality indicators in infant/toddler care. One of the most important developmental tasks for infants is to form secure attachments to primary and secondary caregivers. As Carollee Howes (1987) notes:

> The child who experiences many different caregivers may not become attached to any of them and thus will fail to be secure in child care. The loss of an attachment figure can be very painful to a young child. The child who forms attachments to a series of caregivers, all of whom leave, may find it too painful to continue the cycle and conclude that human relationships are to be avoided. (82)

In an article detailing the steps necessary to create and sustain a high-quality group care program for infants and toddlers, Lally, Torres, and Phelps (1994) suggest that every child be assigned a primary caregiver with whom to build a close and special relationship. These researchers also suggest that the assignment be carried over an extended period of time—beyond standard age groupings. Child care programs that follow these principles do not switch a child's primary caregiver when that child "ages out of" a specific group but rather enable the child to be cared for by the same individual over time.

Lally, Torres, and Phelps (1994) also identify the task of meeting the individual needs of each child within a group setting as an essential component of quality infant/toddler care. Flexibility is the key for developmentally appropriate practice in infant/toddler programs. Children in this age group should be allowed to remain on their own schedules rather than forced to comply with externally determined schedules. Thus, infants and toddlers should be fed when they are hungry, changed when their diaper is wet or soiled, put down for a nap when they are tired, played with when they are alert and happy, and soothed when they are frustrated. In order to foster a sense of security, infant care providers in particular need to be responsive and sensitive to their charges' cues and bids for attention (Rubenstein and Howes 1983).

Rubenstein, Howes, and Boyle (1981) found that infants and toddlers in child care programs where they received a lot of attention and verbal stimulation from the staff tended to speak earlier than those in programs that were less verbally rich. In later studies, Rubenstein and Howes (1983), and Phillips, Howes, and Whitebook (1992) found that infants and toddlers under the care of more proficient and capable caregivers overall were more socially competent. McCartney and her colleagues (1982) also noted the importance of skilled caregivers. In their study, children who were enrolled as infants in verbally rich centers were less anxious as preschoolers than children who had been enrolled as infants in centers with low verbal interaction. Research conducted with infants and toddlers who were enrolled in family child care homes of varying levels of quality revealed that higher overall levels of quality were associated with higher levels of children's play with both objects and adults.

One of the few longitudinal studies of the effects of early child care was conducted in Los Angeles by Carollee Howes and her colleagues. This study tracked both a sample of children who were enrolled in high- or low-quality programs as toddlers and a matched group of toddlers who were home with their mothers. Initial findings revealed that the toddlers who were in high-quality centers were more compliant and self-regulated than those in low-quality centers (Howes and Olenick 1986). When researchers saw these children next, they were in a preschool setting. Those who had been enrolled in high-quality centers as toddlers were observed to engage in more social pretend play and to have a positive affect with their peers, whereas the children who had been in low-quality centers as toddlers had more difficulty interacting with peers than either the high-quality group or the maternal care group (Howes 1990). In kindergarten, the children who had received high-quality toddler care were better adjusted to school than those who had been in low-quality programs as toddlers, and the children who had been in low-quality programs were more destructible, more hostile, less task-oriented, and less considerate of others (Howes 1990). Thus, the effects of infant and toddler care, whether of high or low quality, appear to last into kindergarten, if not farther into the school-age years.

In the same study, the researchers also found that the children who entered high-quality child care as infants did not appear different from the children who entered high-quality care as older children. The mere fact that children were enrolled in child care earlier did not put them at a disadvantage, *as long as the early care program was of high quality*. The long-term positive effects of high-quality infant/toddler care revealed in the study led Howes to conclude: "Children and their families can benefit from high-quality center child care for infants and toddlers. The centers that had good adult-child ratios and stable trained caregivers provided care that enhanced the development of the children and supported the families that use the care" (1987, 86).

In early research on the topic, controversy surrounded the question of whether or not early enrollment in child care negatively affects the development of secure attachment relationships. Belsky (1987, 1988) maintained that full-time infant care prior to the first birthday puts children at risk for developing insecure maternal attachments that cause later developmental problems. However, Phillips and her colleagues (1987) maintained that much of the studies upon which Belsky based his conclusions did not reflect the importance and diversity of infant care quality. Subsequent research has shown, as we will note later, that Belsky was both right and wrong in his claim.

There was also the issue, discussed earlier, that the use of traditional attachment measures was inappropriate in the attempt to ascertain the effects of infant care. Howes (1989) has argued that the few research studies that have measured attachment with a more appropriate instrument have found no differences in attachment between employed and nonemployed mothers. Howes has also asserted that infants in high-quality care are more likely to form secure attachments to their caregivers and that these attachments may compensate for the effects of an insecure maternal attachment (Howes 1989). Howes based her argument on the evidence she and her colleagues collected in a research project examining relationships between mother-child and caregiver-child attachments (Howes et al. 1988). Results from this study revealed that children who had concordant secure attachments (both attachment to mother and attachment to caregiver were secure) were the most socially competent, whereas the least socially competent children had concordant insecure attachments to mothers and caregivers. Interestingly, children who had secure attachments to their mother but not to their caregivers were classified as less competent than those who had secure attachments to their caregivers but not to their mothers. Thus, a secure attachment to a caregiver that was fostered in a high-quality infant care setting may serve to modify the negative effects normally associated with having an insecure maternal attachment.

Further evidence from this study suggested that parents of children with insecure maternal attachments were more likely to enroll them in lower quality child care settings, thus compounding the potential for later developmental problems (Howes et al. 1988). Several other studies have identified a link between family characteristics and the quality of child care parents choose for their children (NICHD 1997). Parents who are more competent and confident in their child-rearing practices and who are under less stress tend to select higher quality child care than those who are stressed and use less than optimal child-rearing styles (NICHD 1997; Howes and Olenick 1986; Howes 1990).

## Effects of the Child Care Environment During Preschool Years

Data from the National Day Care Survey of 1990 (Hofferth 1991, 1996) reveal that employed mothers adopt different care arrangements for preschool-age children (ages 3–4) than they do for infants and toddlers. The percentage of children being cared for by a parent or by a relative decline dramatically after the infancy/toddler years. The percentage of children in family child care homes also declines. At the same time the popularity of center-based care soars; well over one-third of all preschool-age children with working mothers attend child care centers.

The range of center-based care is wide and includes nursery schools; for-profit and non-profit centers; church-operated or church-based programs; child care centers located at worksites; schools or parent cooperatives; and early intervention programs such as Head Start, few of which have day-long services. Parents enroll their preschoolers in these programs not only because they need to work but also because they believe these programs can provide their children with stimulation, learning, and an opportunity to interact with other children and adults (Clarke-Stewart, Allhusen, and Clements 1995).

Because center-based programs for 3- and 4-year-olds have been in existence for a longer time than have infant/toddler programs, and because they have been so popular with both employed and nonemployed mothers, the body of research examining the best type of group care program for preschoolers is much richer than that examining infant/toddler programs. Overall, the research has revealed that preschool-age children do better when they are cared for in fairly small groups with a sufficient number of caregivers to ensure safety and to allow a significant amount of individual attention. In low-quality programs, where children are cared for in large groups with an insufficient number of well-qualified staff, children tend to wander aimlessly and to compete with other children for toys and for their caregiver's attention (Vandell and Powers 1983). In contrast, preschoolers in programs with smaller group sizes and better staff/child ratios tend to be engaged in meaningful activities such as playing with various toys and playing roles (e.g., playing dress-up, playing with kitchen items, cash registers, and workbenches), looking at books, listening to stories, building structures with blocks, and practicing their large motor skills on climbers and riding toys. These children also tend to interact more positively with their peers and their teachers (Clarke-Stewart, Allhusen, and Clements 1995; Rubenstein and Howes 1979).

The research focusing on programs for preschoolers has revealed much the same pattern of effects as that which focused on infants and toddlers. In a study of 100 randomly selected children in ten Pennsylvania child care centers, Kontos and Fein (1987) found a strong correlation between high-quality care and social competence. Holloway and Reichhart-Erickson (1988) found a similar relationship. Their study documented that 4-year-olds in high-quality centers or nursery schools were more likely to exhibit higher social problem-solving skills than those in programs of poorer quality. In a study that indicated that preschoolers in high-quality centers were more likely to engage in positive behavior and positive interactions with adults, Vandell also notes a pattern of positive social effects (Vandell and Corsaniti 1990; Vandell and Powers 1983).

One of the most significant studies focusing on the effects of child care on preschoolers was conducted in Bermuda. The 166 children in this study were enrolled in one of the nine child care centers on the island of Bermuda, with the centers representing a wide range of quality. Findings indicated that the quality of the center predicted social behavior in preschoolers (McCartney et al. 1982). After collecting further data, McCartney (1984) reported that children in the higher quality centers performed better on four separate tests of intellectual and language development than children in lower quality centers. Extending this study, Phillips and her colleagues (1987) also found that high-quality care was related to higher levels of intelligence, considerateness, sociability, and task-orientation in the children, as rated by both parents and caregivers. These findings from the Bermuda study illustrate clearly that developmental outcomes are linked closely to the quality of child care during the preschool years.

Longitudinal studies of children enrolled in preschool child care programs have been few, but the ones that have been done indicate that the positive effects of high-quality preschool care last well into the elementary school years (Howes and Hamilton 1993; Vandell, Hendersen, and Wilson 1988). Vandell, Hendersen, and Wilson (1988) conducted a follow-up study of the children who had participated in the 1983 Vandell and Powers study. At age 8 the children who had been enrolled in lower quality child care centers during preschool were less socially competent, as rated by both parents and peers. These 8-year-olds also rated themselves more negatively than the children who had been enrolled in either moderate or excellent quality centers.

## Effects of the Child Care Environment During School-Age Years

School-age children (ages 5–12) with employed mothers are in a wide variety of care arrangements during their non-school hours, or they are left alone at home in what has come to be called "self-care." The National Child Care Survey (Hofferth 1991) documents markedly different patterns of care for 5-year-olds in comparison to those ages 6 and over. Twenty-nine percent of 5-year-olds are in center-based care, and 13 percent are in family child care. For those children older than 5, 18 percent are in some type of center-based care, and 8 percent are supervised in family child care homes. This pattern is probably indicative of the fact that most 5-year-olds are enrolled in kindergarten classes at public and private schools, and, for the most part, these school programs cover only three to four hours of the day. Thus, most parents also must find some type of wrap-around care for the hours before and/or after kindergarten.

---

BOX 3.3    School-Age Children: Basic Facts

The National Center for Out-of-School Time in Wellesley, Massachusetts indicates that:

- Children spend less than 10 percent of their waking hours in schools, since schools are typically open for only part of the day, and for less than half of the days in a year.

- Children spend more of their out-of-school time watching television than in any other single activity.

- Nearly 5 million children spend time without adult supervision during the week. These children are at risk for truancy from school, stress, poor academic grades, excessive risk-taking behavior, and substance abuse.

- Children who attend school-age child care programs during the hours when their parents are working experience positive effects on their development: They get better grades in school; they are exposed to learning opportunities and have a chance to develop positive friendships. There is an enormous need for school-age programs; it is estimated that 17 million parents need care for their school-age children during their hours of work.

---

The data from the National Child Care Survey show that among school-agers the likelihood of being enrolled in any type of formal child care arrangement declines as age increases. Data also show that after age 5, families are increasingly likely to mention various extracurricular activities such as lessons, clubs, and/or sports as their primary source of care for school-age children. Seventeen percent of 6- through 9-year-olds and 27 percent of 10- through 12-year-olds participate in sports, join clubs, or take lessons, but they are not in any form of supervised child care. Just as enrollment in extracurricular activities increases with age so does the incidence of children in self-care, from a low of 1 percent at age 6 to a high of 14 percent at age 12. According to the Children's Defense Fund 5 million children between the ages of 5 and 14 are left to care for themselves during non-school hours (CDF 1998). Since parents may underreport the amount of time their children are in self-care (Seligson and Fink 1989), the number of children who are home alone before and after school may be even higher.

Determining the exact number of children in each different type of care arrangement is difficult because most parents of school-agers depend on a hodgepodge of arrangements. During the school year one child might be home by herself before school most mornings, might attend an after-school program run by her church most afternoons, and might participate in special interest programs during some school vacations. Another child might depend on a heavy schedule of after-school activities—playing soccer at school on Mondays, taking swimming lessons at the Y on Tuesdays, being tutored in math on Wednesdays, visiting his father on Thursdays, and going to Boy Scouts on Fridays. Still another child might attend a drop-in program at the local Boys and Girls Clubs during the week. On days when school is closed for teacher in-services and local holidays, she might spend the day at her mother's office, doing her homework, playing with the photocopy machine, and talking to friends on the phone. During the summer, she might attend a residential camp program for two weeks, day camp for one month, and then visit her grandmother for the final weeks before school starts.

Schedules like those described above are quite common but very difficult to arrange. Gaps and scheduling breakdowns are usually filled with periods of self-care. Cain and Hofferth (1989) have suggested that most parents rely on self-care mostly for their older school-age children, and then only for a very few hours per day. In their study, 64 percent of the children in self-care before school were alone for less than one hour and 88 percent of those in self-care after school were alone for less than two hours. Steinberg (1986) has found that parents monitor their child's activities in self-care by checking in with frequent telephone calls. Still, a significant number of school-age children—5-, 6-, and 7-year-olds as well as older children—are left home alone for extended periods of time without any adult supervision (Seligson and Fink 1989). Todd, Albrecht, and Coleman (1990) have reported that parents often send their children to community agencies and libraries, even though no supervision is taking place. Seligson and Fink (1989) make the same point; they note that town libraries, community centers, and shopping malls are often destinations for school-age children in self-care.

Research on school-age child care is a relatively young field. Only in the past few years have standards of quality emerged (ASQ 1995; Albrecht 1991; National Association of Elementary School Principals 1993). As was true with both infant/toddler and preschool child care programs, higher quality school-age programs have smaller group sizes and higher staff/child ratios. Kay Albrecht (1991), of Project Home Safe, recommends ratios no lower than 1:10 and group sizes no larger than twenty for 5-year-olds in group care, ratios no lower than 1:12 and group sizes no larger than twenty-four for 6- to 8-year-olds, and ratios no lower than 1:13 and group sizes no larger than twenty-six for those 9 years of age and older. For children ages 5 and 6, the National Association of Elementary School Principals (1993) recommends ratios no lower than 1:10, and for children over age 6, ratios no lower than 1:12—with no groups larger than twenty-five.

The quality of the physical environment in school-age programs is a particular area of concern, since so many after-school programs do not have dedicated space. Many programs operate in a school cafeteria, gymnasium, or all-purpose room and thus face a challenge in having to set-up each day.

The environment of high-quality school-age programs should not appear institutional or barren but should offer cozy home-like areas with rugs, cushions, and comfortable furniture (Albrecht 1991). The space should be designed to include a variety of interest centers (e.g., a woodworking area, science corner, homework table, etc.) as well as a number of private areas where children can curl up with a book or talk quietly with a friend. Access to outdoor space where children can play sports, ride bicycles, or examine bugs is also essential (Albrecht 1991).

In terms of curricula and staff qualifications, Michelle Seligson and Dale Fink put it best: "Quality school-age child care is neither baby-sitting nor more school" (1989, 50). Staff of school-age programs need to have formal education and training in child development, education, recreation, or a similar field. They need to be able to design flexible programming that excites the interest of both younger and older school-age children. The best programs actively involve the children in the planning process. After all, "school-agers vote with their feet. . . . Many will ask to stay home alone rather than attend a program whose activities are geared, in their opinion, for 'little kids'" (Albrecht and Plantz 1993, 15).

Some parents, teachers, and school administrators have argued that after-school programs should be an extension of the school day. In their eyes, the main purpose of a school-age child care program should be to improve academic achievement by reinforcing curriculum from the school day. This fairly common opinion prompted the National Association of Elementary School Principals to discredit specifically the notion that school-age child care programs should be focused exclusively on academics, homework, and cognitive development: A good school-age child care program is not simply a longer school day. Good programs should be different in both structure and content, since children need to shift gears after school as much as adults do after work (National Association of Elementary School Principals 1993, 2). The National Association of Elementary School Principals does recommend, however, that staff of school-age child care programs develop partnerships with both teachers and parents to benefit children's academic, physical, social, and emotional development. Caregivers are sometimes the only link parents have with the school. Most employed parents interact with caregivers more frequently than they interact with their child's teachers.

Because the field is still developing, research into the effects of school-age child care has not yet reached the second wave mentioned above: Only a few studies (e.g., Goyette-Ewing 1992) examine the quality of care in school-age child care programs. For the most part, researchers are still asking: Do children benefit from being enrolled in school-age child care programs? Are children harmed by self-care? Do significant differences exist between school-age children cared for by their parents, school-age children in child care programs, and school-age children in self-care?

Whether self-care harms or benefits children is a controversial question. Some people think that self-care can be beneficial and teach children independence. However, the research indicates otherwise. A study comparing children in supervised programs and children in self-care found that children left alone reported feeling afraid three times more frequently than those left with siblings, and they reported feeling afraid twenty times more frequently than those left with adult caretakers (Long and Long 1984). Children in this study were primarily afraid that someone would break into their home while they were alone and hurt them, but a significant number also reported fearing their siblings would hurt them. Steinberg (1986) found a direct negative correlation between the amount of supervision children received after school and their susceptibility to peer pressure for vandalism. More recently, Posner and Vandell (1991) reported findings that indicate children's participation in after-school programs can result in enhanced self-esteem and improved academic and social competence. However, other studies, measuring self-esteem, social competence (Rodman, Pratto, and Nelson 1985), fear, school adjustment, and academic achievement (Galambos and Garbarino 1985), found no differences between school-age children in self-care and those being closely supervised by an adult. Once researchers begin to take the varying quality of adult supervision into account when designing studies comparing self-care and adult-care groups, perhaps some of the inconsistencies in these findings will be resolved.

Two studies focusing on either end of the age spectrum revealed interesting results about the potential and importance of school-age child care. In a study that compared kindergartners enrolled in a high-quality after-school program with a matched group of kindergartners who were not, Howes, Olenick, and Der-Kiureghian (1987) found that the children who had attended a child care program in addition to their regular kindergarten program were more socially competent and popular with their peers than those who had attended only kindergarten. Another study surveyed over 1,000 eighth-grade students and their parents about the amount of time the students spent unsupervised after school and about their substance use. The researchers reported that across all socioeconomic, gender, family structure, and academic achievement categories, students who were in self-care for more than eleven hours per week were twice as likely to have used alcohol, tobacco, and marijuana (Richardson et al. 1989). Despite the differences in the design of their studies and the results reported, the authors of both studies concluded with a recommendation that communities develop more child care programs for two underserved populations—kindergartners and young adolescents.

After-school programs also can have an impact on juvenile crime. Data compiled by the FBI and the National Center on Juvenile Justice indicate that the peak hours for violent juvenile crime are between 3:00 P.M. and

8:00 P.M., when children are likely to be without supervision (Fight Crime/Invest in Kids 1997), and that the availability of after-school programs can actually reduce juvenile crime (Riley et al. 1994).

## The Quality-Availability-Affordability of Care

The more recent, second wave research has show that high-quality child care does not harm children and that in some cases it enhances their development. Quality child care prepares children for academic success by fostering reasoning abilities, creativity, and communication skills. It enhances self-esteem and self-control. It promotes positive social development by teaching children to share and to empathize and to respect others. Children from low income families, in particular, have been shown to benefit from high-quality care (Clarke-Stewart and Fein 1983; Zigler and Gordon 1982). Research indicates that the other half of the story is that poor quality care is developmentally detrimental, just as good quality care can benefit children (Helburn 1995; Helburn and Howes 1996).

According to Clarke-Stewart and her colleagues (Clarke-Stewart 1982; Clarke-Stewart, Allhusen, and Clements 1995), a third wave of child care research has emerged. This phase asks the question, How do child care environments interact with family factors to affect children's development? Much like Bronfenbrenner's (1979) theory of nested environments, third wave research assumes that home and child care environments are linked and mutually influential. The few researchers who have examined the effects of children's experiences across the two care settings have found that they are additive and interactive. For example, Clarke-Stewart, Allhusen, and Clements (1995) found that a combination of home and child care variables predicted developmental outcomes better than either did alone. In a review of several studies, Gamble and Zigler (1986) found that infant care is more likely to have negative effects on children from highly stressed homes. Howes (1988) reported that children with a history of high-quality care both at home and in a child care setting were better able to adjust to first grade than those who had "less fortunate child care and family histories" (222). With regard to infants in child care, the NICHD (1997) study found that the quality of child care had a small but nevertheless statistically significant relation to infants' cognitive and language development. Equally important, however, was the finding in the same study that "family characteristics and the quality of the mother's relationship with the child" are more important predictors of the infants' development than the child care factors (NICHD 1997, 21).

If we know that low-quality child care contributes, in part, to a child's risk of developing poorly, we should ensure that all child care programs are of high quality. After all, we know what high-quality child care looks like. As we indicated earlier, quality programs are those with warm, well-trained, well-compensated, and stable staffs; low child-to-caregiver ratios; small group sizes; and developmentally appropriate activities and environments. All families and children deserve access to such child care. However, high-quality care is scarce and more expensive than lower quality care. The quality, availability, and affordability of child care are linked. Unfortunately, the higher the quality of care, the less affordable and available it generally is.

Currently the state of child care quality in the United States is pretty dismal, as we indicated in the opening of the chapter. Of even more concern, it appears that the quality of care has been declining in recent years. For example, group sizes and child/staff ratios have increased since the late 1970s, with many programs not meeting state regulations, let alone the National Association for the Education of Young Children's (NAEYC) quality standards (Kisker et al. 1990). Staff turnover has soared from 15 percent in 1977 to 41 percent in 1988, while child care wages, when adjusted for inflation, have fallen more than 20 percent (Whitebook, Phillips, and Howes 1990).

Researchers have begun to recognize that the prevalence of low-quality care may have contributed to some of the early first wave findings that indicated harmful effects from child care. For example, the National Center for Clinical Infant Programs (NCCIP) convened a summit meeting of researchers to discuss the effects of infant care on children and arrived at a consensus statement that read in part:

> When parents have choices about selection and utilization of supplementary care for their infants and toddlers and have access to stable child care arrangements featuring skilled, sensitive, and motivated caregivers, there is every reason to believe that both children and families can thrive. Such choices do not exist for many families in America today, and inadequate care poses risks to the current well-being and future development of infants, toddlers, and their families. (NCCIP 1987, 6)

Thus the quality of child care *as currently experienced in the United States* is a risk factor for poor developmental and educational outcomes (Helburn 1995). We know that high-quality child care is good for children; we know what constitutes high-quality care; and we know that most child care settings are not meeting the necessary quality standards. Taken together these facts should make an effective argument that we need to use all means available to improve the quality of care available to families throughout the United States.

# 4 Schools' Role in the Provision of Nonacademic Support Services: The Debate

$S$CHOOLS THAT HAVE EXPANDED the scope of their efforts to include early care and education and other child and family support services demonstrate the feasibility of the approach and provide a glimpse of the potential inherent in school-based/school-linked services. However, in the absence of a national policy to enable the implementation of such services, interested school districts face several challenges. Perhaps one of the greatest challenges is the disagreement over the role of schools. As you will see in this chapter, there is consensus that, as a nation, we need to address the lack of good quality services for children and families, but there is no agreement that schools should assume this responsibility.

## Concerns

### Schools Are Not Social Institutions

The expectation that schools should assume a new or expanded role is not new. Indeed, schools have changed dramatically during this century, expanding to include such services as counseling, the immunization of children, as well as the provision of food and other services. As Jehl and Kirst (1992) indicate, "a common response to many social problems [over the years] has been to either add . . . to the school curriculum or add new staff (such as school nurses)" (96). The current expansion of the school's role to include early care and family support services is also a response to the social problems we elaborated upon in previous chapters. Nevertheless, several concerns have been voiced about these current changes in the role of schools and in the ways schools operate.

**Schools Are Not Equipped for the Task.** Some opponents argue that schools should not assume responsibility for anything but the traditional mission of the school, namely, to teach children ages 5 to 18. The rationale underlying this argument varies. Referring in particular to the provision of services to preschool children, David Elkind (1988) contends that schools should not be used to solve social problems, since they are not equipped to carry out the task. He argues that the demand for some services for young children is due to the need for quality child care while parents work. According to Elkind, schools that provide programs for preschool children do so for the wrong reasons, often responding to parents' need for child care rather than to convictions about the benefits of early education: "Today's parents—and to some extent teachers and educational administrators—do not fully appreciate the nature and value of early childhood education" (23). Child care for young children and opportunities for preschool experiences are important and needed, according to Elkind, but should not be provided by schools.

Sigel (1991) also voices an opposition to school-based services, making a distinction between preschool experiences for young children (that is, a part-day nursery school) and child care. He argues that preschool is an educational enterprise that is independent of child care: "In a sense," he writes, "issues of the goals and content of preschool can get confounded by social concerns about child care" (87). Admittedly, child care has become a social issue that needs to be addressed. However, as far as the children's experiences are concerned, these are—or should be—reflected in the goals and content of a program, and on that basis there is no distinction between preschool education and child care. Caldwell (1985) makes this point and advocates the use of the term *EDUCARE* to draw attention to the fact that in good quality programs child care and early education share similar content goals; children cannot be well cared for without learning, and they cannot learn unless they are appropriately cared for (Mitchell 1988).

**Conflicting Missions.** The Committee for Economic Development (CED 1994) argues that schools should not assume broad responsibilities for the various needs children and families may have. In its report, *Putting Learning First,* CED (1994) points out that despite a great deal of effort and numerous school reform initiatives, little has been accomplished in terms of student achievement. Not only are students performing no better today than they did in 1970, but they continue to lag far behind children in other countries in such subjects as mathematics and science. The report indicates that whereas schools were designed to educate a relatively stable population of students, they are now challenged by many students who are ill or lack access to health care, who come from dysfunctional families, and who experience violence, drugs, and poverty. Much of the burden for dealing with these social problems has been placed on the schools rather than on parents and others in the community, making it hard for schools to accomplish their academic mission: "No organization can tackle such a swamp of conflicting missions. . . . Yet, most schools in urban areas and many in suburban areas and rural communities are pursuing, willingly or not, everexpanding social and ideological agendas" (4). According to the report, schools don't have the financial or human resources, nor the time, to address social problems and should focus only on academics:

> Our first message for those who set policy for our schools and run them on a daily basis is: Clear away the extraneous and the secondary. No institution can be everything to everyone, and no institution can succeed if it has too many competing goals. The primary mission of public schools is to provide children . . . with substantial knowledge and sound academic skills. (6)

Some educators (e.g., Geiger 1994) agree with CED's message. Others point out that since many educators are already concerned about adding to their responsibilities they may not support the idea of expanding the role of the school. Without such support at the school building level, efforts are likely to fail (Sarason 1995). However, there are those who argue that the CED report misses the point and that if its recommendations are adhered to it will exacerbate the problem, ultimately harming children. According to Davis (1994), the CED report is based on the erroneous assumption that children can block out the difficult conditions they experience and that they can learn and succeed in school despite problems they face at home. He contends that although it appears simple for policymakers to state that schools should focus only on academics, the life circumstances of many students today present barriers to learning, and these realities need to be identified and addressed rather than ignored by schools. Davis argues further that the CED report conveys a narrow vision of education, assuming that it is only about cognition and the imparting and acquisition of academic skills. He agrees that academic achievement is an important goal but believes that if children are to be able to learn, schools must first address some of the problems the students face that stand in the way of their ability to profit from instruction:

> Schools and teachers are finding it increasingly difficult to meet the learning and academic achievement needs of large and growing numbers of students because of the complex health and social problems many of these children and youth have. But the real solution to this dilemma is not, as *Putting Learning First* suggests, for schools to seek to absolve themselves of any real responsibility for children's health and social well-being. The real solution may lie in reassessing what the number one mission of schools should actually be." (39)

Tirozzi (1996) agrees that schools' mission is to enable children to succeed in school, but he disagrees with the contention in the CED report that addressing students' nonacademic needs is not part of this primary mission. Schools that provide support services do so explicitly because they want students to succeed academically and feel that unless they take steps to intervene during the children's critical developmental years, many students would not be able to keep up academically and would eventually be placed in remedial and special education classes. Tirozzi regards both services for children from birth through age 5 and other support services such as health or child care for school-age children not as appendages to school's responsibility but as educational components that are essential if schools are to succeed in their mission to teach children and ensure that they acquire academic skills. A report of the Carnegie Corporation of New York (1996) makes a similar point and underscores the importance of providing preschool programs as well as other services such as those promoting students' health, noting that one of several reasons for low academic achievement is schools' failure to deal adequately with children's nonacademic needs.

## Overburdened or Inappropriately Trained Staff

Another concern about the role of the school in the provision of nonacademic services is that teachers would assume additional roles and cannot be expected to be "everything for everyone," a point made in the CED (1994) report noted above. However, in a counterargument to this position, Hamburg (1994) and others—the authors of this book included—note that in reality, teachers assume additional roles and responsibilities when no provisions are made for needed services. In such cases, teachers often have to find out why the child misses school, what assistance the parents need, whether the child should be referred to health or other services, or what happens to the child once school is out and, whether because of lack of child care the child stays in the school or elsewhere waiting for his or her parents to get off work. In schools that officially assume responsibility for nonacademic services, additional staff is generally available to address these issues, thus freeing the teachers' time and enabling them to focus on the academic curriculum. The two purposes of imparting academic knowledge and also assuming responsibility for ensuring the health and social well-being of students can coexist in the school, a point that will become evident in the next chapter. It does not mean necessarily that teaching staff take on additional roles but rather that additional staff members are designated to carry out or coordinate nonacademic initiatives.

A related concern is that schools will give the task of teaching and caring for young children to teachers who are qualified to teach school-age children but not, necessarily, very young children. This is a legitimate concern. As we have shown in the previous chapter, the quality of care is higher in programs where the staff has an educational background in early childhood development and access to regular training. Another aspect of quality services is an appropriate staff/child ratio given the age of the children, which provides opportunities for the staff to attend to the individual needs of each child.

**Staff Qualifications.** Teachers who are certified to teach elementary school students may not have an understanding of the needs of younger children, nor an awareness of appropriate teaching methods in early childhood, and they may thus have the tendency to have inappropriate expectations of young children. The teachers may also focus on an academic curriculum that would be more appropriate for older children. Fromberg (1989) contends that some elementary school teachers assigned to kindergarten classes undertake teaching styles that are more applicable to older children, and the concern is that the same thing will occur in school-based programs for preschool children. Although this is a potential problem, it is not necessarily an issue in all schools providing services to a preschool population, nor is it a problem confined to the provision of child care in the school building. A national survey of preschool programs has shown that some community-based child care services did not hire appropriately trained staff, whereas about half of the programs that were school-based included staff with expertise and educational background in early childhood (Mitchell 1988). Also, the National Education Association (NEA 1990), in a position statement on early childhood services in public schools, draws attention to the importance of appropriately trained staff in programs serving preschool children and points out that in many cases school districts require certification in early childhood education as a minimum education for teachers serving young children. Generally, no such requirements exist for many early childhood programs sponsored by for-profit or non-profit organizations or for others providing care for young children, so the NEA contends that the public school early childhood workforce may be regarded as the most highly credentialed workforce in the field of early care and education. The NEA points out further that schools are used to certification requirements for the academic teaching staff, so that it is likely that the majority of the schools will have certification requirements for the teachers of young children as well.

Although it is apparent that in at least some school-based programs teachers have an educational background in early childhood, there are still those who maintain that teachers in school-based programs for young children are professionally isolated from others in the early childhood field and that they are outnumbered in the school building and therefore potentially influenced by the practices of the teachers in the primary and upper elementary grades (Rust 1989). However, our experience has been that the direction of influence can go the other way as well; in many of the schools we work with on the implementation of early care and education programs, primary grade teachers changed their practices to reflect those of the preschool staff, thus providing continuity of experiences for the children.

**Academics at an Early Age.**   At the heart of the arguments over staff qualifications is the concern that teachers in school-based early childhood programs would be unable to meet the needs of the young children in their care. It is important to have staff trained in early childhood who would be able, presumably, to provide developmentally appropriate programs for young children. The prevailing view is that young children benefit from an informal, child-centered approach to education, where they can take the initiative to play, explore their surroundings, and establish social relationships with adult caregivers and with their peers. However, schools are traditionally associated with more direct academic instructional orientations, and there are fears that children in school-based early childhood programs will be subjected to formal didactic instruction in academic skills at younger and younger ages. Beyond the potential emphasis on academics and didactic instruction in preschool programs that are based in public schools, there is concern about the children's transition to kindergarten and first grade. Opponents argue that even in schools that provide developmentally appropriate, child-centered programs, children will have difficulty once they are in the primary grades, where they are exposed to vastly different instructional methods. A suggestion presented by some groups is that an ideal situation—as indicated in *Right from the Start*, a report prepared by the National Association of State Boards of Education (1988)— would be for developmentally appropriate practices to govern the education of children from ages 3 to 8.

The tension between a child-centered, developmentally appropriate focus and an academic orientation has a long history, as has the concern that many young children find it difficult to make a transition from the informal preschool environment to a more formally structured regular classroom (Goffin 1992). However, the emphasis on academics at an early age is not a problem that is unique to school-based programs. Mitchell (1988), in a national survey of school-based preschool programs, found that the quality of these programs varied but not any more so than in other child care facilities in the community, suggesting that variations in quality and a focus on academics can exist regardless of program sponsorship; that is, some preschool and child care programs that are not based in or otherwise associated with schools focus on academics and formal instruction and some school-based programs are child-centered and nonacademic in their approach. A study on the cost, quality, and outcomes of child care programs in four states contains additional evidence that school-based child care should not be a source of concern. The findings indicate that, in general, the majority of the programs were of poor to mediocre quality and that the better quality programs—that is, those that provided appropriate services to young children—were based in or were in some ways linked to universities and schools (Helburn 1995).

Dunn and Kontos (1997) reviewed the research on developmentally appropriate practices. They note that such practices create a positive classroom climate that is conducive to children's development, but they indicate that the majority of early childhood teachers, although they philosophically subscribe to developmentally appropriate practices, fail to implement these practices: "Unfortunately . . . few early childhood education classrooms exemplify developmentally appropriate practice—as little as one third to one fifth of the programs studied" (4). Stipek (1992) makes a similar point; she found that staff training in early childhood does not necessarily guarantee adherence to a developmentally appropriate, child-centered curricular approach. According to Stipek, many teachers with appropriate training "teach" children basic skills. Stipek, Rosenblatt, and DiRocco (1994) found that an increasing number of preschool teachers with training in early childhood ask young children "to recite the alphabet, count to 100, and fill out ditto sheets" (4). The pressures from policymakers as well as from parents, and not the lack of appropriate training in child development and early childhood education, is behind this trend. As the researchers note, policymakers at every level are concerned with student achievement and mastery of basic skills, and in the short term, didactic, teacher-directed programs can raise children's performance on achievement tests. Parents, many of whom are concerned about their children having an educational edge over other children, also influence curricular decisions in early childhood programs, whether these are sponsored by schools or by other organizations.

Developmental experts are concerned that exposing children at an early age not only to academics but also to a teacher-directed, didactic approach might inhibit intellectual, social, and emotional development. However, for some populations of children a didactic approach may be useful, depending on the program's goal. Stipek and her colleagues (1995), for example, found that children in didactic classrooms performed better on reading tests than children in child-centered classrooms, although no differences were found between the two groups on knowledge of numbers. However, they also found advantages to the child-centered approach: Compared with children in didactic classrooms, children in child-centered classrooms rated their abilities higher; they had higher expectations for success on school-like tasks; and they showed less dependence on adult approval and permission and more pride in their accomplishments.

## Revised Guidelines for Developmentally Appropriate Practice

Although the above-noted studies indicate advantages to both the didactic and child-centered approach, more research is needed. We should also note that those who contend that schools are likely to emphasize a didactic rather than a child-centered orientation often use as their guiding principles a set of developmentally appropriate practices that have been criticized and are now obsolete. The developmentally appropriate practice guidelines (Bredenkamp 1989) focused almost exclusively on play and social development, and many teachers thought the guidelines implied that teachers should not have goals for or expectations of young children and should let children choose how they wanted to spend their time and what activities they wanted to pursue. On the basis of these guidelines, many teachers believed that developmentally appropriate practice meant that they should not be providing any directions at all to the children; the role of the teacher amounted to no more than that of monitor (Farran, Silveri, and Culp 1991).

The guidelines also were presented in a way that made them appear as a singular concept, when in fact developmental appropriateness has multiple meanings and takes into account children's individual differences in learning styles, temperament, and experiential background, as well as variations in the ages during which children achieve developmental milestones. As Farran, Silveri, and Culp (1991) note: "The search for a single, all inclusive definition [of developmentally appropriate practice] may be fruitless; what teachers need to know is how to recognize when children are learning and responding to the social and physical environments provided . . . and how to change those environments if they fail to stimulate the children" (71).

Critics of the developmentally appropriate approach point out further that although young children should not be expected to sit still for long periods of time or participate in skill drills, the original developmentally appropriate guidelines are too extreme and portray as unnatural even simple learning activities that many young children may enjoy, such as learning colors and letters (Hirsch 1996).

In response to criticism, the early childhood field has come to accept recently that neither the child-centered nor the academic approach is appropriate if practiced to the extreme, and the guidelines to developmentally appropriate practice have been revised (Bredenkamp and Copple 1997). The new guidelines, which represent a working document to guide continued discussions on the topic, include broadly conceived goals for children at each age level, as well as more emphasis on the role of teachers in providing children with guidance. As such, the guidelines enable teachers to include formal subject areas such as science and math in ways that are appropriate for young children (see Box 4.1), making the link between play and education more discernible and concrete (Carnegie Corporation of New York 1996).

## Cultural Issues

Additional concerns about the role of the school in the provision of nonacademic support services stem from the contention that schools are

---

### BOX 4.1   New Developmental Guidelines

As the Carnegie Corporation of New York (1996) makes clear, new guidelines for preschool curricula do not rule out the offering of challenging content in which children explore not only shapes and colors but also fundamental concepts. Although previous guidelines denounced any formal academic teaching, the new developmental guidelines provide examples for combining developmentally appropriate practices with the academic content areas. For example, social studies may take the form of block-building or a trip to the railroad station and may engage children in projects that lead them to ask thought-provoking questions, such as: How do we know that people were living on earth a long time ago? Simple math can be taught as part of a cooking project or through the use of manipulative toys. Teachers can encourage preschoolers to explore the physical properties of familiar things like water, sand, a rolling pin, or marbles and to pursue inquiry-based approaches to science that enable them to explore their own assumptions about the physical world. For example, using blocks, children can construct ramps of different heights, roll toy cars down them, and predict which one will go farthest. Then they can check and record how far each car actually traveled. In the process, they develop spatial relations, prediction, observation, charting, and cooperative learning skills.

---

unable to serve the needs of minority populations. Moore and Phillips (1989) contend that the public school system as a whole does not have an impressive track record of fostering academic achievement among African-American school-age children. African-American children are twice as likely as other children to be placed in special education classes and to be suspended from school; they are more likely to experience corporal punishment; and only a small percentage of African Americans go on to college. Moore and Phillips (1989) contend further that, in general, no racial diversity exists among the faculty in most public schools and that African-American children thus do not have opportunities to identify with teachers of similar backgrounds. Their concern is that children will be subjected to these inequalities at a younger age if schools assume responsibility for providing services to preschool children.

Other concerns about school-based programs and minority populations focus on parents. The National Black Child Development Institute (NBCDI 1988) points not only to inequality issues that exist in pubic schools' treatment of children but also to the fact that parents of minority children may feel too intimidated by the school. NBCDI is concerned that these feelings of intimidation would result in failure to enroll children in early childhood programs based in schools, or that they could cause rifts between the home and the school. NBCDI recognizes the vast potential that exists in the use of public schools for nonacademic services, as well as for care and education for preschoolers, but suggests that safeguards must be put in place to ensure that minority families are served appropriately. The safeguards include assurances that teachers come from the community and are racially and ethnically representative of the children they serve, that parents should be involved in decisions about curriculum and policy, and that the programs for preschoolers also include parent education opportunities (NBCDI 1988).

### Community Versus School Sponsorship

Besides concern over the provision of school-based services to young children, there are concerns that schools will be unable to provide comprehensive services that address the various needs children and families may have. Powell (1991) points out that families need not only early care and education programs but also various other support services that, he contends, schools would be unable to provide. The potential limitation of schools is also noted by Halpern (1995) in his treatise on the history of neighborhood initiatives in the United States. He notes that earlier in this century there were attempts to use schools in poor neighborhoods to house social services, but these efforts did not materialize because although schools proved useful for recreational activities, "they were [not well-suited] to organizing the residents of poor neighborhoods to address social and economic concerns" (40).

Opponents of school-based services also contend that schools, as relative newcomers in the provision of nonacademic support services such as child care, will put community-based organizations out of business (Neugebauer 1996). For example, there is concern that schools will compete for clients by offering child care services at lower fees and/or that they would attract the best teachers by offering higher salaries. Although it is noted that higher staff salaries are essential if the quality of care in programs for young children is to be attained (Whitebook, Phillips, and Howes 1990), there is nonetheless the fear that schools' presumed ability to offer higher staff salaries would spell the demise of many community-based programs.

These and other concerns have led to proposals to use the schools in a more limited way through school-linked—as opposed to school-based—services, with schools being one of several partners in a coordinated effort to address the needs of children and families (Center for the Future of Children 1992). Chaskin and Richman (1992) contend, however, that even in such an approach schools should not be the primary site for the delivery of support services, nor should they assume even a primary coordinating role. Chaskin and Richman note that in either a school-based or school-linked approach there are likely to be problems, perhaps most importantly, the problem of failing to attend to all children's and families' needs. Chaskin and Richman point out that children and parents have diverse needs that can be met only within a broad system that includes not only specialized services for children and families at risk but also an array of activities, facilities, and events that "make up the fabric of children's organized social world" (109). Chaskin and Richman feel that such needs can be met best in a "local community system" that links services together.

Although Chaskin and Richman (1992) support the idea of schools' participation in the community system, they (among others, such as Gardner 1992) argue against building a system that too strongly favors any one organization, especially the school, contending that "too strong an institutional bias runs the risk of missing a substantial number of children in need; to serve all children, multiple access points are essential" (110). They argue further that school is the last place the disenfranchised will turn to for help, that schools are too rigid and will be unable to change and promote such important principles as parental involvement, and that in many cases schools do not draw students from a geographically circumscribed area. Rather, because of busing practices, the emergence of magnet schools, and other developments, any one school is likely to serve students from several communities, making it difficult to provide linkages to the home, for example, or to make referrals for some of the services the children and their parents may need.

## Advantages in the Use of the School

These and other concerns notwithstanding, many schools have implemented school-based services successfully, and there is widespread support for such efforts. Many educators and other professionals point out several benefits inherent in the use of the school for the provision of nonacademic support services. Hausman and Weiss (1988), for example, analyzed several state-sponsored child and family support initiatives. They found many similarities among such initiatives, regardless of the sponsoring agency, and they noted that often the decision of whether to provide services in schools or in other agencies or organizations in the community is dependent in part on who the formulators of the initiatives are and what their professional affiliations may be. They also noted that although some of the initiatives are thus defined in terms of "education" (for example, to prevent later *educational* failure or to promote future school success) or in terms of "support" (for example, to prevent future welfare dependency), they are otherwise indistinct; that is, any effort to prevent welfare dependency must necessarily focus on ensuring that children succeed academically, and educational efforts designed to promote academic success also have as the ultimate goal a desire to ensure eventual economic self-sufficiency among the children served.

## Benefits to Children

**Universal Access.**   Though the various initiatives Hausman and Weiss (1988) studied were similar in content, they found several advantages associated with those based in the school. One of the advantages to the school-based approach is universal access, which means that all families can participate with equal standing and anyone who needs or wants services has access to them.

Universal access is important for several reasons. First, as we noted in previous chapters, all families need some kind of support at one time or another during the course of raising children, but categorical programs that target only a specific group of children and families are unable to capture such needs in the same way that universal programs do. Also, inherent in universal access is the concept of primary prevention, in which attempts are made to meet the needs of children and families "holistically and promptly" before the problem becomes exacerbated and reaches a crisis situation (Morrill 1992). As numerous studies have shown, it is much simpler and more cost-effective to prevent problems than it is to later provide ameliorative treatments (Albee and Gullotta 1997). Cost-benefit studies associated with the Perry Preschool Project have perhaps made this point best; the studies found that for every dollar spent on providing home visits and preschool experiences to children, $7.16 was saved in the later costs of grade retention, special education, and social services, as well as the costs of welfare and crime (Weikart and Schweinhart 1997). Although community-based organizations can provide such services to a target population of children and families identified as being dysfunctional or at risk, schools can provide the services to a broader group not yet considered at risk but nonetheless needing support.

The attempt to reach all children and families is important. However, most schools, no matter how homogeneous, are likely to have some students who have more extensive needs than the rest of the students or who come from poorer or more dysfunctional families and may need more intensive services. Educators must identify such children and families and provide or refer them to additional services (Payzant 1992). In such cases, universal access provides the opportunity for recognizing the needs of at-risk populations, and, importantly, it also allows educators to serve children and parents within the context of heterogeneous groupings in order to "maximize the modeling and learning" that can occur in a mixed group (Hausman and Weiss 1988, 13). In such heterogeneous groupings, certain families can serve as child-rearing models to some of the families that need help in this regard (Hausmann and Weiss 1988), and children can model positive social interactions to other children (Hauser-Cram 1991).

We also have learned over the years that when programs target only some children and families, labeling, stigmatization, and alienation can re-

---

BOX 4.2    Growing Popularity of School-Based Services

Although numerous concerns have been raised regarding schools' provision of child care and family support services, the advantages of the approach are clear and include:

- *Universal access,* meaning that all children and families can participate with equal standing and anyone who wants or needs services has access to them

- *No labeling or stigmatization,* as can occur when programs serve only a targeted group of children and families

- *Continuity of care,* enabling children to become familiar with the school environment before they enter kindergarten

- *Greater parent involvement,* which, as the research has shown, occurs because parents develop a trusting relationship with educators and come to regard the school as an institution that addresses their needs

- *Cost-efficient approach,* building upon a system that already exists as opposed to creating a whole new system

---

sult, setting apart those who need help rather than helping and nurturing them. "When a program focuses only on those most in need [as opposed to universal access], there is increased risk . . . [of] treating the children and families served as somehow deficient (Center for the Future of Children 1992, 13). Also, as Hauser-Cram (1991) notes, in categorical programs that serve only a targeted group of children and families, such as those who are low income or developmentally disabled, the "stigma associated with such programs can drive away the very individuals the programs are attempting to serve" (26). According to Hauser-Cram, schools are better suited than other organizations to serve broad groups of children, since all children, including those with special needs, are required to attend school.

**Continuity of Care.**    Another benefit associated with the use of the school for nonacademic services is continuity of care. Continuity of care is important for young children who need to become familiar with a stable environment. The younger the children, the more imperative it is to avoid multiple transitions involving several different settings. When schools provide child care for preschool as well as school-age children, children do not have to attend programs in several different locations. Also, preschool children who attend school-based child care services become familiar with the school environment and thus have less anxiety when they begin kindergarten or first grade. Ladd and Price (1987) also found that children who attended school as preschoolers had more positive views of school than those who did not participate in such programs.

## Benefits to Parents

**Promoting Parent Involvement in Schools.**   The benefits associated with the use of the school for nonacademic support services extend to parents as well. When schools reach out to families during the child's infancy or preschool years, parents who might otherwise have been critical of the school develop a trusting relationship with educators and begin the process of communicating with teachers. For example, an evaluation of the Parents as Teachers home visitation program found that the home visits provided by the schools encouraged parents to become involved in their children's education once the children were enrolled in school (Winter and McDonald 1997; Pfannenstiel, Lambson, and Yarnell 1991). As we indicated in previous chapters, parent involvement is an important aspect of children's success in school; the more involved parents are in their children's schooling and the more interested they are in what happens to the children during the school day, the more likely that the children will take learning seriously. In studies of schools providing child care for preschool as well as school-age children, parents indicated that they appreciated the services provided by the school and were more likely as a result to become supportive of schools as a whole (Finn-Stevenson and Gillette 1996; Finn-Stevenson, Gillette, and Brown 1997).

**Responding to Parents' Needs.**   Also important is schools' ability to reach out to parents and encourage them to continue their education (Smith 1991). This two-generational approach is especially important with young mothers who have dropped out of school. The PACE program, initiated in Kentucky and implemented in various other states as well, seeks to serve not only children but also their parents, offering the latter child care and other assistance so they can work on completing their high school education. In another example, some Schools of the 21st Century in poor, urban communities provide not only various child care and other support services but also literacy training for the parents of the children (Zigler, Finn-Stevenson, and Stern 1997).

## Building upon an Existing System

There are other benefits associated with the use of the school for the provision of early care and education and family support services. A school-based approach to the provision of services is associated with easier access to children and families, since schools, more so than any other organization, are conveniently located in all communities and also known to and utilized by families with children (Levy and Shepardson 1992). Jehl and Kirst (1992) also underscore the importance of involving the school in the provision of services, noting that "the durability and stability of schools make them an essential participant in [such] efforts" (97). The use of the school for the provision of nonacademic support services also builds upon a system that already exists (Zigler 1987), as opposed to creating a whole new system that, in view of today's fiscal restraints, is unrealistic. Building on an existing system provides an opportunity to make use of an already existing administrative and management structure (Child Care Action Campaign 1993) and can result in considerable financial savings and the streamlining of services (Zigler and Finn-Stevenson 1996).

Some concerns about the use of the school for the provision of early care and education and family support services is evident, but so is a great deal of support for and excitement about the promise of these school-based services. Although there is opposition to the approach at some level, many schools, as well as community-based organizations working with schools, are looking for ways schools can provide support services that meet the needs of families, beginning at the birth of the child. However, the implementation of school-based support services is not an easy task. As we discuss in the next chapter, whether schools succeed in implementation is often dependent on educators' commitment to change and careful consideration of policy and other issues that need to be addressed at the outset.

# 5 Implementation

THE ADVANTAGES ASSOCIATED WITH SCHOOLS' ROLE in the provision of early care and family support services can be realized only if: (1) the programs are well implemented at the local level and (2) they achieve widespread dissemination. These two issues are related aspects of the development of school reform initiatives and will be discussed here primarily within the context of the School of the 21st Century. As we described in Chapter 2, the School of the 21st Century is a school-based child care and family support program. This program is particularly well suited as an example in this chapter on implementation for three reasons. First, it is a broad initiative that encompasses not one but several programs, as well as a range of services such as health and nutrition, the provision of which is important if children are to develop optimally and grow up able to benefit from schooling (see Box 5.1). Second, the program has been implemented in about 600 schools in seventeen states, representing various circumstances, resources, and needs. The wealth of information we have drawn from the implementation of the program in a variety of different communities is sufficiently representative to allow us to generalize and apply the experiences to schools in other communities as well. Third, the program has been in existence for over ten years, demonstrating a staying power that few other initiatives can claim and enabling us to draw lessons about the different phases of a program's growth and development. How have schools in different communities approached implementation? What were some of the challenges they faced? What factors facilitated successful implementation? These are some of the questions we will address in this chapter. In addition to examining the program's implementation at the local level, we also will examine the strategies used to achieve widespread national dissemination of the program. Although we will focus primarily on schools that implemented the School of the 21st Century program, we will highlight lessons learned in the course of the implementation of other initiatives as well.

## Setting the Stage

When schools adopt any reform initiative they do so because they want to bring about change, and they focus most often on enabling students to do

---

BOX 5.1    Programs and Services Included in
the School of the 21st Century

- School-based, year-round child day care for children ages 3 to 5
- School-based before- and after-school and vacation care for children up to age 12
- Comprehensive preventive health care
- Home visiting by trained parent educators
- Support and training to family child care providers
- Nutrition programs and education
- Information and referral

*Some schools may also provide:*

- Social services
- Teen pregnancy prevention
- Adult and family literacy
- On-site prenatal services
- Outreach to community child day care providers
- Intergenerational programs

*(See also Box 2.1)*

---

better academically. However, if implementation of an initiative takes place, other changes will occur—in the way the school operates and in the relationship between parents and educators and among educators in the school building. Fullan (1992) makes this point in his discussion on successful school improvement in general. He notes that often the implementation of an innovative program is more important than the idea itself and that it is essential for educators to consider what changes are likely to occur and what policy issues need to be addressed in order to facilitate implementation.

### Anticipating Change

**Operational Issues.**   Some of the changes are logistical, but they are important to understand at the outset because they will affect the way the school operates. In the School of the 21st Century, for example, the provision of child care services means not only that the school begins to work with children early in life but also that the school day begins as early as five or six in the morning and that the school remains open until late in the evening. Furthermore, the school has to remain open during staff development days, school vacations, snow days, and so on. Decisions such as who will open and maintain the school will have to be made, and other issues will have to be thought through and addressed.

For example, since traditionally schools are closed in the summer, many do not have air-conditioning; provisions have to be made to address this potential problem. Often at least one school in the district may be air-conditioned, so during the summer, when the school is not used for academic purposes, services can be consolidated in one such school. If none of the buildings are usable during the summer, provisions may be made to make one of them air-conditioned or to use alternative space in the community.

Another issue is related to maintenance. In cases where school buildings are cleaned in the evenings, early mornings, and during the summer, policy decisions regarding maintenance schedules have to be made. In one district this has meant that to prepare all the schools for the academic year services are not provided during the last two weeks in August; but in other districts the services remain open in all schools year-round, with maintenance occurring while the services are ongoing. None of these and other operational issues are difficult to address, but it will be easier to deal with them if they are anticipated and considered at the outset so that potential problems are circumvented.

**Relationships with Parents.** Another change likely to take place when schools implement nonacademic support services is related to the relationship schools have with families. D. R. Powell (1991) writes that traditionally there has been a considerable distance between the school and the family, in part because of the desire of schools to protect their autonomy and their traditional role. According to Powell, "optimal social distance" between schools and families "sustains the social structure of the school through its expectation that experts (teachers) handle uniform tasks and non-experts (parents) handle nonuniform tasks" (309). Once the school broadens its role to include various family support services, problems may arise unless educators "recognize the family's perspective" (D. R. Powell 1991, 310). Powell concludes that in the abstract the provision of school-based support services may not have a negative impact on the relationship between schools and families, but he cautions that some people may perceive that schools are encroaching on the family's authority and that the services that schools offer are an intrusion into the relationship between the parent and child.

This negative perception may surface when a school announces its plans to address the needs of children and families beginning at a young age. There is often an opposition to school reform, especially to an initiative that expands upon the traditional mission of the school and provides services that go beyond academics, with some opponents claiming that schools are attempting to interfere with family life. One way to address the issue is to emphasize that the services are voluntary and noncompulsory and that the school is not serving in any surrogate role, nor is the school interested in assuming the responsibilities of parents. Rather, the school's role is to support parents and provide them with knowledge and services that will facilitate their children's growth and development. This change in service does represent a change in the relationship between schools and families, but it is a positive change and is something that schools should strive toward, creating opportunities for educators and parents to work in partnership. Wagstaff and Gallagher (1990) suggest that the relationship between educators and parents may be compared to the right and left hemispheres of the brain; input from both the teacher and the parent is vital, and each must complement the other if children are to develop optimally and achieve academic success.

Not only educators but also parents should anticipate, as well as work to create, positive changes in the relationship. Such change is likely to happen if parents find that the school is responsive to their needs. Often when school-based support services are implemented, parents come to realize that the school is not the same that it once was. The school not only operates at different hours but also assumes a two-generational approach, focusing on the needs of children as well as the needs of parents. This approach is especially clear in the case of child care. As indicated in Chapter 3, good quality child care is essential if we are to ensure the optimal development of children and their ability to profit from instruction. Child care is equally important, however, as a service to parents; access to good quality, affordable child care eases the pressure parents have when looking for child care and the stress and guilt they experience about leaving their children in substandard facilities (Finn-Stevenson, Desimone, and Chung 1998; McCabe 1995).

In Independence, Missouri, the School of the 21st Century program has been in place for ten years, providing parents with preschool and school-age child care, nutrition education, and a range of other services associated with the School of the 21st Century. Over the years, many of the parents have come to regard the school as user-friendly, often asking the principal and program staff for help in meeting various other needs. The same thing has happened in other Schools of the 21st Century. In Arkansas and Colorado, for example, parental demand prompted the implementation of child care for infants and toddlers in addition to the child care for older children because there was no suitable program for infants in the community.

The importance of responding to parents' needs and also of encouraging them to participate in their children's programs is a fundamental aspect of school reform and of the success of early interventions, regardless of whether such programs are based in the school or elsewhere in the community. However, some schools fail to reach out and communicate with parents, in part because they neither recognize nor accommodate the realities of family life. Louise Iscoe (1995), writing about the implementation experiences of a School of the Future (the program, in four schools in Texas, seeks to bring health and social services to schools), notes that although parent involvement is an essential aspect of the program, it has been hard to achieve for several reasons: Many parents in the community are single, working parents who have little if any time, and others are poor, unemployed, do not speak English, and generally mistrust the school. Iscoe points out that to be successful in gaining the trust of parents, educators need to recognize the family's circumstances and needs.

Iscoe also suggests that schools adopt new means of communicating with parents. In a brief example, she notes that it was standard practice for the staff to communicate with parents through the children, who were given flyers or messages to take home: "Often, the flyers or messages were considered unimportant and tossed aside, if they ever made it home to begin with" (32). In contrast to this experience, a school in Norfolk, Virginia, also serving a very poor, minority population, has successfully achieved parent participation and involvement within the context of implementing the Comer/Zigler (CoZi) initiative (in part, a School of the 21st Century). Their success in encouraging parent involvement and participation is attributed to two practices.

First, the school does not limit parental involvement to the school day but also offers activities in the evening in order to accommodate the needs of parents who are working or in training. Second, rather than attempting to communicate with parents through children, the school relies on direct communications with parents. For example, in conducting a needs assessment the school recruited ten individuals from the housing project where most of the families lived to canvass the area door to door, telling parents about the proposed program, asking them if they would be interested in the initiative and what other services they might need. This effort not only provided vital information that helped shape the program and establish priorities about which aspect of the program to implement first, it also inspired parents, who felt at the outset that they were important players in the process of the program's development. From the inception of the program, parent involvement has been a strong part of the effort, as has the support of parents, who, seven years later, continue to assist the teachers and others in the school in advocating and fund-raising for the program. The point we underscore and that should be recognized by educators implementing programs is that just as families and schools change, so should the relationship between them.

## Staffing Issues

Another change that should be anticipated is related to staff relations. When schools are providing school-based services such as child care, there is a need to hire additional staff. Besides policy decisions regarding staff qualifications, schools have to make an effort to treat the entire staff as a whole rather than treat the child care staff as separate from the academic faculty. Such separation—which considers the support services merely as an add-on—can stand in the way of the programs becoming part of the very core of the school's operation (Jehl and Kirst 1992). If educators and administrators make no attempt to conceive of the programs as part of the school, the support services can indeed function autonomously within the buildings, simply using the physical space made available in the school. However, the services are more likely to realize their potential and have positive outcomes if they are an integral aspect of the school's operations and culture.

If the provision of early care and family support is conceptualized as an integral facet of the school, then there will be a reason to involve the entire staff as early in the program planning process as possible and to make provisions for regular whole-staff meetings. This level of staff involvement will help in:

- Facilitating interactions among the staff; and
- Instilling the notion that the academic as well as the nonacademic support services are important functions of the school as a whole.

Although staffing issues are usually considered at the school building level, it is important to understand that the change associated with the implementation of nonacademic programs also involves educational administrators with different responsibilities in the central district office, as well as the custodians and others who work at the school whose support of the effort may be crucial. In some Schools of the 21st Century, for example, the principal or program coordinator has responsibility for opening and closing the schools early in the morning and late in the evening. However, in some of the schools this is the responsibility of the custodial staff. To ensure the support of as many of its academic and nonacademic staff as possible in the implementation of the School of the 21st Century, one school district established a policy that enabled the children of anyone on its staff, even if they lived out of the district, to participate in the program, and this proved to be an important benefit to many of the faculty and other staff members.

**Training and Orientation.**   In addition to informing the staff of plans, seeking their input in the planning process, and accommodating their needs, schools also should provide staff orientations early in the program's development to ensure that all players both understand the rationale behind the provision of services and support the initiative. Teachers who have not participated in such orientation might assume that early education or after-school child care are extraneous efforts that drain educational resources and, as such, stand in the way of their ability to teach academic subjects. In such cases, not only resentments but also continued in-fighting over space and materials can result. But if the teachers are made aware, for example, that children who are left home alone after school present behavior and academic problems and that the provision of good quality early care ensures that children come to school ready to learn, then teachers would understand the relevance of the programs and their potential to facilitate rather than inhibit teachers' ability to teach.

**The Role of Teachers.** Fullan (1992) underscores the importance of orientation and staff development workshops, noting that these should be aspects of any reform strategy. He emphasizes, however, that even when all players participate early on in the process of change not all of them necessarily understand the significance of the effort, nor are they all entirely supportive of it immediately, so provisions for continued staff development opportunities should be made. In reference to a study of several reform initiatives, Huberman (1992) also notes that initially staff commitment to the programs was fragile, in part because not everyone understood the significance and relevance of the efforts: "It was only when teachers had undergone a few cycles of experimentation . . . that they got on top of the [programs] in conceptual terms," he writes. "This, in turn, strengthened their technical mastery and heightened their commitment" (10).

In school-based programs where the academic teachers do not directly provide support services, their role is nevertheless critical to the success of the initiative:

> Teachers have a critical role in any school change initiative. By understanding the philosophy behind the School of the 21st Century, and working with full knowledge of the scope of its programs and services, teachers can help each student and each family to make the most out of the available services and programs. Teachers provide the machinery to make school reform a reality. No meaningful efforts to make schools better can succeed when imposed from the outside. It is only with the enthusiasm and involvement of teachers in each classroom that schools can be . . . made better. (The Bush Center in Child Development and Social Policy 1995, 11)

## Adopting a New Philosophy

Besides anticipating some of the changes likely to take place, it is important that educators recognize that the implementation of early care and family support programs is often one aspect of a broader effort to reform schools. The past two decades have seen the emergence of and experimentation with numerous strategies, some more elaborate and comprehensive than others, but all aimed at improving the nation's schools and ultimately enhancing student achievement. Some of these strategies have entailed curriculum changes; others have focused on recruiting and retaining exemplary teachers by increasing salaries and changing district and building-level decisionmaking and other policies. Although many of these strategies are effective, in and of themselves they are insufficient because they fail to address the realities of family life; for many children, the stress associated with poverty, dual working parents, and a lack of good quality child care, among other problems, create barriers to learning. These barriers need to be addressed if reform is to succeed, a point we made earlier in the book.

However, simply providing such services may not be sufficient in a school that is dysfunctional due to poor staff relations, lack of motivation, or failure to meet the needs of individual students. In such cases, not only the provision of early care and support services but also other reform initiatives that focus on changing the culture and management of the school may be necessary. Fiske (1992), in his descriptions of numerous initiatives, notes that although each of the efforts is exemplary, each school implements one reform initiative when in fact several are needed if there is to be a positive impact on students and families.

Additionally, if early care and support services or other reform efforts are to become an integral aspect of the school, they cannot be perceived only in terms of the implementation of programs or services. There has to be a broader philosophy that governs the effort and redefines the school and the responsibilities of educators. This point is evident in a report on the community school initiative developed in New York City in order to provide a range of services such as after-school child care, health, and education for the community at large:

> When we talk about the community school, there is a tendency to focus on the services they make available to children and their families. But there is a broader philosophy that governs [these schools] and defines what makes a school a community school. . . . It [means] transforming our schools to revolutionary new institutions . . . [that] provide an arena for the community to come together to resolve its . . . problems. (Children's Aid Society 1995, 34)

When we assist schools in adopting the School of the 21st Century program, we point out that the emphasis has to be not just on the implementation of various services that children and families may need but also on assuming responsibility for continually monitoring the status of children and families and ascertaining if the programs are meeting their needs, if modifications are in order, or if additional services are called for. With this philosophy governing the program, the staff, as well as local school and district leadership, are involved not only at the inception of the initiative but throughout its implementation and operation.

# Starting Implementation

## *The Planning Process*

The preceding section highlights the reorientation in philosophy and practice that must take place as educators consider implementing early care and family support services. The implementation of such services in the school is often more of a complex undertaking than is the case with many other reform initiatives (for example, curriculum or salary changes). These new services require additional staff, the establishment of procedures and policies, space modification, public awareness, and community support, as well as funds that are often not earmarked in the school budget. Also, as noted earlier, such efforts are two-generational, focusing on both students and parents, and may entail more than one program. In the School of the 21st Century, for example, there are several components, each of which is a program unto itself. Whether the components are implemented simultaneously or are phased in, they will all be part of the School of the 21st Century. This overall design brings all components together and provides a conceptual umbrella that enables everyone in the school to understand that they are working toward the same goal—the optimal development of children.

However, each of the components must be developed so that it is part of the overall design but can also stand alone. As such, the implementation of each of the components requires consideration in terms of:

The scope of the service to be provided
Start-up funds and other resources that will be needed for implementation
Staffing needs
Policies that need to be established
Operational budget requirements
The schedule for completing the implementation
Plans for evaluation

**Action Plan.** Although educators should consider and plan each component separately, it is essential to have a plan for the overall development of the initiative as well. The plan should be considered a working document that provides an overall sense of direction. It does not have to abide by any specific format; it needs simply to detail what the school wants to achieve ultimately and to provide a realistic timeline for accomplishing short- and long-term objectives. Fullan (1992) acknowledges that complex changes such as the implementation of several programs or services in the school require careful planning, but he warns against overplanning, noting that after a certain amount of goal and priority setting, it is important not to get "bogged down" in the process by continually discussing goals or creating a complex plan: "Recent evidence in both education and business indicates that effective leaders have an overall sense of direction and start into action as soon as possible [by] establishing small scale examples" and by adapting, refining, and expanding upon these over time (88).

Fullan (1992) summarizes the strategy as "thinking big and starting small." It is a useful phrase that speaks to the fact that to be effective, implementation should be undertaken in small dosages. For example, in the majority of the Schools of the 21st Century, the intent is to provide access to early care and education to all the children in the district, which would necessitate services in most of the district's elementary schools. School districts vary in size: Some are relatively small and have three or four elementary schools, whereas others serve large, urban cities or entire counties and may have over 100 elementary schools. Regardless of its size, a district may implement the services first in one or two school buildings and then refine and elaborate upon them in these schools before later implementing services in the other schools. Within each of the schools, the services also may be phased in, starting with the implementation of one or two components and later adding additional ones. Given financial constraints, gradual implementation is often a practical decision, but even if funding is not an issue, we have found that programs are stronger and of better quality if implementation is phased in over three to five years.

In developing a plan of action, schools are advised to respond to a few questions, the answers to which will provide the basis for the planning document:

### What Do We Want to Accomplish?

- short-term objectives?
- long-term objectives?

### What Is Our Road Map for Getting There?

- how do we decide on priorities?
- what do we want to do first?
- what can wait until later?

### What Obstacles Are We Likely to Encounter Along the Way?

- how will we get around these?

### How Will We Measure Our Progress and Success?

**Organizational Audit.** The actual plan is the outcome of the planning process, which includes several steps, one of the first being an organizational audit. The purpose of such an assessment is to determine what strengths, resources, and capabilities the school district and individual schools have and what remains to be addressed in order to facilitate implementation.

The School of the 21st Century National Center, which we discuss later in the chapter, often facilitates an organizational audit meeting for schools planning the implementation of the program. The audit is a probing process, and the questions are formulated on the basis of the ultimate goal of the program and the reasons educators express for wanting to implement it. The reasons for implementation and the overall goal are often similar among the Schools of the 21st Century, but since each program is developed for a specific community, local staff should articulate these reasons and goals.

Participation in the audit meeting should be limited to a few key individuals who will have responsibility for implementation, including the superintendent, other administrators from the central office, some teachers, and the principals. There is no specific format for the audit since many of the questions are unique to the direction the school district wants to take. However, it is important to have a knowledgeable facilitator whose role is not only to ask questions but also to probe intently, because often the answers are not obvious.

We begin the audit by asking each individual in the group what his or her understanding of the program is and what he or she sees as the goals of the program. Additional questions are related to the district's previous experience with implementing innovative programs, the strengths the district has that will facilitate implementation, and some of the problems the program can expect to encounter. These questions provide not only a sense of the direction the school wants to go but also an indication of the staff's understanding of and commitment to the program and their ability to work as a team.

If it becomes apparent that group members differ in their understanding of the program or in what they see as the overall goal, implementation will be hampered and may have to await more consideration about how to proceed. In some cases it becomes apparent that one principal, for example, does not see a need for the program in his or her school, or perhaps he or she perceives more difficulties than benefits. There may be another principal in the same group who acknowledges potential difficulties but sees the need for the program as immense and portrays not only excitement but also a willingness to work hard to overcome obstacles. The superintendent will be well advised to pilot the program in that principal's school.

Other aspects of the organizational audit entail identification of what financial resources are available, the district's capability in raising additional funds that may be needed, and financial or other resources in the community that may be accessed. Human resources also must be considered: Who will be responsible for program planning and administration? Who will staff the program, and what funding is available for staff salaries? The answers to some of these questions are not always apparent immediately, hence the need for a knowledgeable and probing facilitator.

For example, educators in a district wanting to implement child care for preschoolers indicate initially that no money is available for staff salaries, but eventually, because of the probing questions of a facilitator, teachers note that the school is eligible for Title 1 funds and that these can pay for the teachers to operate the program during the school day. In this case, less money is required to staff the wrap-around child care portion of the program. In another example, one team undergoing the organizational audit indicates a need for services for preschoolers but, given the lack of space in the elementary schools, abandons the idea. A modular unit is not feasible. However, in the course of the meeting, the team, with the help of a facilitator, established that the district's high school is centrally located, has space as well as additional benefits such as child development courses. The child care for 3-, 4-, and 5-year-olds can be implemented in the high school, and high school students can participate as interns or work after school under the direction of the head child care teacher.

## Appointing a Program Coordinator

There are numerous other examples of questions and answers that, in the course of the organizational audit, provide the direction for the next steps in the planning process. One of the most critical of these is related to the appointment of an individual to assume responsibility for coordinating program planning, implementation, and operation.

Some school districts are able to appoint a program coordinator early on in the process, but others hire a program coordinator later and start by designating a lead person on staff, freeing a portion of that individual's time for major responsibilities associated with the planning process. Regardless of the approach, it is imperative to have a designated individual assume responsibility for the project in order to ensure that meetings are scheduled and that decisions are followed up. In the absence of such leadership, the planning process may never be completed, even though meetings and discussions occur.

In the event that someone on staff takes responsibility for coordinating the planning process, the district will have to appoint a program coordinator to oversee the implementation and operation of services once the planning is complete and the implementation of the program is imminent. A full- or part-time (depending on the scope of the effort) program coordinator may be needed in each school implementing the program, and if a district-wide approach is planned it is also advisable to appoint a district-level program director who will oversee the program's development in all the schools planning implementation. The appointment of a program coordinator and district director should be considered carefully since the success of implementation often depends on these individuals' leadership potential, their ability to handle ambiguity (which often occurs when a program is first initiated), and their administrative proficiency, since tasks such as fee collecting are often new to the school (see Chapter 6).

The program coordinator in particular also must have the ability to work across various sectors. This ability is important since the coordinator often has to win the support of the staff within the school as well as work collaboratively with other agencies and organizations. Iscoe (1995) highlights the critical role of the program coordinator in this regard. She also points out the various responsibilities of the coordinator, which in some cases entail not only overseeing operations but also proposing various policies and procedures, assuming budget responsibilities, fund-raising, and writing proposals.

Besides considering the coordinator's skills, it is also important to appoint or hire a coordinator whose educational background is relevant to the proposed program. Although this consideration is essential in any reform initiative, it is especially important in programs serving young children. In order to ensure the provision of good quality services, such programs must hire a coordinator with a background in early childhood care and education. Ideally the coordinator should have a master's degree in early childhood education; and either independently or in conjunction with the building principal, the coordinator will have to hire appropriately trained teachers to run the program. The child care staff should have an educational background in early childhood or child development, and although some staff members may have a bachelor's degree, other possibilities include an associate's degree or the Child Development Associate (CDA) credential, which is a competency-based credential signifying knowledge and experience in working with preschool children.

**Needs Assessment.** One of the activities the coordinator will undertake in collaboration with others on the planning team is a needs assessment. The assessment should be conceptualized by planning group members, each of whom should be aware of the function of the assessment, when it should be administered, and what approach should be adopted to ensure that complete and accurate data are collected. Timing is also important; assessing needs too early in the process is futile since families move in and out of the district and services change, rendering the information collected obsolete.

A needs assessment should be designed for each one of the components being considered for implementation. An assessment is made up of two parts. The first part establishes needs on the basis of available information, with the focus on two major questions:

- What services currently exist in the community?
- What are the characteristics and needs of the population to be served by the services being planned?

The information may be compiled from existing data sources, that is, from what is available at the school or in existing municipal and state agencies, as well as from other organizations such as the Chamber of Commerce and information and referral services. It is important to compile information not only about what services exist but also about whether or not the existing services meet the need. For example, in order to gauge the need for additional child care services, a school planning child care would need to know not only the number and location of existing licensed child care facilities but also if there are any waiting lists. For other components, the need might not be ascertained easily, and the school might need to develop good relations with other agencies and organizations in the community and work collaboratively with their staffs.

The second part of the needs assessment should seek to establish what parents perceive as their needs and, if programs were to be implemented, whether and to what extent parents would participate. Approaching parents in this regard should be one of the last items on the list of planning activities. Asking parents and others in the community about their needs too far in advance or prior to knowing what the district can realistically offer will only result in raised expectations and possible disappointment. One school district that sent out parent questionnaires before the planning process even began found that over a two-year period it had to go back to parents repeatedly with additional questions. Parents eventually refused to participate or indicate their support, and the program never reached the implementation phase.

Often the needs the school seeks to address are known, since the rationale underlying the desire to implement the program is based on educators' perception of what may be helpful to students and families. However, it is essential to obtain specific information that will guide the planning and development of the program. A school may be aware of the potential need for school-age child care since the majority of the parents are working, and since the first part of the needs assessment that relied on existing data may have indicated a need. However, at the start no documentation exists about how many parents would enroll their children in the proposed program and, more importantly, how many would do so if they had to pay a fee for the service. Parents who leave their children with a relative may indicate that they would enroll their child; but would they enroll their child if they found out later that they have to pay for the service? If fees are to be collected for child care, and/or if subsidies may be made available to eligible families, these facts should be mentioned in the needs assessment questionnaire. The questionnaire also should include questions that will lead to information about, for example, how many children, and of what age, are likely to be enrolled and what hours of operation are best for the parents involved. If a majority of parents are factory workers who begin their shift at 5:30 A.M., then a school-age child care program that begins at 6:00 A.M. is unlikely to meet their needs. These types of questions will provide data that are essential in the overall planning and design of the program and in establishing priorities and a time schedule for the implementation of its various aspects.

**Collecting Data.**    Just as a well-structured parent questionnaire is essential, so is the process used to collect data. As indicated earlier, schools are used to communicating with parents through the students, but this process can severely limit the response rate and jeopardize the accuracy of results. First, some students cannot be counted on to give parents the information. Second, this approach is, at best, useful only for some of the services, such as school-age child care, but not for others, such as those services that target preschool children, since many of them may not have an older sibling at school. Reaching all families in the community can be time-consuming and expensive. However, there are resources that may be put to use in this regard. For example, some schools have worked with the PTA membership to canvass the neighborhood and administer the questionnaire or to ask questions over the phone, whereas others have worked in collaboration with another volunteer organization in their community.

## Promoting the Program

**Building Support.**    Promoting the program to ensure that the community is aware of its existence is essential not only during the planning process but also throughout its operation. The first step in this regard is to reach out to and get the support of others in the community who are working with children and families. Although inherent in the implementation of school-based services is the assumption that service provision will occur within the school or that the school will assume an important role in initiating services, the school cannot separate itself from the larger community and has to establish relationships with other agencies and organizations. Getting to know and working collaboratively with other service providers will:

- ensure that good quality services are not duplicated unless needed
- facilitate awareness of the programs
- result in efficient use of resources

**Steering Committee.**   Some school districts take this first step of building support by creating a steering committee that is composed of school and non-school members. The steering committee, which generally functions during the planning phase, should be a group of individuals who share an interest in and commitment to early care and family support as well as an appreciation for schools' role in the provision of such services. Although it may be tempting to have as many groups, both from the school and from the community at large, and as many parents represented on the committee as possible, too large a group may be a deterrent to action. Arvey and Tijerina (1995) make this point; in the course of planning a program in a large urban area, they found that there were so many groups and individuals represented that it became a time-consuming and ineffective endeavor just to hold a meeting.

**Advisory Group.**   Since limiting the membership of the steering committee is advisable, some schools provide another means for individuals and organizations to participate by creating an advisory committee, or advisory council. The advisory group differs from the steering group in that it is established once the program is implemented and operational, whereas the steering committee's input is sought during the planning and pre-implementation phase. The function of the advisory group is to advise the staff on ways to facilitate implementation and operation of the program. The specific activities of the group may include fund-raising, information dissemination, coordination with existing community programs and other resources, and public relations. This latter activity is essential and should be ongoing, since continued support for the operation of the program, as well as for its expansion, will depend on the community's perception of its effectiveness and benefits.

## Challenges and Opportunities

The previous section describes some of the steps leading toward implementation. Although in most instances we have used examples drawn from the implementation of Schools of the 21st Century and other programs that focus on early care and family support services, the steps are generic and apply to the planning and implementation of other school reform initiatives as well. Also, what we have discussed is only an outline of what schools experience in practice; when schools are implementing such programs, many other issues arise, calling for more decisions. For example, schools have to:

- Define the role of school board members and their involvement in the program
- Establish an organizational structure

- Establish and implement policy decisions regarding resource allocation, fee assessment, and staff salaries, as well as the day-to-day operation of the program
- Address possible legal issues concerning the use of buildings, the assessment of fees, and the acquisition of grants

These are some of the many considerations and decisions that anyone initiating reforms will have to make, depending on the particular district and the scope of the program envisioned.

## Challenges

There are also numerous challenges to overcome. Staff resistance to the program, logistical hurdles, limited vision, and lack of commitment are some potential problems that we have discussed already. Some of these challenges may be anticipated at the outset and addressed as a means of averting potential problems.

**Funds.** There are additional challenges, not the least of which is funding. You will see in the next chapter that a major portion of the School of the 21st Century is designed to operate on a fee-for-service basis, but schools still need funds for start-up expenses, for the financial support of those services for which fees cannot be assessed, and for child care subsidies for families who are not able to pay. The challenge is not only to find funds but also, if successful in this regard, to coordinate the various different funding sources.

There are two issues regarding funds for nonacademic services in the school. First, public funds are limited, so those seeking reform must look into private sources of funding. Second, the public funds that are available come from disparate sources. Hence Lisbeth Schorr (1997) notes that federal subsidies for early childhood alone come from "ninety different programs located in eleven federal agencies and twenty offices" (241). The disparate character of these programs and agencies and offices not only makes it difficult for schools to know about the numerous public funds but also, once a school is successful in getting grants, requires that the school attend to innumerable details in order to meet the various guidelines and reporting procedures (Iscoe 1995). Larger school districts may have personnel who have time to make sense out of the disparate funding opportunities, but smaller districts have to rely on the entrepreneurial and creative skills of the superintendent, principal, or program coordinator.

We should emphasize that although the funding issue places a burden on educators implementing reform initiatives, the availability of money in and of itself will not always ensure success. The Annenberg Challenge initiative, for example, funded several schools with over $500 million over a five-year period. The central assumption was that giving money to educators at the local building level would result in needed change. Within the first three years, however, it became apparent that although money is necessary, it is not sufficient to bring about effective implementation (Olson 1997).

**Turf Issues and Opposition.**    Another challenge is dealing with the opposition. Schools are institutions embedded in the community, from which they draw their strengths. But as embedded institutions, they not only derive positive feedback about their efforts from the community but also are susceptible to criticism. Schools are, as Peshkin (1995) points out, contested institutions, continually having to defend practices and programs, especially when implementing early care and family support services, the provision of which is relatively new and outside the traditional conception of the American public school. Many people in the community, especially young families, are likely to want and be supportive of early care and family support services and would welcome the school's role in providing such services. However, there may be a small but vocal group opposing such programs, creating challenges to implementation. As we noted earlier, opposition also may come from within the school and from other organizations in the community serving the same population. Dryfoos (1994) notes that although such opposition is distracting, it rarely stalls the reform process, if it is anticipated and addressed at the outset.

**Space.**    Finding space for the services is another challenge. The space issue is not new to school districts; educators respond routinely to changes in enrollment, sometimes building new schools to meet the demand and at other times closing buildings when enrollment is down. Currently, enrollment in many elementary schools is high and space is at a premium. Further, many school buildings across the nation are old and in need of major repair. The issue of enrolling even more children or housing various support services in the school is therefore not addressed easily. Nevertheless, various solutions have been found: Using modular buildings, putting to new use previously abandoned school buildings, and renovating unused space within existing buildings are some approaches utilized by the School of the 21st Century and other similar programs.

How a school addresses the space issue is in part a reflection of the school's commitment to the program. Dryfoos (1994) notes that not all schools have adequate space for school-based services and at times place these in unsuitable and depressing places within the building: "The sense of hopelessness conveyed by a program tucked away next to the boiler room," she writes about a school-based program for teen mothers, "is hard to overcome. . . . It [has] the effect of hiding [the participants and] conveying a strong message that they [aren't] worthy of anything better" (156). This kind of situation is always a possibility, but when the entire staff is excited about the program, they often find ways to make other provisions and to make a statement in support of the program. For example, the Norfolk CoZi school we discussed earlier brought in two modular classrooms when the preschool child care services were planned. The modular units would have been suitable for the younger children, but, in order to convey the message that the new services are an integral part of the school, the school staff decided collectively that fourth and fifth graders would utilize the modular units and that the preschoolers' classrooms would be on the first floor of the school building. When the entire staff is in charge of making this type of decision, schools will not only achieve desired outcomes but also foster positive feelings about reform.

## Characteristics of Successful Schools

Given space and funding limitations and the likelihood of opposition to the effort, at least initially, it is a wonder that so many school districts have succeeded in implementing early care and family support services. What is even more impressive, however, is that in many Schools of the 21st Century, the programs have become institutionalized: Some of the programs have been operating for nearly ten years and have been both expanded and refined continually. What accounts for the success stories? In examining the process of implementation and the history of several Schools of the 21st Century, we have found several attributes that are predictive of successful implementation. We already have discussed some of these attributes:

- Schools that anticipate and address potential problems at the outset are more likely to succeed than others.
- Educators who regard the program as an integral aspect of the school are more likely to be successful than those who simply conceive of the effort as an add-on that is unrelated to the academic mission of the school.
- When educators follow a rational planning process that entails thinking through existing needs and available resources, they are able to design programs that are responsive to students and families, and such programs are likely to succeed.
- When educators "plan big but start small," they envision the program as they would like to have it in three to five years, but they phase in implementation and thereby aid success by building a strong foundation.

**Leadership.** Besides these and other attributes that may be found in earlier sections of the chapter, there are two other characteristics that distinguish successful schools. One is entrepreneurial leadership. The superintendents, school board members, and principals who want to implement early care and family support services are visionary, recognizing that such services represent an investment that will eventually pay off in terms of enhanced student achievement. Although the need for and potential benefits of early care and family support services are becoming recognized by more and more people, many remain ignorant of these needs and benefits. Indeed, as we noted earlier, often some people oppose the schools' role in the provision of such services. In successful schools, the leadership team "sells" the program to others within and outside the school and builds enthusiasm for the effort, as well as looks for the initial funds that may be needed.

**Commitment.**   The second characteristic is commitment. As with any endeavor, the implementation of early care and family support services is a difficult task, and participants in the planning process usually have many other duties and tasks to accomplish. If they succeed, they do so because they have a commitment to the effort, and such commitment is essential at every level.

We noted earlier that the role of the teachers is critical to the success of reform initiatives and that their support and involvement are needed. Also critical is the support of the board and superintendent and their commitment to the program. This point became apparent in the Annenberg Challenge initiative discussed earlier. The whole idea behind the initiative was to give money directly to schools, with the hope that they could avoid red tape and get right to the business of creating change through effective implementation of reforms at the building level. Despite the substantial amounts of money they were given, the schools failed to achieve the goal: "As Annenberg Challenge reformers [in New York City] and in other cities have learned, without the support of the existing district structure, progress can be difficult if not impossible" (Olson 1997, 30). Fiske (1992), in a review of several reform efforts, also notes that if such efforts are to succeed and survive, they need political protection and the support of the central office.

Also critical is the support of the principal and his or her commitment to the program. The role of the principal, especially during the planning phase and early in the implementation and operation of the program, is so critical that we advise schools against implementing new initiatives in schools where the principal's commitment is not apparent. Not only verbal commitment is essential, but also active participation in planning and implementation. Additionally, principals facilitate implementation by helping staff overcome difficulties and take positive actions. In evaluations of the School of the 21st Century program we have found that schools where the principals reported devoting at least 20 percent of their time to the program during the first year were far more successful than schools where the principals reported spending 5 percent or less of their time.

Fullan (1992), in his review of several studies on the implementation of school reform initiatives, makes these same points. He notes that the principals' actions "carry the message as to whether change will be taken seriously" (82). He notes further that among schools implementing the same program, the degree of implementation differs depending on the extent that principals participate. According to Fullan, principals should not be expected to operate the program and handle daily routines; nonetheless they must have direct and frequent communication with the staff, foster staff development, and share staff enthusiasm about, commitment to, and vision for the effort, not only within the school building but with others in the district and the community as a whole.

In summary, the work involved in implementation at the local level seems enormous and, to some, intimidating, a point made by Fullan (1992). He notes that when educators first consider reform programs, the task "looks enormous, complex [and] daunting—just too much" (56). Yet, in the majority of instances, educators and those who support and assist them—parents, consultants, and other professionals—rise to the challenge, becoming involved in and excited about the implementation. It is this excitement and commitment that enables them to overcome hurdles, capitalize on strengths, and work toward creating effective change.

## Widespread Implementation

Although we have learned much about the implementation process and the factors that lead to success at the local level, schools that have implemented early care and family support services or other innovations are still the exception rather than the rule. Schorr and Elias (Schorr and Schorr 1988; Schorr 1997; Elias 1997) make this point; they contend that although effective programs and services exist, such programs often represent isolated instances of excellence and are not widely implemented. This problem is not new. At issue is not only lack of widespread implementation of innovative reform efforts but also, in some cases, either the lack of consistency in or the outright failure of implementation (Elias, Gager, and Leon 1998).

The implementation of poor quality programs or, over time, of programs that in fact dilute intervention is another problem that afflicts efforts of reform. Schools implementing early care and family support programs are especially vulnerable in this regard because often financial constraints can lead to program changes that affect quality. A parent education program such as Parents as Teachers, for example, has yielded positive outcomes such as the promotion of parent involvement and higher academic achievement once children are in school. These positive outcomes are associated with regularly scheduled and frequent home visits, as well as with group interaction opportunities for parents and developmental assessments for the children. A lack of funds, however, may force a program like this to provide only occasional home visits, to increase the workload of each home educator, and to shorten the home visits or otherwise cut corners, thereby placing the program's integrity in jeopardy and risking failure. Similar problems may arise in the implementation of child care and early education programs if, due to financial difficulties, an insufficient number of staff or untrained staff are employed.

Both the failure to implement programs widely and poor quality implementation are problems common with innovations that have proven effective on a small scale but face challenges as the attempt is made to scale up. In part, difficulties in scaling up arise because of the way programs are generally developed, whereby far more attention is paid to the idea and initial design of a program than to its implementation beyond the model demonstration or pilot site. Program developers tend to put all their energies and resources into one school to demonstrate the effectiveness and feasibility of the initiative; they then evaluate the effort and claim success only to find out later that such success is limited to the demonstration site: Many of the conditions that factored into the success of the program—especially the constant attention and the coaching, nurturing, and financial and other resources that program developers offered to educators during the implementation process—cannot be replicated, and since the program is not widely implemented or replicated expanded efforts of reform do not resemble the original program and fail to produce positive outcomes (Elias 1997).

## Ensuring Widespread Implementation

In conceptualizing the school of the 21st Century, our intent at the outset was to ensure widespread implementation, since our goal was to address the need, across the United States, for good quality and affordable child care. Rather than limit our work to one demonstration site, we developed the School of the 21st Century National Center and enhanced our staff capacity to enable us to treat all schools interested in implementation as demonstration sites and to provide each with technical assistance, training, and individualized coaching.

**Technical Assistance and Training.**   Our approach is twofold. First, we provide on-site technical assistance and training as well as opportunities to attend national and regional training conferences. The technical assistance staff, who we refer to as implementation associates, are based at Yale and have a designated number of schools in their region; an associate works with each of the schools intensely for about two years. As the schools become more proficient and implementation is under way, the associates assume an advisory role and provide only occasional assistance, usually by phone.

*Peer Training.*  The implementation staff is assisted by superintendents, principals, program coordinators, and others who have successfully implemented the School of the 21st Century. We have found that pairing experienced 21C educators with their counterparts in schools beginning the implementation is an effective and efficient training approach that not only enables educators to learn from one another but also provides an informal support system that can be an invaluable source of strength during the initial phases of implementation. This peer approach to training is especially effective when we pair educators from similar districts or those likely to experience similar problems.

*Training Conferences.*  Peer training opportunities also exist at the National Academy, which is an annual, four- or five-day orientation and training conference, as well as at smaller training events held in several regions around the country. The latter training and informational events are usually made by arrangement at the invitation of several schools or a university interested in learning about the approach. Several schools that have implemented 21C also have arranged such regional training events as a means of solidifying their relationship with each other and nurturing their ability to network. Such regional training events provide opportunities for more staff to participate since they are closer to the school.

Participation in regional training is at present voluntary. However, each district interested in implementing the program must participate in the national training at least once. The faculty at the national training is made up of experienced 21C educators as well as invited guest speakers. The conferences serve newcomers as well as those who have already implemented the program and provide the latter with the opportunity to further their growth and to showcase their efforts.

**National Network.**  The second aspect of our effort to facilitate widespread implementation is the establishment of a formal School of the 21st Century National Network. Schools that have implemented the School of the 21st Century—as of 1998 they numbered close to 600—have participated in an informal network and have helped other schools implement the program through peer training and presentations at national and regional conferences, described above. However, as the program continues to grow nationally, it has become imperative to ensure that services at the local level maintain a high level of quality. The National Network entails the development of standardized professional materials and services, the codification of procedures for working with schools, as well as a tiered, fee-based membership structure (see Box 5.2). The latter provides opportunities for schools to: (1) continue to be formally affiliated with the program even when they have successfully completed implementation; and (2) work

BOX 5.2   School of the 21st Century
Network Membership Options

## Affiliate Member

*Eligibility*   Any school or organization that would like information and regular updates on 21C and school-based family support services

*Benefits*   Subscription to *21Community News,* the network's quarterly newsletter packed with essential information on best practices, funding, research, publicity, and so on

*Cost*   $100 annually

## Associate Member

*Eligibility*   Any school currently implementing the 21C/Family Resource Center

*Benefits*   Quarterly newsletter, *21Community News*

25 percent discount on tuition at 21C conferences and training events

Sampler packet including three free copies of all 21C publications and a 25 percent discount on additional copies

Regular consultation and guidance from 21C Network staff, including at least one site visit

*Cost*   $1,000 annually

## Contract School

*Eligibility*   Any school new to the 21C Network that requires intensive support and technical assistance

*Benefits*   *Associate membership benefits, plus:*
Intensive mentoring and coaching from 21C Network staff

Customized training

*Cost*   Contract schools enter individualized, three-year agreements that specify the support they will receive from the Yale Bush Center. Contracts start at $10,000 per year. A limited number of schools are selected to receive contracts.

---

**Demonstration Site**

*Eligibility*  Schools that have fully implemented the 21C/FRC Model

Selection every two years through a *competitive application process*

*Benefits*  *Associate membership benefits, plus:*

National recognition

Invitation for selected staff to become part of the 21C National Faculty

*Cost*  All membership benefits are free. Demonstration site status must be renewed every two years.

---

toward refining their efforts, eventually becoming eligible to apply to become 21C National Demonstration Sites.

These approaches to widespread implementation have enabled us to respond to the interest schools have in implementing the program and in maintaining enthusiasm for the effort once the program has been implemented. This national orientation is an essential ingredient of scale-up efforts that have been adopted by other initiatives, such as Success for All (Slavin, Dolan, and Madden 1994). However, this national orientation in and of itself is not sufficient. Practical information about program implementation—what difficulties to expect, how to overcome them, and what specific steps to take—and an understanding of the local level described earlier are also important (Fullan 1992). Such information and understanding can be obtained only when program developers work with several schools, when they "immerse themselves into the local settings and contexts . . . and extend their ranks through participation" in implementation (Elias 1997, 261). Through the dual efforts of program developers and local-level implementers, a program can achieve widespread implementation and ensure that quality is maintained.

# 6    Program Funding

A QUESTION THAT COMES UP in any discussion of program development and implementation is, How will it be paid for? Funding is such a critical aspect of implementation that we need to devote an entire chapter to its discussion. As we stated previously, child care and family support services are essential to the educational success and improved life outcomes of many children. However, such services fall outside the traditional academic realm and at this point are unlikely to be included in a school district's budget. In the absence of a national funding plan, the many schools now providing such services have had to find various ways to pay for them. In this chapter, we describe how some of these schools currently finance the operation of the programs, and we also present a funding proposal that would increase the number of schools able to offer the services. It will become apparent in the course of the chapter that our proposal is one of several possible funding strategies and that regardless of the strategy there are challenges and obstacles that have to be overcome.

## Funding and Financing of the Human Services System

Before discussing specific proposals, we should note that the financing and funding of child care and other family support services—and, for that matter, of schools in general—are important. We say this not only for the obvious reason that resources are needed for operation but also because the methods for financing affect the delivery of services and the nature and outcomes of programs (Farrow and Joe 1992). Financing issues have been discussed for many years. In recent years, however, they have captured increased attention, and in response there have been widespread calls for school finance reforms and for massive changes in social and health services—not only in the way they are funded but also in the way they are delivered.

### Inadequacies in the Current System

**Fragmentation of Services.**   Indeed, the delivery of services is intricately related to and dependent on the way they are funded. Current funding strategies, which were developed in a different era and have evolved over

103

the years, seem to be obsolete today and cause numerous problems. Morrill (1992), in a review of the human services delivery system, analyzes the three components—education, health, and social services—that make up the system. He emphasizes that the system is so vast and complex that it defies a simple description; but for clarity, he notes that each of the components that make up the system is very different in terms of organizational structure and delivery of services, and that each also has its own "programmatic relationships to federal, state and local governments through a variety of programs" (Morrill 1992, 32). In social services in particular, Morrill (1992) and others (e.g., Schorr and Schorr 1988; Schorr 1997) note that this "system" results in fragmentation and at times duplication of services; and it prevents efficient delivery of services and contributes to the inability to reach children and to effectively respond to children and families with multiple needs. Perhaps even more critical, despite years of program interventions, many problems that children and families experience persist, and some are getting worse (Levy and Shepardson 1992; Schorr and Schorr 1988; Schorr 1997) and cost more to address (Larson, Gomby, and Behrman 1992; Lewit 1992).

**Inadequate Funding Base.**   Huge amounts of money are spent each year (to provide an idea of how much is involved, Morrill [1992] estimates that in 1989 close to $280 billion in federal, state, and local funds and tax expenditures were spent in human services for children), but the system as it currently operates is nevertheless underfunded and has not kept pace with changes in child and family needs. Rather than change how the system is funded and how the money is distributed among agencies and services within these agencies, new programs are developed, but these operate within the existing framework. Given limited spending, such new programs often target crises rather than prevent problems and are short-lived, and often there is not enough money to serve all those who are eligible. Not only do we fail, as a result, to adequately serve children and families, we continue to have a patchwork of small-scale, temporary services rather than long-term programs that are "systematically developed and funded" (Farrow and Joe 1992, 56).

This state of affairs is frustrating because we have come to recognize that the traditional response described above rarely helps children in need, and exacerbates the problems of fragmentation and inadequately funded services. Scientific knowledge about children's development and about prevention and intervention strategies (Weissberg, Kuster, and Gullotta 1997; Gullotta 1997) has fueled a desire to overhaul the system. However, the need for more money within each of the components of the system has been a critical factor as well. Although there have been numerous proposals for change, they have been tried only on a small scale and have represented minimal change, as opposed to an overhauling of the way the system operates.

Kagan and her colleagues (1995) note that there has been experimentation with comprehensive funding and financing reforms across various human service agencies. One experiment combines such services as health, mental health, and job training with early care and education, thereby serving not only children but their parents as well (Smith 1991). Another experiment links education with human services. As we described in Chapter 2, school-linked services attempt to better serve children by having various agencies work together, as well as use the school building as "an easily accessible physical plant . . . that can be . . . [the] center of positive community activity" (Levy and Shepardson 1992, 46).

Although there is agreement that various human service agencies, including schools, need to be involved in the provision of services, some people question whether these services need to be located at the school. In any case, regardless of the type of school-linked services proposed, it is an essential aspect of all such proposals that individuals from different agencies are willing and able not only to work together but also to pool their financial resources. The financial resources of any one agency are simply too limited to address the problems of children and families (Farrow and Joe 1992). However, although a handful of communities have tried to put the idea of interagency cooperation and the pooling of resources into practice, and though much has been written about this idea, it has yet to be put into practice systematically for a sustained period of time.

**Inequities in Funding.** A related problem is inequities in funding that result in differential support, dependent on where children and families live. Kirst (1994) mentions studies that have shown that in several states there are huge inequities in spending for health and social services; some counties in a state may spend less than $1 a year per child for such services, and another county in the same state may spend nearly $50 per child. Such inequities—which occur for different reasons, depending on the community in question—do not seem to be related to need. A county spending more per child does not necessarily have fewer children who need services. Such inequities are significant but have not attracted much attention. Inequities in school financing, however, have been much debated for some time, and efforts have focused on the view that equalizing the amount of money spent on children in poor districts and on those in wealthier districts will result in better educational outcomes.

Admittedly, equalizing the resources of schools in different locations, or at least providing poor districts with adequate funds, is a helpful strategy, but it should be considered only as a basic first step; simply equalizing financial resources without considering how districts will use the money may not result in improved educational outcomes for many of the students. The problem might not simply be that some school districts have less money and therefore fewer resources than others, but also that these same poor districts have more students with multiple problems who need *more* services. As we point out in Chapter 1 and in other writings (e.g., Zigler and Finn-Stevenson 1994), there are factors outside of the school and circumstances that occur from the birth of the child throughout childhood that influence educational outcome and ability to profit from instruction.

More and more, legislators and the courts in several states have called for redefining equity in education not only in terms of finances but also in terms of programs that need to be provided if children are to achieve acceptable levels of academic achievement. In states such as Kentucky and New Jersey, court-mandated services include the provision of early care and other programs for children considered at risk for educational failure. Such actions have meant that, at least in some schools, partial funding is available for the provision of nonacademic support services.

## Problems with Child Care

The court-mandated and state-legislated programs often focus on school readiness issues and on the provision of preschool experiences for part of the day. As such, they do not address the need for all-day child care for preschool children and for before- and after-school and vacation child care for school-age children. Obviously, any infusion of money and associated services is helpful, but again, these efforts represent only a partial, temporary solution (and only in some states) and fail to address issues related to the need for and funding of child care.

We discussed issues related to child care in Chapter 3 and noted that in child care, as in other social services, what exists is a non-system—a patchwork of non-profit, for-profit, and individually operated child care facilities. Not only are services fragmented and unequal—some children have access to good quality services, others do not—there are also concerns about the availability and accessibility of child care services for children from birth though age 12 and about the quality of these services.

Although it is difficult to estimate accurately parents' share of the cost of child care, we know that it is substantial and that it takes up a considerable portion of the family income. For low income parents in particular, child care expenses amount to as much as 27 percent of their earnings (Hofferth 1996). And regarding the overall cost of child care, some researchers estimate that in the United States parents pay as much as 80 percent of the cost (Helburn and Howes 1996); others estimate approximately 70 percent (Stoney and Greenberg 1996). The variation in the estimate is due to the fact that it is difficult to ascertain exactly how much parents pay for child care, in part because many parents and providers may not fully disclose the amount.

Federal and state governments also assume part of the child care cost. Federal spending for child care and early education amounts to about $11 billion, which subsidizes the cost of care for low income children and funds some programs directly (U.S. House Committee on Ways and Means 1996); a very small percentage of that amount is spent on program quality issues such as staff training. The fragmentation of services makes it difficult to ascertain exactly how services are funded and how the money is actually distributed, and it is unclear how much is spent for all-day child care, since the phrase "early care and education" is all-encompassing and includes part-day preschool programs as well as full-day child care. However, it is estimated that in the early 1990s, the majority of federal spending for child care and early education targeted low income, at-risk families (through the Child Care and Development Block Grant, AFDC Child Care, Transitional Child Care, and At-Risk Child Care) and that some assistance was also provided to middle-income, working families through tax-based subsidies. These subsidies include tax credits, tax deductions for employers, and child care payments made with pretax dollars, which, in effect, reduce the amount of taxes parents pay (Mitchell and Dichter 1993). These initiatives are designed to help parents with the cost of child care and, in a small way, encourage employers to address their employees' need for child care (Stoney and Greenberg 1996).

Besides these public efforts to fund child care and early education, the federal government and, to a much lesser degree, the states also provide funding for children from birth to age 5 who have special needs; this funding includes money for child care services for this population of children. Kagan and Cohen (1997) note further that there are non-public institutions—religious institutions, volunteer organizations, and businesses—that fund child care and early education by contributing either cash or in-kind support. Although such contributions often make a difference to individual programs, collectively they amount to a very small percentage of the total cost of child care.

The actual cost of child care per child has remained relatively stable for many years, in large part because staff salaries have remained low (Hofferth 1996). Additionally, despite the seemingly large amounts of public money spent on early care and education, the federal and state share of the cost has decreased over the years and parents' share of the cost has increased. Some researchers note that the amount of public spending in the early care and education field is much lower than the need for services, so that states are unable to provide subsidies to all the low income children who are eligible (Adams and Poersch 1997). Kagan and Cohen (1997) note further that the government's "investment" in early care and education not only fails to meet the need but also is much lower than the amount spent on public education. When children enter school and until they are 18, public spending amounts to an average of $5,800 per child, which is made up of local, state, and federal governments' contributions. This amounts to about $5 an hour per child. Government spending for the care and education of children under age 5, however, amounts to about $2 an hour per child (Kagan and Cohen 1997; Mitchell and Dichter 1993).

The government's role in child care and the amount of public money devoted to such care reflect current priorities, which are a matter of national, state, and local policies. The difference in spending per child between child care and education results in lower wages for individuals who care for young children than for teachers of older children, and these wages have implications for the quality of care children receive.

The quality of care children receive is critical since it directly affects children's developmental outcome. As we noted in Chapter 3, the various issues related to child care—the cost of care, the lack of accessibility and the lack of availability of good quality care, as well as the attendant issues of staff training and staff/child ratios—are all intricately related. Thus addressing the issue of cost in the child care field is not simply a matter of infusing additional money. We also need to build a sound infrastructure that can ensure that we have staff training, sufficient services to meet the need, and universal access to good quality and affordable services, which means ensuring that all children have access to such services.

## Our Response: The School of the 21st Century

As things now stand, only some affluent families are able to purchase good quality child care; the majority of working, middle-class families are unable to do so, and subsidies for the cost of caring for low income children are inadequate. From a policy perspective, a major aspect of the child care problem is the lack of a coherent system. What we have in place, as we stated in Chapter 3, is a patchwork of services, some delivered by individuals out of their homes, others operated by non-profit and for-profit groups in a variety of settings. A few of the services are of good quality; the majority are not. Although some people argue that additional funds alone can address the child care problem, it is our contention that, given the lack of a system, even with additional money we will be unable to make any improvements with any assurance that they will be implemented and sustained.

### Toward a Realistic Solution to the Problem

Attempts to address the above-noted problems have resulted in calls for both lesser and greater government involvement in child care. Some people have advocated limiting the role of government to tax credits, whereas others have argued for increased government spending and involvement in such issues as the regulation of child care facilities. These and other views were represented in hundreds of bills introduced in Congress and culminated in the passage of the 1990 Child Care and Development Act. The law makes funding available to the states in the form of block grants, allowing allocation decisions to be made at the state level. To some extent, this method of funding represents an opportunity since each state can respond more readily to its population's needs. However, in light of both the non-uniform standards for child care that exist across the United States (Young, Marsland, and Zigler 1997) and the diversity of services within the existing non-system, this legislation does not address the need to establish a comprehensive, accessible, quality *system* of child care; it merely provides some additional funds, and even these are insufficient.

The majority of states are unable to fully address even basic needs for child care subsidies because the funding still falls far short of meeting the needs of all low income families (Adams and Poersch 1997; Blank 1994; Ebb 1994). Even if additional funds were made available to meet the needs of low income families for subsidies, no provisions exist for addressing the needs of working- and middle-class families. Recall from Chapter 3 that Hofferth (1996) indicates that children from the lowest and highest income families have the highest quality care, and that the children of working- and middle-class families receive lower quality care. Although tax-based initiatives such as credits, deductions, and exemptions help some parents with the cost of care, such initiatives do not address the quality of care issue nor the availability of services.

Given the scope of the problem, we contend that we must build a stable, reliable, good quality child care system that is integrated with the political and economic structure of society and is tied to a recognized and easily accessible societal institution—the public school. This need for such a coordinated, accessible child care system led to the conceptualization of the School of the 21st Century program. The program, as we noted in Chapters 2 and 5, calls for implementing a child care system within the already existing educational system, making use, where possible, of school buildings and various administrative support services of local education agencies. Although several support services are included in the School of the 21st Century program, its focus is on the provision of good quality, affordable child care for children from ages 3 to 12. The strength and ultimate potential of the program stems from its integration with the education system. From a developmental perspective, the program embraces and actualizes the view that learning begins at birth and occurs in all settings, not just within the classroom. This view encourages the necessary consistency and enrichment opportunities for children to realize their academic potential.

## Financing the School of the 21st Century

From a cost perspective, the program, which makes use of the already existing educational system, provides an efficient means by which to address the need for good quality, affordable child care. Since many schools already have implemented the program, we can discuss how the schools manage to operate the program in absence of any supportive government policy, and later we will present a proposal for an ideal funding situation. In both the current and the ideal financing plan, parental fees for services represent an important core element. However, the ideal plan calls for different levels of government to assume some responsibility for supporting a system of child care, as they do for public education.

**21C Schools: Current Funding Practices.**   Currently, school districts that have implemented the School of the 21st Century finance the program in a variety of ways, but in all cases, the child care components operate on parental fees for service, with a sliding scale that ensures low income children have access to the services. The fees tend to be about the same as, or slightly below, other child care fees in the community, but they prove to be sufficient because unlike other child care centers, Schools of the 21st Century do not pay rent for the use of the building. Admittedly, some not-for-profit centers make use of donated space. However, unlike the School of the 21st Century, they lack an overall administrative structure and still may have to pay for custodial and/or utility costs, insurance, and secretarial and administrative expenses that are provided by the school district in 21C schools. The advantages of linking child care with an existing educational system extend beyond the ability of the existing system to cover overhead operational expenses, but this coverage is critically important.

Schools need start-up funds to support building renovations that may be necessary to accommodate young children, as well as to purchase materials and to operate the program during the first year. The majority of schools have been able to secure start-up funds from community foundations and corporations or from enabling legislation (for example, in Kentucky and Connecticut, discussed later in this chapter). After the first year, many schools are able to operate and even make a profit on the basis of parental fees for the child care services and the school district's in-kind support (the profit is put back into the program to support various other components and also to provide staff training and to upgrade staff salaries). In cases of low income children, some schools arrange for public subsidies; or sometimes a consortium of businesses in the area near the schools donate money to a scholarship fund that is used to offset tuition costs for needy families. In Figures 6.1 and 6.2 we break down sources of start-up support for a School of the 21st Century in an urban and a suburban area, respectively. In Figures 6.3 and 6.4, again for an urban and a suburban site, we show sources of revenue that cover operating costs during the second year of implementation. In many districts, the second year is still considered a start-up period, but, as is evident in the figures, parental fees begin to assume a greater share of the cost.

FIGURE 6.1    Sources of Revenue for a School of
the 21st Century in an Urban District: Start-Up Costs

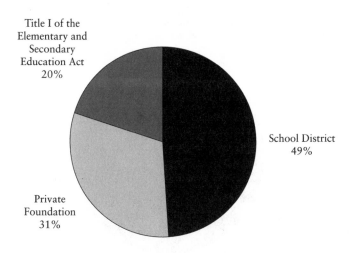

Title I of the
Elementary and
Secondary
Education Act
20%

School District
49%

Private
Foundation
31%

- Start-up costs totaled $140, 000.
- The program serves 65 preschool and 100 school-age children.
- Of these children, 92 percent are eligible for free or reduced-cost lunches
- Start-up costs included the purchase of two mobile units (donated by the school district), a coordinator's staff time, and the renovation of four preschool classrooms.
- Upper grades have moved into the mobile units, and preschoolers occupy four classrooms in an early childhood wing of the school.

As we indicated earlier, child care is the core of the School of the 21st Century, and often schools have to find the means to support the other components, as well as any additional services that may be needed. To fund these additional services, some schools use part of the surplus from the child care revenue, and others use various public and private sources of support. In Table 6.1, drawing on the collective experiences of several Schools of the 21st Century, we show the various sources of revenue that support the operation of child care and all other components of the program.

In general, the program has been implemented as a grassroots effort at the initiative of local school districts' leadership. However, in two states, financial support for the program is available through state funds. In Connecticut, legislation enacted in 1988 to implement three demonstration programs was broadened in 1989 and was later supplemented by a three-

FIGURE 6.2    Sources of Revenue for a School of the
21st Century in a Suburban District: Start-Up Costs

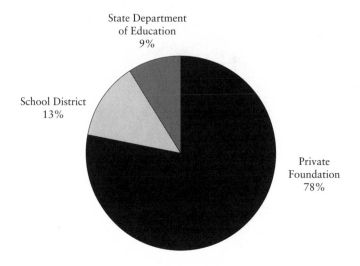

State Department
of Education
9%

School District
13%

Private
Foundation
78%

- Start-up costs totaled $160, 000.
- The program serves 69 preschool and 100 school-age children.
- Of these children, 20 percent are eligible for free or reduced-cost lunches.
- Start-up costs included the renovation of four classrooms (paid for by
  foundation grants), the in-kind contribution of a coordinator's staff time
  (donated by the school district), and staff training modules (paid for by the
  state Department of Education).

year federal grant and by school readiness legislation so that now over
sixty schools in the state operate Family Resource Centers, as the program
is known in Connecticut and Kentucky. In Kentucky, the program is part
of the 1990 Kentucky Education Reform Act (KERA), which provided
funding for the development of Family Resource and Youth Services Centers; the legislation phased these programs into school districts over a five-
year period.

**Special Education and Title I.**    Schools of the 21st Century also supplement parental fees for child care by having several slots for special education children, since public funding is available for the education and care
of these children, beginning at preschool or even earlier. In these cases, the
special education services are inclusive, meaning that the children participate in the same program with all other children. Some programs also use

FIGURE 6.3    Sources of Revenue for a School of
the 21st Century in an Urban District: Operating Costs

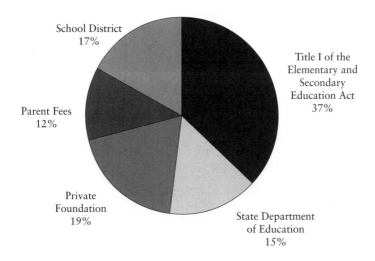

- The total annual budget for ongoing operations is $362,000.
- No fees are charged for the preschool program. The district has not yet used child care subsidies for its low income preschool and school-age children but is in the process of making available such subsidies.
- Certified teachers and paraprofessionals are used in the preschool classrooms. Average group size is 16 children with one teacher and one teaching assistant (8 to 1 ratio).
- Teachers are given an additional stipend of $15 per hour to work in the before- and after-school program and the vacation program. Parents pay nominal fees for these programs.
- Title I dollars are used to pay for the teachers in three of the four preschool classrooms. The school district pays for the fourth classroom.
- The district also provides in-kind support in the form of custodial, food, office, and administrative services (not depicted in the chart).

Title I funds; these funds enable schools, particularly those in urban settings, to pay for the child care teacher salaries.

**Linkages with Head Start.**    Head Start is one of the most popular programs among policymakers, so the idea of linking Head Start to child care as a means of addressing the child care crisis is at times discussed. However, Head Start's focus is on children from low income families, and the amount of federal money appropriated for Head Start, although relatively substantial, meets only a percentage of the need. Additionally, Head Start

FIGURE 6.4    Sources of Revenue for a School of the
21st Century in a Suburban District: Operating Costs

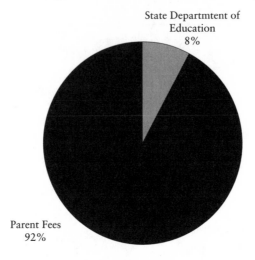

State Departmtent of
Education
8%

Parent Fees
92%

- The total annual budget for ongoing operations is $379,348.

- Operating costs for the child care and after-school components are supported almost entirely by parent fees. In fact, the fees for child care subsidize
  other 21C service components.

- The district offers sliding-scale fees to parents: 50 percent of preschoolers
  and 20 percent of school-age children receive some reduction in fees.

- Sliding-scale fees are possible because occupancy costs such as rent, utilities,
  insurance, and some administrative costs are covered by the district in the
  form of in-kind donations (not depicted in the chart).

- This program uses preschool teachers and assistants rather than certified
  teachers. The preschool staff members are paid at rates comparable to the local market rate, although benefits and regular raises are provided, which
  should reduce turnover.

- In its second year of operation, this 21C program is just breaking even finan-
  cially. Grants from federal, state, and foundation sources will be necessary if
  services other than child care are to be offered.

is, with a few exceptions, a half-day program, and there are other factors
unique to the program that would make its adaptation to a universal child
care system problematic.

   Although there is no formal policy for linking 21C and Head Start, some
of the 21C schools, with the full knowledge and approval of the Head Start
grantor, have made this link at the local level in several ways. In some
school districts, for example, Head Start is fully integrated; the Head Start
children attend the same program as the child care children, but only for
part of the day.[1] In this case, the funding associated with each child attend-

TABLE 6.1    Revenue Sources Used to Fund the Child Care and
Parent Outreach Components of the School of the 21st Century

| Component | Funding Source |
|---|---|
| Before- and after-school and vacation child care for school-age children | Sliding-scale fees (paid by parents)<br>AFDC vouchers<br>State grants<br>Foundation grants<br>Drug-Free Schools grant<br>Employer subsidies for child care<br>Family Resource Center grants<br>(in Kentucky and Connecticut) |
| Preschool child care | Sliding-scale fees (paid by parents)<br>Special education funds<br>AFDC vouchers<br>State grants<br>Head Start (in cases of 21C–Head Start integration)<br>Foundation grants<br>Child Care and Development Block Grant<br>Town council<br>Employer subsidies for child care<br>Title I of Elementary and Secondary Education Act<br>Department of Education funds<br>Family Resource Center grants<br>(in Kentucky and Connecticut) |
| Parent outreach | State grants<br>Department of Education funds<br>Department of Human Services grants<br>Foundation grants<br>Title I of Elementary and Secondary Education Act<br>Drug-Free Schools grant<br>Child Care and Development Block Grant<br>Family Resource Center grants<br>(in Kentucky and Connecticut) |
| Family child care provider network | Support by other components<br>Child Care and Development Block Grant |
| Information and referral | Partnership with local child care resource and referral agencies<br>Supported by other components<br>State grants<br>Foundation grants<br>Title I of Elementary and Secondary Education Act<br>State Department of Education funds |

ing Head Start becomes part of the operating money for the child care components. In other schools, primarily those that operated Head Start before also implementing 21C, the program is separate but is under the overall 21C umbrella, facilitating such activities as joint staff training. In at least one school district, a partnership was established between the school and a community-based Head Start grantee; the school district contracted with the latter to plan and implement the early childhood child care component of 21C.

**Medicaid.** The use of Title I funds, the inclusion of special education children, and the collaboration with Head Start programs are some of the ways that schools have been able to expand the scope and reach of the program once it is implemented. Several schools also have established a Medicaid case management system by training staff nurses to identify children eligible for Medicaid and to document which services in the school are supplied to Medicaid eligible children. Because such services are reimbursable, the school district can use Medicaid funds to pay for these services (Farrow and Joe 1992). Although such funds may be redirected to any of the various programs and services within the district, these funds have the potential for assisting in the financing of the School of the 21st Century, and indeed this has been the case in some 21C schools (Lubker 1995).

## Funding the School of the 21st Century: The Vision

At this point, many of the Schools of the 21st Century are relatively new, but in all sites progress in implementation is evident. Among the more mature sites—that is, those in operation three or more years—the program is expanding to include (1) more schools within the district, (2) increased participation among children and families, and (3) additional services that address families' needs. Regenstein, Silow-Carroll, and Meyer (1995), as part of an overall study on early education models, conducted an independent study of one school district's School of the 21st Century and concluded that the School of the 21st Century

> proves that a high-quality, affordable preschool program can be successfully implemented in a public school setting. Indeed, a number of Schools of the 21st Century have begun in the past several years in urban, suburban, and rural areas, demonstrating the program's replicability and adaptability to various settings. Significant participation rates indicate that the program does not have to be free in order to attract enrollees. For many families, reasonable user fees are not a barrier to enrollment. (46)

Schools of the 21st Century not only provide good quality child care, they also address inequities in early experiences by ensuring that every child, regardless of the family's income, has access to preschool services as part of the child care component. In this way Schools of the 21st Century follow the example of several industrialized nations, such as France and Italy, where school enrollment begins in the preschool years.

Although the schools implementing the School of the 21st Century program constitute a good start and have provided invaluable lessons on various implementation issues discussed in the previous chapters, the concept of linking child care and education is not likely to be expanded on a national scale without changes in policy and funds specifically dedicated to the program. The policy and funding changes needed are included in our vision for financing the School of the 21st Century, a discussion of which follows. The financing plan, although presented as a vision, is grounded in reality. We acknowledge that radical changes in how the nation regards child care are needed if we are to reach the ideal wherein citizens see good quality child care, like education, as the right of each American child and agree to finance it accordingly. At the same time, we realize that such changes will occur only incrementally over time. Nevertheless, changes need to be initiated now, and these changes are the focus of our plan for financing the School of the 21st Century.

The plan calls for supporting the School of the 21st Century on the basis of parental fees for services combined with financial support from the state, local education agencies, and the federal government.

**The Role of States.** The states' major role in the development of the school of the 21st Century is to stimulate and coordinate the development of the program statewide. We propose that each state invest in the program by supporting start-up costs in each school district and, later on, by supporting the state Department of Education's ability to evaluate and coordinate the program and to provide schools with technical assistance and training in early care and education. Many state education agencies already have an early childhood division that could be expanded to include additional staff to coordinate the School of the 21st Century.

In our projections for funding the School of the 21st Century statewide, we looked at the potential costs in one state and have identified several assumptions that are based on information derived from a state where the various population statistics are a reasonably close match to national averages:

- There are 120 school districts in the state.
- Approximately 20 percent of the children in the state are in poverty.
- 30 percent of school-age children receive free or reduced-cost lunch.

- In 20 percent of the school districts, more than 50 percent of the children participate in free or reduced-cost lunch.
- The total population of 3- and 4-year-olds in the state is about 250,000.

Our projections take into account two options, both of which may be considered as an adaptation of Kentucky's efforts in the development of Family Resource and Youth Services Centers. In Option I, the state would provide a one-time start-up grant to each school district, based on a formula that favors districts with more free and reduced-cost lunches. Various formulas are possible. In our example, the base grant per school district is $75,000 plus $50 for each student that receives a free or reduced-cost lunch, for a maximum of $250,000 for the start-up grant. In this scenario, the start-up period is considered to be one year. In addition to the start-up grants—which would be phased in over a five-year period so that an increasing number of schools participate—the state would need to appropriate funds for:

1. the administration of the program and the provision of technical assistance and training, which we calculate at an annual appropriation of 5 percent of the grant program for five years
2. evaluation, which we calculate at the rate of an annual appropriation of 1 percent of the grant program for five years

We propose that the grant program be administered by the state Department of Education. The total investment for the state under this option is approximately $26,000,000 over a five-year period.

Option II is based on the same assumptions and follows the same recommendations but regards the start-up period more realistically as a longer period of time and thus calls for a three-year diminishing allocation grant for each school district. For example, a district may receive $200,000 the first year, $150,000 the second year, and $75,000 during the final year. This diminishing allocation will enable the school district to build a strong foundation for its School of the 21st Century and to provide the time to make a transition from state to local and parental support. As in the first option, a formula would be developed to favor schools on the basis of the number of students who receive free and reduced-cost lunches. Administrative and evaluation costs are calculated as in the first option, and we again allow for a phase-in approach that sees an increasing number of school districts participating each year. However, since the start-up period is three years as opposed to one year, the overall grant program would be in effect for seven years, and the total investment would be approximately $54,420,000 (see Table 6.2).

TABLE 6.2 Total Costs to the State for the Start-Up of Schools of the 21st Century[a,b]

| | Implementation Phase | Grants | Evaluation | Admin. | Total Costs |
|---|---|---|---|---|---|
| Year 1 | Planning | $0 | $60,000 | $300,000 | $360,000[c] |
| Year 2 | 25% of districts | 6,000,000 | 60,000 | 300,000 | 6,360,000 |
| Year 3 | 50% of districts | 10,500,000 | 105,000 | 525,000 | 11,130,000 |
| Year 4 | 75% of districts | 12,750,000 | 127,500 | 637,500 | 13,515,000 |
| Year 5 | 100% of districts | 12,750,000 | 127,500 | 637,500 | 13,515,000 |
| Year 6 | 100% of districts | 6,750,000 | 67,500 | 337,500 | 7,155,000 |
| Year 7 | 100% of districts | 2,250,000 | 22,500 | 112,500 | 2,385,000 |
| Total State Expenditures | | $51,000,000 | $570,000 | $2,850,000 | $54,420,000 |

[a]Including start-up grants, evaluation, and administrative costs.
[b]Based on assumptions about the state role as outlined in pages 117–118.
[c]This is the planning year for the overall state grant program. During this year, the state would develop the administrative structure that would govern the School of the 21st Century program, issue a request for proposals, select the first cohort of school districts to participate, and devise plans for the overall evaluation of the statewide 21C program.

In either scenario, the state grants would facilitate the implementation of the program in one or two schools within a district. It has been our experience with existing sites that each district starts with one or two schools and is eventually able to provide the services in every one of the elementary schools. Dryfoos (1994) provides similar examples, showing how in some areas, such as Seattle, a state grant for one school-based health clinic served as a catalyst for district-wide clinics that were funded through a special tax.

**The Role of Local Education Agencies.** The state start-up grant would enable local school districts to initiate implementation of the School of the 21st Century and to prepare the program for operation. After the start-up period, parents who can afford it pay for the child care services. Low income parents might be eligible for child care subsidies. Both parental fees and subsidies cover operational expenses incurred by the child care service component of 21C. On average, parents pay about $3,000–$4,000 a year for child care for preschoolers in the School of the 21st Century. The fees vary, depending on market rates in the different communities, as well as on other factors. The fees and subsidies should be supplemented by the local school district, which, in addition to assuming the costs of some of the operational expenses such as maintenance and utilities, should support every child in child care.

For example, for school-age children, the per-child annual spending of school districts is, on average, $5,583. These funds are derived as follows:

6.6 percent from federal sources, 47.3 percent from the state, and 46.0 percent from localities.[2] If school enrollment would begin earlier, at age 3, the $5,583 per child would supplement parental fees, raising the amount available per child in child care to approximately $8,000 to $9,000, which is about the cost of high-quality child care. Admittedly, schools can operate the program on user fees only, but with a greater number of schools involved, it would be essential to ensure good quality care; the additional funds would be used for staff training, salaries for certified staff, and for creating career ladders, all of which are essential aspects of the professionalization of child care and the provision of good quality care.

**The Role of the Federal Government.**   We envision a dual role for the federal government. First, the federal government should support the care of low income and handicapped children, as it does currently. However, with regard to child care subsidies in particular, this support should be expanded to enable states to provide subsidies to all eligible children, which is not currently the case. Additionally, federally supported targeted programs such as Head Start, although not linked fiscally to the School of the 21st Century program, should become—if the grantee organization is the local school district—part of the overall School of the 21st Century. Other federally funded programs, Title I of ESEA in particular, should be expanded. Their use in preventive (as opposed to remedial) services should be encouraged so that it is more widespread. This expansion would enable some school districts with a high proportion of at-risk students to supplement the state start-up grant and the operational revenues from such federally funded programs.

Second, the federal government should play a prominent role in promoting the concept of linking child care and education. This promotion could be accomplished by providing incentives to states to create an infrastructure that would support the training and professionalization of School of the 21st Century staff (discussed in more detail in the next chapter). For example, the federal government would appropriate $2 million a year to be used as incentives for states to develop a training infrastructure. Additionally, the federal government would appropriate funds to support a National Center of the School of the 21st Century. The National Center would provide leadership and direction on key policy issues relevant to the School of the 21st Century; review, conduct, and disseminate research pertaining to aspects of the program; serve as a clearinghouse of information regarding local practices; and provide training and networking opportunities for policymakers and for teachers and administrators of the School of the 21st Century.

## Discussion of the Financing Plan

This plan represents a practical approach to financing the School of the 21st Century and relies on a combination of user fees and local, state, and federal support. The plan is based on our experiences with existing Schools of the 21st Century, which have shown that the majority of parents are willing to use and are able to pay moderate fees for child care in the school. The plan is also based on the way education is financed currently. A review of educational spending conducted under the auspices of the Finance Project (Gold and Ellwood 1995) shows that spending for elementary and secondary education is estimated at about $246.3 billion, of which $115.2 billion is provided by the states, $144.1 billion by localities and non-federal sources, and only a small portion, $17.0 billion, by the federal government.

We see the role of the states and localities in this plan as an investment. The states' role is limited for the most part to supporting a start-up period to help schools initiate the program, although it also includes the states' share of the per pupil spending. In the hypothetical example that we used to project the costs, there are approximately 530,000 children under age 6. We estimate that 215,000 of them are ages 3 and 4 and that 65 percent of these 3- and 4-year-olds would need child care and be enrolled in school. If the state's share of per pupil spending is $2,640,[3] the increase in state spending would be $368,940,000 per year.

The question is, Where would the money come from? The American people in general do not believe that government should support social services, and many even doubt the government's ability to address social problems. However, the general trend is to require all levels of government to operate efficiently, and the concept of an investment in start-up rather than on-going support should appeal to the public. Nevertheless, we are not necessarily recommending an infusion of new funds for the start-up grant program; rather, we believe that the redirection of funds is an approach that is applicable in many states.

The funds to be redirected could be derived from various sources in the state. As an example, we propose that, where applicable, states would use funds currently targeted for pre-kindergarten programs. In a review of states' services, the Children's Defense Fund (1994) has found that an increasing number of states have invested in programs that seek to help at-risk, pre-kindergarten children succeed in school. The amount of money invested by each state varies (and a few states do not spend anything), but the total spending among the states in 1992 was about $665 million. This total does not take into account the spending on initiatives that focus primarily on parents or those that provide early interventions for children with disabilities. Nor does the total include spending in two states, California and Wisconsin, where schools offer kindergarten beginning at age 4, as opposed to age 5. A few of the states use the pre-kindergarten funds to supplement federally supported programs such as Head Start, but in the majority of cases the spending is for state initiatives that provide educational services to pre-kindergarten children.

The annual amount spent on pre-kindergarten initiatives is relatively extensive in many of the states (Children's Defense Fund 1994). However, the initiatives have limitations. First, since the initiatives are dependent only on the state for revenue, no state has been able to serve all the eligible children. Many of the states did not provide the comprehensive array of services children need if they are to be prepared to succeed in school, nor did many of the states provide staff training in early childhood education, which is an essential aspect of the provision of good quality services for preschoolers (Ripple et al. in review). Perhaps even more important, in most states, the pre-kindergarten services are provided for only part of the day, so that eligible children whose parents both work have no opportunity to participate.

We should point out that the types of experiences provided to preschoolers in the School of the 21st Century are essentially the same as those provided to children in a good nursery school (Finn-Stevenson et al. 1990; Regenstein, Silow-Carroll, and Meyer 1995) and as those that should be provided in state-funded pre-kindergarten initiatives, if these are to meet their objectives. Schools implementing 21C are not only providing child care but also, in effect, working to meet Goal 1 (readiness) of the Goals 2000 initiative (National Education Goals Panel 1995). Therefore, the use of the pre-kindergarten funds to support start-up for the School of the 21st Century would not represent a philosophical change in direction. Indeed, since 21C schools include various services besides child care, they can better address the overall goal of pre-kindergarten initiatives, which is to prepare the children for school success.

Pre-kindergarten funds still would be used to ensure that at-risk children are ready for schooling, but these children would not be segregated; rather, they would be served with other children who need child care and whose parents pay for the services. What we are proposing, in effect, is to leverage the use of existing pre-kindergarten funds. This is a fiscally efficient approach and has the added benefits of serving all children, as opposed to segregating some of them (see Chapter 4). Additionally, in states not currently investing in pre-kindergarten, the focus on all children as opposed to just children at risk, as well as the focus on a limited time period for the state investment in start-up grants for the School of the 21st Century, could well be more politically attractive and result in appropriate legislation.

To avoid being misunderstood regarding the broader use of already existing pre-kindergarten funds, we should reiterate our intent. Our goal is to achieve universal access to good quality child care. However, this care is noncompulsory; we do not mean to suggest that all children should attend the program. Rather, parents who need good quality child care should have access to it; and the voluntary nature of 21C means that parents should pay for it if they can. Also, the proposed wider use of pre-kindergarten funds should not be understood to mean that children should be exposed to formal schooling at an early age. Rather, they should be provided with opportunities for play and social interactions and cared for by loving adults (see Chapters 3 and 4).

The additional state funds needed to support the states' share of per pupil spending could begin after the start-up grant, so that the initiation is phased in over a five- or eight-year period. In the majority of cases, state revenues from income and other taxes and from lotteries are used to fund education (Mitchell and Dichter 1993). At the local level, property taxes are the main source of revenue for per pupil spending. We believe that each state can decide how to raise the additional revenue needed. And with regard to the increased number of children in school as a result of starting enrollment at age 3, we believe that each state should respond to such fluctuations as they have in the past; fluctuating enrollments are nothing new. What we are proposing is not so far fetched. Mitchell and Dichter (1993) list communities in states such as Colorado and Iowa that have a dedicated sales tax or a local options sales tax, part of the proceeds of which is used to fund child care services.

Since the local share of per pupil spending is not required until after the start-up period, when parents and others in the community have had an opportunity to see the merits of the School of the 21st Century, it is likely that many people will be willing to support the program through bond levies or increased property or local taxes if necessary.[4] But in many cases, this kind of funding may not be necessary. The number of 3- and 4-year-olds who would be enrolled is limited to those who would be using the child care services,[5] which would be, at most, approximately 65 percent. To illustrate potential costs, we looked at our hypothetical example of a state with about 215,000 3- and 4-year-olds, approximately 65 percent of whom would need child care, or a total of 139,750 served by 120 school districts. In each school district, the increased enrollment would be approximately 1,165, and the local share of increased per pupil spending would be just over $3 million.

Although, as we have shown, the spending for creating a child care system that is linked to education is fiscally feasible, from a policy perspective, a change in orientation is essential; the School of the 21st Century should be regarded as an investment in human capital, not as a cost to be assessed in terms of present value. The long-term benefits school districts and society stand to realize by investing in this program include: improved grade retention rates, reduced use of special education and other special services, fewer graduates on welfare, increased rates of college attendance, and decreases in delinquency and social problems (Barnett 1995; Weikart and Schweinhart 1997). In terms of costs and benefits, a conservative estimate indicates that for approximately every dollar invested in high-quality, developmentally appropriate preschool programs, a subsequent seven dollar savings will be realized (Barnett 1993a).

## Opposing Views

Our proposal to link child care financing and service delivery with the public education system has witnessed both opposition and support. Some of the opposition focuses on logistics such as lack of space, which we discussed in Chapter 4, but some of it is directed at the funding plan we propose. For example, although our proposal is based in part on parental fee for service, Goldberg (1996) contends that it goes against the prevailing ideology, which is one of personal responsibility rather than government intervention. He also notes that although the start-up funds we propose may be feasible, there would be problems with ongoing financing, since in our proposal it is tied to school financing, which is fraught with problems and generally regarded as inadequate. On this point we agree; we have noted earlier that it is vital to make an (ultimately financial) commitment to the early childhood years, as years of critical importance for school success.

Others oppose the plan because it represents a change from the way child care services are currently delivered. Schultz (1996), for example, argues that "it seems clear that [the] plan is to centralize the governance, delivery, and management of child care services within the public schools" (141) and that if this were to happen, then our present mix of for-profit, non-profit, and home-based services would not survive. We disagree with Schultz and believe that just as we have a mix of public and private schools, we will continue to have private and community-based child care centers along with school-based child care.

## Other Proposals

Our plan for funding the School of the 21st Century does not cover the cost of care for children from birth to age 3. This aspect of child care can be addressed in part through paid parental leave (Zigler, Hopper, and Hall 1993). Zigler and Lang (1991) also suggest using social security benefits to cover the cost of infant care or paid leave from work, depending on whether parents choose to work or stay home with the baby.

Cunningham (1990) proposes to change the structure and management of local governments, including school districts, as an approach to better serve and finance services for children. He proposes a focus on the well-being of children that would encompass not only K–12 schooling but also child care, physical and mental health, adult education, counseling, job training, libraries and museums, among other services. With this central focus on well-being, he calls for reconstituting local governments and creating "local districts for well-being" (Cunningham 1990, 146). Although he does not fully describe the functions, roles, and responsibilities of the proposed new local districts for well-being, he believes that the broad mandate concerning well-being would result in the provision of services to all individuals, not just those considered at risk, and that it would enable people to see schools, for example, as institutions that provide services from the birth of the child forward, focusing not only on cognition but also on physical, emotional, and mental health. Cunningham notes further that his proposed reconstitution of local government would be authorized by state legislatures through enabling legislation, but he stresses the importance of local vision and responsibility and the fact that his proposal allows us to "break away from traditional patterns of finance, many of which are marked by inequity and unintended negative consequences" (Cunningham 1990, 148).

Other proposals focus on maintaining the way services are currently delivered but include suggestions for various ways to raise the additional funds needed if we are to have good quality services. Whereas Cunningham's proposal acknowledges the importance of local governance, Kagan and Cohen (1997) review an opposite view that focuses on the role of the federal government. They note that the funds needed for quality early care and education should come from the federal government for several reasons: The federal government has the ability to raise funds across richer and poorer states and communities; early care and education represent services that are "collective goods," that is, they benefit society at large and thus should be funded by the federal government; and the federal government can require states to match the funds, in this way providing an incentive for states to invest in early care and education.

Other suggestions include proposals to keep the current non-system in place but to require that people with higher incomes contribute more toward early care and education and that multiple funding mechanisms be instituted to raise funds; these funding mechanisms would include cutting other expenditures and creating opportunities for a partially paid parental leave that would be funded using Temporary Disability Insurance (TDI) (see Kagan and Cohen 1997).

There are other proposals for raising money or redistributing existing money. However, none—including the one for funding the School of the 21st Century—are popular, given the high cost involved as well as the requirement that we make a commitment to long-term change.

We do not propose to simply maintain the status quo, nor do we propose radical change. Rather, given the current political-economic climate, we believe that developing and implementing a comprehensive child care system must be based in part on user fees, and that the system needs to be regarded as a state rather than federal responsibility. This latter stance is not without precedent, since child care, like education, is not mentioned in the Constitution. Therefore, as with public education, child care could be perceived as a state and local responsibility. Of course, in the funding plan proposed for the School of the 21st Century, the federal government would still have a role to play, namely, to subsidize the cost of care for low income children and children with developmental disabilities. Additionally, as we elaborate in the final chapter, the federal government should support national training and dissemination efforts to ensure that all schools have an opportunity to learn about and implement the program.

## Notes

1. In the case of Head Start children who need full-day child care, either tuition or a subsidy is required for the additional hours the children are in child care.

2. Note that these are average statistics and that spending per child and the relative share of federal, state, and local sources vary greatly from state to state. The statistics presented were compiled by the Finance Project (Gold and Ellwood 1995).

3. This figure is based on annual averages.

4. At some existing 21C sites, community support has been extensive. Parents utilizing the services constitute a core of enthusiastic voters in favor of schools, so that bond levies pass more easily.

5. Some families with only one parent working may not need all-day child care but may want to send their children to the program for part of the day. However, we do not know how many such children are represented, so they are not included in our calculations.

# 7 Evaluation

THE IMPLEMENTATION OF ANY PROGRAM must include an evaluation component so that the effort may be monitored to ensure it yields desired outcomes. The provision of early care and family support services may seem at first glance to be a matter of social policy, the value of which is self-evident; after all, if children are to develop optimally, they need appropriate health, nutrition, social interactions, and a safe, stimulating, and nurturing environment. Since these are the basic elements of good quality school-based child care and family support services, some educators and service providers may question the need for evaluation. However, simply knowing that programs and services are essential for optimal development or that they are generally associated with benefits is only the starting point and is usually the reason we implement programs. Once we begin implementation, additional questions must be addressed: Are we meeting our goals? Are we making a difference in the lives of children and their parents? Are their needs being addressed and, if not, what can we do to improve our efforts? The answers to these and other related questions are derived from process and outcome evaluations and program monitoring procedures that we discuss in this chapter. Since so much can be written about evaluation, we limit the discussion and only outline some of what is known about the topic. Our goal is to provide educators who implement child care and family support services with an understanding of why evaluation is important and of their role in the process.

## Potential Program Effects: What We Know from the Research

It is important at the outset to review briefly some of what we know from the research about the outcomes associated with the provision of early care and family support services, since this knowledge in part forms the conceptual underpinnings of the program being implemented. With programs such as the School of the 21st Century and other school-based or school-linked services, conclusive evaluation findings are not yet widely available because the programs are relatively new and, as will become clear later in the chapter, must achieve stability before we can assess their outcomes. Also, such programs entail not one but several different components that are phased in over time, are characterized by flexibility and variability, and change and evolve in order to continue to meet the needs of the children and families they serve. These characteristics contribute to the strength of the efforts, but they pose challenges to evaluation, which may become, as a result, quite complex. Schorr (1997) points out that besides the lack of outcome evaluation findings regarding comprehensive programs such as those provided in schools, "the fact that intervention in human and social development [is in itself] so complex" exacerbates the problem (Schorr 1997, 132).

## The Benefits of 21C: Preliminary Findings

Nonetheless, researchers have made progress on program evaluation, and their work will eventually enhance our understanding of the effects of programs like 21C on participants. For example, we have conducted preliminary studies that have yielded not only information about the process of implementation but also insight about the program's impact on children and families. In a study of the first school district to implement the School of the 21st Century program—Independence, Missouri—we looked at the implementation process and the benefits of some of the components and found that children's participation in the program was associated with several trends: higher achievement test scores; the identification of children's learning problems at an early age (which provided opportunities for follow-up interventions); and increased readiness for kindergarten (Finn-Stevenson, Desimone, and Chung 1998). A preliminary study of the program in another school, in Norfolk, Virginia—which, unlike the first one, served predominantly poor children—reported similar findings (Desimone, Finn-Stevenson, and Henrich 1999). An evaluation of the School of the 21st Century program in yet another district has shown that the provision of school-based, full-day child care for children ages birth through 5, as well as of care for school-age children, was associated with decreases in stress among parents (McCabe 1995).

We are still awaiting findings of a more comprehensive evaluation of the School of the 21st Century, an evaluation that looks not only at some of the individual components of the program, as noted above, but also at the effects of the integration of various of the 21C service components, as well as at the value each of these components added to the school. For the time being, however, in addition to reporting preliminary findings, we can draw from extensive evaluations that have been conducted with single-focus programs associated with the model.

## Parent Involvement

Parent involvement, for example, is one of the required aspects of 21C. We described the potential benefits of parent involvement in Chapter 2. We

BOX 7.1    Benefits of the School of the 21st Century

Through both process and outcome evaluations at several 21C sites, the Yale University Bush Center in Child Development and Social Policy has gathered ample evidence of the efficacy of the School of the 21st Century (21C) model. Moreover, the 21C model builds on individual components that have been successfully evaluated on their own. The findings from both sources provide compelling evidence that the 21C program benefits children, parents, and the school as a whole.

### Findings of School of the 21st Century Evaluations

The following benefits of 21C are based on findings from:

- the first phase of a longitudinal outcome evaluation conducted by the Yale Bush Center in Independence, Missouri, the first school district to implement 21C

- an independent study of the 21C program in Leadville, Colorado

- implementation evaluations of the CoZi program (a variation on 21C that combines James Comer's School Development Program and Edward Zigler's 21C model) in schools in Norfolk, Virginia, and Bridgeport, Connecticut

### Benefits for Children

- Children participating in 21C for at least three years evidenced higher scores in mathematics and reading achievement tests than children in a control, non-21C school.

- Children who participated in 21C beginning at age 3 started kindergarten ready to learn, as evidenced by their scores on kindergarten screening tests.

- According to teachers, the 21C preschool program helped identify and address children's special learning needs early in the educational process.

- Availability of 21C child care services enabled parents to provide consistent adult supervision and high-quality, out-of-home care, vital factors in healthy child development.

### Benefits for Parents

- Parents in 21C schools, in comparison to parents in non-21C schools, reported that:

    They experience significantly less stress, as measured by the Parental Stress Index.

    They spend less money on child care.

    They miss fewer days of work.

- According to teachers, 21C programs helped parents form an early and positive relationship with the school.

*(continues)*

*(continued)*

- Parents gave their school higher marks for academic focus, caring and sensitivity, school-community relations, and collaborative decisionmaking than did parents at the comparison school.

### Benefits for the School

- Principals in 21C schools report:

    substantial reduction in school vandalism

    increased parental involvement and parent appreciation for the school

    changes in teaching practices in first and second grade to reflect developmentally appropriate practice and provide greater individual attention

    positive public relations because of the expanded services offered by the school

- In the first-year evaluation from the CoZi site in Norfolk, Virginia, teachers reported significantly higher school climate levels than their counterparts at the non-CoZi school on almost every dimension of school climate (i.e., leadership, achievement, motivation, collaborative decisionmaking, parent involvement in decisionmaking, teacher involvement, school-community relations, staff expectations, and teacher collaboration). Research shows that there is a strong correlation between school climate and academic performance: Students are more likely to do well academically if they are in schools that have a positive climate.

noted that studies have shown that parent involvement, either in and of itself or in conjunction with a service focus on children, is related to increased self-esteem among parents as well as enhanced academic achievement and motivation to succeed among their children (Epstein 1992; Epstein and Lee 1995). By becoming involved in the educational process and expressing an interest in education, parents convey to children "their aspirations and expectations for educational attainment," thereby encouraging the children to succeed (Scott-Jones 1995, 79).

Evaluations of the home visitation program Parents as Teachers (PAT)—also part of the School of the 21st Century—studied both low- and high-risk families participating in the program. Researchers found that the program increased children's school readiness, intellectual achievement, language skills, and social development, and that it enhanced parents' knowledge of infant and child development. The PAT studies also found increased involvement in school among parents who had participated in the program during their children's first three years of life (Winter and McDonald 1997; Owen and Mulvihill 1994; Pfannenstiel 1989).

## Benefits to Preschoolers

In the area of child care, discussed in greater detail in Chapter 3, we can draw upon studies of quality preschool interventions that have proven to be effective in promoting the optimal development of children. The High/Scope Perry Preschool Program's longitudinal evaluation has demonstrated that program participants outperformed their peers academically and socially not just immediately after participation in the program but for many years later, through age 27: Program participants were 50 percent less likely than non-participants to be involved in criminal activities; they had significantly more earnings and were more likely than non-participants to make a commitment to marriage (Berrueta-Clement et al. 1984; Weikart and Schweinhart 1997). In reviews of studies of other preschool programs, researchers note that when such programs are of high quality they are associated with positive effects on children's intellectual and social competence; researchers note also that program participants are less likely than non-participants to be placed in special education classes or to be retained in grade by the time they are in middle or junior high school (Haskins 1989; Barnett 1995).

The benefits associated with early care are especially apparent among low income children who are compared with a similar group of children who do not receive such early care or preschool experiences. Another way to think about potential benefits of child care for preschool children is to look at the research about the effects of poor quality care. As we noted in Chapter 3, national studies provide evidence indicating that many children from middle-class families are in poor quality child care environments that have a negative developmental impact on the children. By providing all children access to good quality services, schools are ensuring that the children will not experience developmental harm.

## Benefits to School-Age Children

Potential benefits are also associated with the school-age child care component. As we noted in Chapter 3, Richardson and his colleagues (1989) found that students who are in supervised, after-school programs are less likely to abuse drugs and alcohol than those students who are home alone after school. This finding held regardless of the students' socioeconomic background. More recent data were submitted in a report to the U.S. attorney general, indicating that nearly half of all violent juvenile crime takes place during after-school hours, between 2:00 P.M. and 8:00 P.M. (Fight Crime/Invest in Kids 1997). The same report presented evidence of a 75 percent decline in juvenile arrests after a school-age child care program was implemented in one neighborhood, and a separate study found that sixty-four school-age child care programs in one city were associated with

BOX 7.2   Other Benefits of the School of the 21st Century

**Related Research**

Substantial research has been conducted on many of the components of the 21C model. The following is a brief summary of some of the findings of these independent evaluations:

*Benefits of Quality Preschool*

- The best long-term study of preschool effects to date, the High/Scope Perry Preschool Project, has revealed that for every dollar spent on preschool programs, taxpayers reap a benefit of over seven dollars. Participants are more likely to be employed and married, and less likely to be delinquent or to have committed a crime. Another major benefit is the reduction in the number of special education placements (Schweinhart, Barne, and Weikart 1993).

- Numerous other studies attesting to the benefits of preschool are reviewed in *Starting Points: Meeting the Needs of Our Youngest Children,* a 1994 report by the Carnegie Corporation of New York.

*Guidance and Support for New Parents*

- At age 3, children who had participated in Parents as Teachers were found to be significantly more advanced in language and social development, as well as problem solving and other intellectual tasks, than comparison children (Pfannenstiel and Seltzer 1985).

- Another study examined whether Parents as Teachers augments the effects of Head Start and Title I pre-kindergarten. Results showed that the Parents as Teachers children had significantly higher cognitive, language, social, and motor skills than non-participants. These higher skills led to lower remedial and special education costs for first grade. The Parents as Teachers participants also had substantially reduced welfare dependence and half the number of child abuse and neglect cases (Drazen and Haust 1994).

*Benefits of School-Age Child Care*

- Several studies have shown that high-quality, school-age child care programs that offer structured, developmentally appropriate activities for children have positive outcomes for both children and families, including improved social skills, reduced problem behavior, and increased academic performance (University of California Cooperative Extension 1993).

- A study of school-age child care that examined whether formal after-school programs have a beneficial effect on low income children in comparison to other types of after-school settings (parental care, informal adult supervision, and self-care) indicated that structured after-school programs do have positive impacts on academic achievement and social adjustment in comparison to other types of after-school care. Moreover, a greater degree of contact time in after-school programs is more beneficial than superficial contact (Posner and Vandell 1994).

- Research has shown that after-school programs reduce vandalism and juvenile crime and are associated with improvements in academic performance and behavior among children who participate (Fight Crime/Invest in Kids 1997).

- Children in after school programs are less likely than those who are unsupervised to abuse drugs and alcohol (Richardson et al. 1989).

### The School of the 21st Century

The School of the 21st Century (21C), also known in some communities as Family Resource Centers, is a school-based child care and family support model that transforms the school into a year-round, multi-service center providing services from morning to evening.

reduced vandalism and improvements in students' behavior and academic performance.

## Evaluating School-Based Programs

### *Why Conduct an Evaluation?*

The above-noted benefits, as well as those discussed in previous chapters, provide some evidence of the potential inherent in the provision of early care and family support services. It is critical not only to think about the benefits of such efforts in general but also to examine specifically the provision of the services by schools. Evaluation in this regard is important because schools' provision of child care and family support services is still relatively new and, as Gomby and Larson (1992) note, such programs are still in a stage of experimentation: "We need to learn as much as we can from these initiatives. Toward this end, [every school engaged in such efforts], no matter the size, should be [involved] in some level of evaluation"(Larson, Gomby, and Behrman 1992). Evaluation efforts may differ, depending on the scope of the program and the resources available, but should at a minimum consist of stating what is expected of the program in terms of its effects on participants and collecting data to ascertain if this has been achieved. On a national level, there is also a need for evaluations that focus on several different school districts' efforts, providing descriptive information about aspects of implementation, as well as information about various anticipated and unanticipated outcomes. Such evaluations can be helpful to policymakers and other schools as they attempt to implement programs, and these evaluations are important in establishing whether and in what ways the programs are effective.

Valente and Dodge (1997) summarize and elaborate on what we have said so far, noting that evaluation at both the local and national level is important for:

- theory development, in that program evaluations can contribute to our understanding of child and family development
- implementation clarity, in that evaluations require that implementation strategies be articulated in detail and that the actual services and activities involved be described as well as measured, thereby enhancing attempts to replicate the programs
- identification of effective programs, in that evaluation findings enable us to determine whether programs work as anticipated and which programs are most effective in addressing certain needs, thereby providing opportunities for practitioners to review and choose among program options
- feedback and improvement, in that a critical feature of a good evaluation is iterative, and the documentation of both successes and shortcomings can be used to improve upon and refine the effort

## What Evaluation Means to Program Implementers

There are other reasons to conduct an evaluation, one of these being to obtain recognition and support for the program. Findings from an evaluation provide educators with the information they need to disseminate to the district leadership, the community, and funders. Additionally, as we noted in the previous section of this chapter, an evaluation provides the means by which to gauge progress toward the program goals and objectives, so that the staff implementing the program can make modifications as necessary. Schorr (1997) notes the importance of this aspect of program evaluation, pointing out that in the excitement of implementing and providing services, the staff might confuse means and ends; in other words, instead of taking the time and effort to ascertain whether these services are contributing to the overall goals of the program, the staff might be tempted simply to document that the services are in fact being provided. Any one of us may have encountered well-meaning educators who are excited about their efforts and describe these in terms of the numerous services they provide. The list of services may be impressive in its comprehensiveness, but it tells nothing about how effective the services are or about their impact on the recipients. However, when educators say, "We have been providing child care for preschoolers for the past three years and have found that the number of children testing well on kindergarten readiness has increased by 30 percent this year," we know not only about the service they provide but also that they are monitoring their effort and its benefits to children.

## Who Should Conduct the Evaluation?

Often, a distinction is made between implementation and evaluation, with the thought that those who implement the program should not be involved in its evaluation. This notion stems from the perceived need for objectivity in the evaluation. Walberg and Greenberg (1998) comment that developers of widely disseminated programs have an understandable bias and thus should not evaluate their own efforts. However, we contend that practitioners in a school or school district do need to evaluate their own programs. Even when an "outsider" conducts the evaluation, there needs to be extensive involvement on the part of practitioners, since the evaluators can know about the program only by working cooperatively with the staff (Herman, Morris, and Fitz-Gibbon 1998).

Having made the point that practitioners need to be involved in the evaluation, we still face the question of who should have ultimate responsibility for developing and carrying out the evaluation. The answer depends on the resources available. When funds are ample or a specific grant is available for the evaluation, an outside evaluator or evaluation team is often hired for the task. However, the majority of schools do not have sufficient funds and must set aside time to do the evaluation in-house, or they might form a partnership with researchers at a higher education institution near their community. It may be useful in this case to designate someone on the staff as the evaluation coordinator, whose task it is to learn about approaches to evaluation and assist the rest of the staff in making decisions about evaluation strategies. In other words, just as an implementation coordinator is essential if program planning is to get under way, so too it is imperative to appoint an evaluation coordinator who will ensure that plans for an evaluation are in place, that someone is assigned to collect and analyze data, and that evaluators write an evaluation report and disseminate it appropriately.

Regardless of who conducts the evaluation, it is an arduous task for those who are also implementing the program. Those with sufficient funds may think that their role in the evaluation is completed at the point of hiring an outside consultant, but in reality they too have to work closely with the consultant in order to answer questions about and explain the program. Also, it is imperative that the implementers of the program be aware of the challenges and opportunities entailed in any program evaluation, as well as of the various approaches to evaluation, so they are better able to assist the evaluators.

## Challenges, Opportunities, and Approaches to Evaluation

**Current Focus on Outcomes.** There are several strategies that may be used to evaluate programs, depending on the scope of the effort. In general, however, the various strategies fall within the two types of evaluation: process and outcome. Process evaluation, which is also referred to as formative or implementation evaluation, describes the implementation of and the various activities associated with the program, whereas an outcome or summative evaluation focuses on the changes brought about as the result of the program. Although for clarity we will discusses these two types of evaluation separately, we perceive the two types on a continuum; there is overlap between the two, and they are both essential in establishing whether and in what ways programs are effective.

Outcomes can be ascertained only some time after the process evaluation begins, since a program needs to be fully implemented and stable before we can begin to ask the question: Is it working? However, we will discuss outcome evaluation first for two reasons. First, the current emphasis on results among policymakers, funders, members of the media, and others is a reality for many who implement programs. This focus on results is welcomed, especially now, when funds are limited and when—whether it is the entire nation, a state government, or a school board—it is important to know that the investment of money is producing intended results. Second, it is important at the outset to think about the outcome evaluation and to know not only what one will be implementing but also how one will know if one is achieving the intended results.

Conducting an outcome evaluation is a challenging task. In theory, it is not enough to point to a change or outcome; we also need to establish that the changes occurred as a result of the program. Traditionally, causation is established by comparing children and families participating in the program (sometimes referred to as the intervention or experimental group) with children and families who have similar characteristics but did not participate in the program (sometimes referred to as the control group). To be absolutely certain that any difference between the two groups can be attributed to the program, certain scientific procedures need to be applied. One such procedure is random assignment, in which children with similar backgrounds or characteristics are randomly assigned to participate in the program or to serve as the control group. Random assignment is usually regarded as the most rigorous method because it "presumably equalizes the two groups initially" (Barnett 1995, 29). However, random assignment is often not an option. It is expensive, and it also raises ethical issues, since it requires educators to withhold services from children and families assigned to the control group. As a result, alternative strategies have been utilized. One example is using children who are on the program's waiting list and comparing them with those who are participating in the program. Another possibility would be to use children from a similar school or neighborhood where the program is not implemented as a comparison group. Such strategies—often also accompanied by statistical techniques to control for initial differences between the two groups (Barnett 1995)—have to be utilized despite the fact that they cannot establish causation with absolute certainty.

Some researchers contend that the use of such alternative strategies is seriously flawed (Rossi 1998; Gilliam et al. in press). They note that in the "real-world" context in which services are provided, various unanticipated events occur, presenting challenges to evaluators. In addition, the alternative strategies are at times difficult to use or to maintain. For example, the comparison school chosen in an early evaluation of one School of the 21st Century program was carefully selected to ensure that the comparison school itself—as well as the children and the families and the community as a whole—had similar characteristics as the program school. However, within several months of the evaluation, educators at the comparison school decided to implement the School of the 21st Century, thus rendering their role in the evaluation obsolete. In other instances, comparison communities underwent drastic changes—the demolition of several homes in the neighborhood and subsequent relocation of families in one case, and the institution of a community-based service center in another—and as a result could no longer be considered as effective comparisons, and several adjustments had to be made to the evaluation design.

Another problem concerns the fact that most of our knowledge regarding outcome studies has come from the evaluation of single-focus programs that include a circumscribed intervention. A home visitation program such as Parents as Teachers is an example of a single-focus program. However, the new breed of interventions or programs—school-based services such as the School of the 21st Century among them—are more complex and involve not one but several types of services, as well as extensive collaborations with other agencies serving the same clients. Such programs are designed to address various needs and circumstances at the local level. As such, they cannot be adequately assessed using the traditional "experimental" approach. Schorr (1997) notes that the mismatch between traditional approaches to evaluation and the new breed of programs not only results in failures to conduct an evaluation and, thereby, to collect outcome data but also creates conflict between evaluators and program staff. Understandably, program staff are often wary of evaluators and concerned that their efforts will be distorted, misunderstood, proclaimed as failures, or subject to programmatic design changes in order to accommodate the evaluation.

New approaches to outcome evaluation are more realistic. Both researchers and program staff now understand that traditional evaluation methods might meet scientific standards but are unlikely to capture the program's impact (Cook 1997). The approach now is to change the evaluation design to accommodate complex programs rather than the other way around. From a pure science perspective, the new approaches utilize study methods that may not be rigorous but that nonetheless provide useful information. Schorr (1997), in a summary of the new approaches to evaluation, notes that although they vary, they share several common characteristics:

- they rely on theory for guidance;
- they acknowledge the importance of involving in the evaluation not only evaluators but also program managers, service providers, and in some cases participants;
- they utilize several study methods that are designed to "build a body of knowledge rather than . . . [provide] simple yes-no answers to what works" (Schorr 1997, 153).

Often, evaluators combine alternative strategies. In an evaluation of community-based family support centers, Green and MacAllister (1998) combined both a theory-based approach to evaluation and a participatory evaluation. They note that in theory-based evaluation, "theory" refers to an understanding of how the program or service is expected to work, which entails identifying service components and linking them to expected outcomes: "These services, outcomes, and the hypothesized links between them are [actually] the basis for developing a program model . . . [that becomes] the framework to guide the . . . implementation and interpretation of the [program's] evaluation" (30). Green and MacAllister (1998) explain further that in the process of establishing a theory-based approach, they rely not only on evaluation staff but on the participation of program administrators, staff, and participating families: "Participatory evaluation involves active collaboration between key stakeholder groups in designing, implementing and interpreting the evaluation" (31). But even such new approaches to evaluation pose challenges similar to the ones noted above. Green and MacAllister note that the challenges include the high cost and extensive time commitment needed in program evaluation, as well as concerns about the objectivity of the evaluator and methodological shortcomings. But one of the greatest difficulties is the fact that programs are never static; rather they change and evolve over time, so the evaluation design also must change.

**Studying the Process of Implementation.**   The new evaluation approaches also underscore the importance of studying the process of implementation. This kind of evaluation, at the most basic level, seeks to address the questions: *What services are delivered, to whom, and how?* Traditionally, such process data would be used primarily to provide a descriptive context within which to better understand outcomes. However, in the new approaches to evaluation, process studies are used to provide critical information that has several uses:

- program improvements and refinement of the program design to ensure it meets the needs of participants
- the collection of information on participants' characteristics, needs, and other factors, and the later use of such information as baseline data to establish any change that occurred to participants
- the assessment of the quality of the services or programs provided
- ascertaining the stability of the effort and its readiness for outcome evaluation

The evaluation of the Family Resource Centers—part of the School of the 21st Century Network—began with a process evaluation that monitored the progress of implementation at three sites: urban, suburban, and rural. The evaluation took place at the end of the first year of implementation. Since these programs were funded by the state of Connecticut, the purpose of the first evaluation was to assess the extent to which the programs at the three sites were meeting the state's goals for implementation and to document any hurdles to implementation and any improvements that needed to be made. As part of the evaluation, site observations and interviews were conducted and enrollment and service data were collected in the aggregate to determine the characteristics of staff and participants and the duration of their involvement in the program. From these data, the evaluators formulated a first-year report that contained recommendations for improvements; these recommendations were shared not only with the policymakers who requested the evaluation but also with program staff to enable them to make necessary changes (Larson, Gomby, and Behrman 1992).

In an evaluation of the Community School Program sponsored by the Children's Aid Society, Robison (1993) also used systematic interviews and observations in order to make recommendations for improvements and as the basis for a case study on the program's implementation. Like the School of the 21st Century program, the Community School entailed extensive collaborations and several different services, not all of which were implemented at the time of the evaluation. Robison, however, took a differential approach to the evaluation, noting that although the services vary in many ways and are initiated at different times, they all experience similar challenges as they evolve from an initiation stage to an implementation stage to stabilization. Her approach was to describe each of the services at its stage of development.

## From Process to Outcome Evaluation:
## Two Ends of the Continuum

Another example that exemplifies not only an initial focus on process but
also the eventual link between process and outcome is presented in a five-
year evaluation of the Iowa Innovative Early Education Program. In 1990
and 1991, the Iowa legislature appropriated funds to enable the Iowa Department of Education to award grants to twenty-five elementary schools
for the implementation of programs and services designed to address the
needs of students at risk for educational failure. The grantee schools implemented a variety of services for students in kindergarten through third
grade, and some families and schools also provided services for preschool
children. Despite the variations among the schools in the type of services
and programs implemented, all twenty-five schools were guided by a common set of criteria that governed and provided direction to the overall
grant program. Each of the schools conducted an evaluation of its own efforts, but the Iowa legislature and the Department of Education also
wanted to have the grant program as a whole evaluated over a period of
several years.

**Identifying Program Goals and Research Questions.**   Evaluators first had
to identify what the overall goal of the legislature was in appropriating the
funds. The identification of the goal is an essential first step in any evaluation. However, this step is often not enunciated clearly. In the case of the
Iowa grant program, since priority was given to schools with a high rate of
poor children who were at risk for educational failure, the assumption had
to be made (and confirmed) that helping these students do better in school
was one major goal.

The evaluators noted at the outset that the schools would first have to
provide programs and services for at least three years before any outcomes
could be realized, so they designed the evaluation to be undertaken over a
minimum of a five-year period, with aspects of the evaluation conducted
each year. The overall evaluation design focused on both process and outcome evaluation, encompassing three major research questions to be answered over time:

1. Are the schools meeting the expectations inherent in the legislation
   creating the grant program?
2. What types of activities, programs, and/or services are each of the
   schools implementing?
3. What impact does the grant program have on participating students?

The evaluators began by seeking answers to the first two questions, thus providing documentation on the process of implementation. The information was presented not only to legislators but also to program staff and the teachers and administrators at each of the schools. By the third year of implementation, evaluators found that the program as a whole was ready for an outcome evaluation, on the basis of the following findings:

- The twenty-five schools, as a group, were meeting the expectations inherent in the legislation.
- Each of the schools had implemented different initiatives, but three practices stood out as common among the group—the hiring of additional staff, thus enabling teachers to attend to the needs of individual students; collaborations with other agencies; and home visitations/parent involvement. Research has established that these practices are effective strategies in interventions for at-risk students and their families.
- There was a high degree of personal and professional satisfaction and agreement about the overall goal of the programs among administrators, teachers, support staff, and parents, as well as extensive collaborations among the staff.

The latter two findings are essential if programs are to be deemed ready for outcome evaluations, because these findings point to stability in implementation and the ability to sustain the future of the program.

In years four and five of the evaluation, the evaluators addressed the third overall question, regarding program impact. Among the students in third and fourth grade, there were indications of upward scores on the Iowa Test for Basic Skills. However, it was too early in the grant program to determine conclusively that the program was associated with long-term student achievement. Often, evaluators point to gains much too early, only to find out that these gains are not sustained over time. Although the preliminary findings in Iowa are encouraging, they are nevertheless preliminary, so it is essential also to examine intermediate indicators. One intermediate indicator—significantly reduced grade retentions in all participating schools—suggests that enhanced student achievement will be sustained over time.

During the fourth and fifth year of the evaluation, students in second through fifth grade responded to a survey designed to find out about the school's overall climate and about how students were feeling about themselves, their school, and their teachers. The responses indicated that the students felt their teachers were supportive of them, and that the students felt comfortable asking teachers for assistance. The students also felt that their teachers and parents expected them to graduate from high school and go on to college, and the students themselves felt that they were doing well in school and would continue to succeed.

These findings are important and provide indications of positive academic orientation and of a path toward success among the students. There were also indications that parents were involved in the educational process. Parents' participation in school activities was found to be low; for the most part, the same group of parents attended school functions, and when students were asked if their parents came to school often or if they often saw the parents of other children in the school, the most frequent responses were "no" or "sometimes." However, when the students were asked if their parents helped them with homework, talked to them about school and academics, and felt good about the school, the responses were overwhelmingly positive, indicating that although not all parents participate in school activities, they nonetheless convey to the children their interest in the children's education.

**Lessons Learned.**   We elaborate on this example of the evaluation in Iowa in order to underscore several critical lessons:

1. An evaluation needs to be conducted in phases over a period of several years, but at the outset, it is critical to know what to examine during each of the evaluation years.

2. When an evaluation is initiated at the same time as program planning, there is an opportunity to collect baseline data that can then be used to chart progress and, later, to establish outcomes.

3. A systematic approach to data collection will ensure that information is collected. In the Iowa example, educators in each of the grantee schools had to complete mid-year and year-end reports (see Box 7.3) that required them to describe their school, the activities they were implementing, and statistics regarding the number of students in the school, the number of students in special education, the number of students retained in grade, and so on. During the first few years, data can be used to provide a descriptive context for the program; later on it can be used to point to program outcomes. For example, decreases in the number of students enrolled in special education or retained in grade are powerful indicators of a positive change. The information also can be used to point to the investment value of the program; since each student retained in grade or in special education costs a substantial amount of money per year, a positive impact on children also can be described in terms of financial savings.

4. It is important to use not one but several methods of data collection. In Iowa, besides the mid-year and annual reports, evaluators also used surveys, site observations, and existing data available in school records. The latter were used in the aggregate so no individual student was identified.

5. Program recipients are children and parents, so often the evaluation focuses only on them. However, it is important also to include program staff, teachers, administrators, and others (for example, staff at other agencies collaborating in the effort) in the evaluation. As we indicated earlier, in order to ascertain program stability it is important to include feedback from everyone involved. Additionally, extensive feedback provides an opportunity to document broad program outcomes that may include not only a positive impact on the children and families but also on the teachers, other staff, and the school and community as a whole. At the same time, if evaluators find no positive results, data collected from the various players might be used to explain the lack of positive findings and to provide direction for programmatic changes: Are the teachers resentful of the effort? Do administrators feel that they have no opportunity for input? Are parents aware of the services the school is providing? Asking students for their perception is also important; their answers can be used to elaborate on or corroborate findings.

6. Having teachers, staff, and parents respond to a questionnaire or a structured interview is often an essential time-saver, but the findings such questionnaires produce can be limited. For this reason the Iowa evaluation also included open-ended questions that asked staff and parents to describe the services, to provide a case study of how one or two children or families benefited from the services, and to give their assessment of the most important outcome of the programs and services. This part of the process enabled the evaluators to use case studies to bring the data to life, and it also provided an insight into some of the unanticipated benefits of the program. For example, it became apparent over the course of the evaluation that resiliency—the children's ability to overcome difficulties and cope with adverse situations—was a possible outcome of the programs in Iowa, and findings from subsequent student surveys confirmed the outcome.

## Getting Started

An evaluation, by its very definition, occurs after the program has been implemented. However, as we noted earlier, plans for an evaluation need to be made much earlier, during the program design and planning stage. Additionally, various aspects of the planning process, especially the needs assessment and organizational audit that we described in the previous chapter, are important not only for programmatic direction but also for evaluation purposes; the information that such activities yield provides baseline data, enabling staff to monitor the progress they are making and later to gauge whether changes have occurred as a result of the program.

BOX 7.3   Sample Year-End Report Questions

1. Year being reported_____.
2. School enrollment: beginning of the year_____; end of the year_____.
3. How many students are on free and reduced-cost lunch?
4. How many students left the building during the year?
5. How many students were absent more than eight days during the school year?
6. How many students were absent more than thirty-seven days during the school year?
7. How many student referral services?
8. How many retentions for the school year?
9. How many families were referred to community agencies for services during the school year?
10. How many agencies were actively involved with this elementary building during the school year?
11. How many parents were involved in building PTA during the school year?
12. How many parents were involved in a school-sponsored parent education program?
13. How many homeless children were served during the school year?
14. How many migrant children were served during the school year?
15. What percentage of children in this building completed all required immunizations for the school year?
16. How many preschool children are served by the school?
17. What services are provided to infants and preschoolers?
18. How many school-aged children participate in school-age child care?
19. If kindergarten screening is required at the school, what percent of the children passed the test?

The compilation of data from several years of year-end reporting can provide an indication of the benefits associated with the program or of places where modifications may be necessary.

## *Action Steps*

There are several steps in undertaking an evaluation:

**1. Articulating the Conceptual Underpinnings of the Program.**   An essential first step is to articulate the theoretical basis of the program. We noted earlier that new approaches to evaluation are guided by theories about why and how a program is expected to yield positive outcomes. Ideally, program planners would articulate the theory at the outset and use it to

---

BOX 7.4   Costs and Benefits

Programs and services are costly to provide, so it is not surprising that school board members and policymakers want to see positive results. To show the investment value of programs, the data need to be collected at the outset. A reduction in the number of students retained each year and in the number of students referred for special education should be translated into *dollar amounts saved*, which, over the years, can offset program costs. To be able to document savings, educators need to be sure to have baseline information on the number of students in special education, the number of students retained each year, and so on at the *start* of the program.

---

guide the design of the effort. But in reality, programs are often planned and implemented because they have been known to work in another school district or have been widely publicized by the media. In such cases it is important even after the implementation has started to understand the link between the theoretical underpinnings of the program and its goals and objectives (National Center for Clinical Infant Programs 1987). This understanding is essential not only for those in charge of the evaluation but for all program staff: "Evaluators who are using theory based evaluation believe it can help people on the front lines to think more rigorously about what they are doing, help them improve their programs, allow others to learn from their successes and persuade the skeptical funder, legislator, and taxpayer that the purposes of the initiative are being achieved" (Schorr 1997, 148).

An understanding of the theory underlying the approach may be derived in part from evaluation findings of similar efforts, as well as from the relevant research. Educators attempting to promote academic achievement among students at risk for educational failure, for example, may be aware that they should provide services at an early age, beginning ideally in infancy, since early stimulating experiences as well as appropriate health and nutrition are essential if children are to be "ready" for school and able to profit from instruction. This research is important and is, in fact, the reason for starting the program, but it is equally important to keep up with the research in the area; new findings can shed more light on why and in what ways early experiences are critical. This is especially evident in current research on the brain, which, through new techniques in neuroscience, has shown that if infants do not receive stimulating experiences the brain will fail to develop properly (Carnegie Corporation of New York 1994). Two important aspects of this knowledge are helpful in practice:

1. the fact that brain development and, therefore, stimulating experiences are critical during the first few months of life
2. the fact that parents and child care providers play a key role in ensuring that infants receive appropriate stimulation

This knowledge helps ensure both that parents and providers are aware of the important role they have in children's ability to benefit from schooling and that good quality services are available for infants and children.

In multi-service programs such as the School of the 21st Century, it is important to be aware of the research background that supports each of the program's components (discussed earlier in the chapter). Also essential is an understanding of how each of the components relates to the other, with the eventual outcome being the optimal development of children. A key understanding in the new breed of programs is that several points of intervention may be necessary and that support to children and families should be provided not only during one critical period but continuously, as needed during the childhood years (see Figure 7.1).

**2. Determining Goals and Objectives.**    Building on the discussion above, we note that program staff must be aware that children's development is complex and that several factors interact to have an impact on their developmental outcome. It is therefore essential not only to articulate the overall goal for the program but also to itemize the objectives and activities for accomplishing the goal. Whereas goal statements are all-inclusive and convey a long-term vision—for example, to facilitate the optimal development of all children or ensure academic success for all children—the objectives are more circumscribed and must be measurable so that they can be assessed. Again, although the statement of goals and objectives is essential in an evaluation, it is also needed in program planning and implementation. You can see, then, that there exists an overlap between the implementation and operation of a program and its evaluation.

Although the importance of having a clear statement of goals and objectives may seem self-evident, it is often overlooked. For example, the Supplemental Food Program for Women, Infants, and Children (WIC) provided dairy products during pregnancy and the early childhood years to needy families. The rationale was to ensure appropriate nutrition to prevent developmental disabilities associated with poor nutrition. However, the overall goal was not articulated clearly, and evaluators assumed initially that the purpose of the program was to eliminate poverty, so the program was inappropriately deemed to be a failure. Subsequent evaluations have shown, however, that although WIC participants remained in poverty, their children benefited from the nutrition, as was evident in their cognitive and social functioning.

Often, widely replicated programs such as the School of the 21st Century have an overall goal, but it is also important for goals and objectives to be articulated at the local level so that there is awareness of as well as agreement on the direction of the program and its ultimate aim. As we indicated in the previous chapter, lack of agreement on the goal and mission

FIGURE 7.1  Outcome Evaluation: The School of the 21st Century Conceptual Model

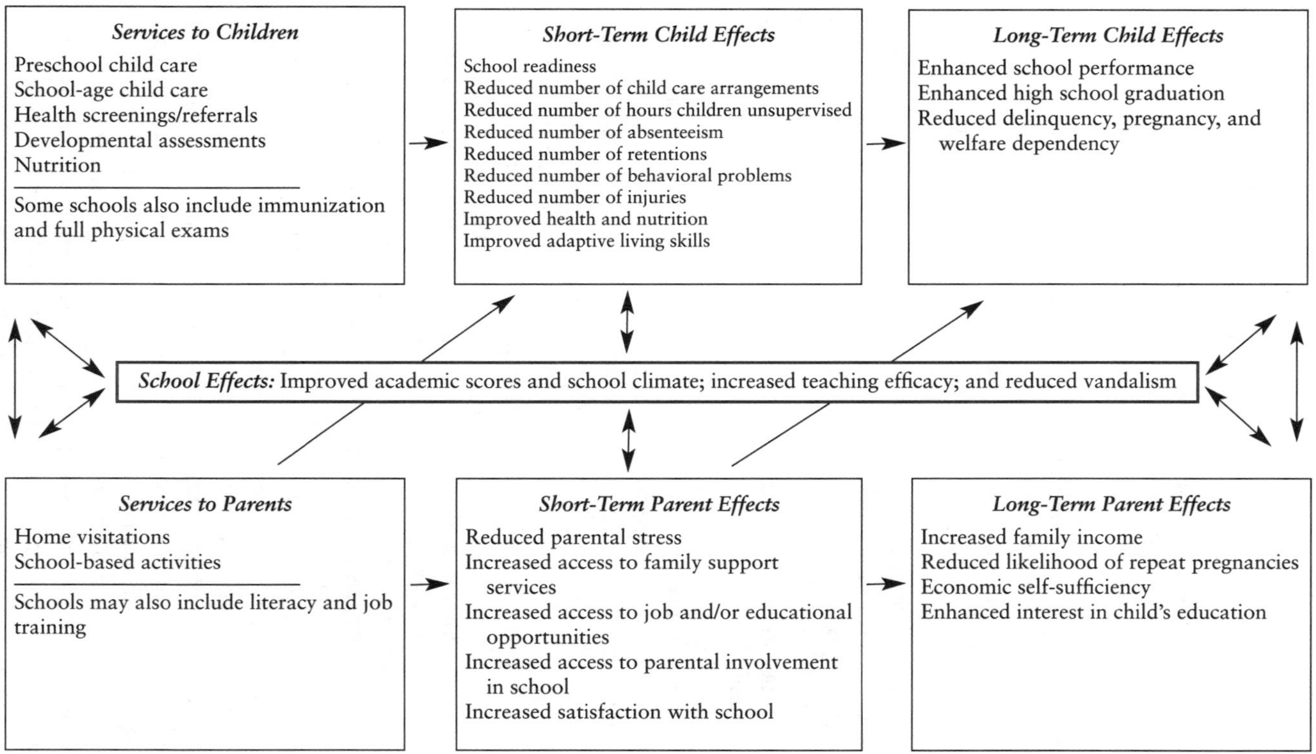

**Services to Children**

Preschool child care
School-age child care
Health screenings/referrals
Developmental assessments
Nutrition

Some schools also include immunization
and full physical exams

**Short-Term Child Effects**

School readiness
Reduced number of child care arrangements
Reduced number of hours children unsupervised
Reduced number of absenteeism
Reduced number of retentions
Reduced number of behavioral problems
Reduced number of injuries
Improved health and nutrition
Improved adaptive living skills

**Long-Term Child Effects**

Enhanced school performance
Enhanced high school graduation
Reduced delinquency, pregnancy, and
welfare dependency

**School Effects:** Improved academic scores and school climate; increased teaching efficacy; and reduced vandalism

**Services to Parents**

Home visitations
School-based activities

Schools may also include literacy and job
training

**Short-Term Parent Effects**

Reduced parental stress
Increased access to family support
services
Increased access to job and/or educational
opportunities
Increased access to parental involvement
in school
Increased satisfaction with school

**Long-Term Parent Effects**

Increased family income
Reduced likelihood of repeat pregnancies
Economic self-sufficiency
Enhanced interest in child's education

of the program is usually an indication of poor implementation and a reflection of internal conflict and confusion over direction (Fullan 1992).

**3. Articulating Short- and Long-Term Program Expectations.** An aspect of the articulation of goals and objectives is an awareness of program expectation, in other words, what we want to ultimately achieve. However, because it may take several years to see any social or academic changes in children, it is important to have both long-term expectations and short-term indicators that the program is on the right track. For example, in the Iowa programs described above, the overall expectation is for academic success. To be a meaningful outcome, we must see that academic success is sustained over time rather than for one year or two. Ultimately, this success may be evident in decreases in school dropout rates and in increases in the number of students who successfully complete high school. However, since the program serves children in the primary grades, it is important to look at shorter term indicators of success, such as decreases in the number of students who are retained in grade and in the number of students who are in special education classes. It would be useful at the outset to list long-term expectations and then, for each one of these, to indicate short-term or intermediary indicators.

**4. Collecting Data.** Both outcome questions—Are we making a difference?—and process questions, which focus on providing a descriptive profile of the program, must be answered on the basis of data that are systematically collected beginning at the planning stage. The needs assessment and organizational audit provide a baseline of information against which we can measure progress. For example, the needs assessment may show a lack of child care for preschool-age children, illustrated in the fact that each of the community's child care centers has a long waiting list. A reduction in the number of children on waiting lists after the opening of school-based child care programs may be an early indication that the programs have made progress in meeting the need for child care. Additional information about the quality of care and other issues (for example, are there now fewer children in the community needing child care, or have other programs opened?) would be needed, but program staff can use this preliminary information to know that they are on the right track.

In the course of program planning, implementation, and administration, the importance of evaluation may be overlooked; even if there is a plan for an evaluation, data may not be collected regularly. For this reason, it is useful to build into the program a systematic means for collecting and compiling data. In the Iowa programs described above, we noted that the grantee schools were required to complete mid-year and year-end reports that provided basic information about their goals and objectives, activities, the characteristics of participating students, as well as additional information related to the goal of the grant program, such as the number of students retained in grade and number of students in special education. Each grantee school also was required to spend at least 1 percent of the grant amount on evaluation. In the case of the Iowa schools, they were required as a condition of the grant award to complete the mid-year and year-end report and submit the information to the state Department of Education, which administered the grant program. Other schools or school districts might adapt this strategy and either analyze the information internally or provide the information to an evaluation consultant.

Other ways to systematically collect data include:

- asking parents to complete an enrollment form for each year the child or family is enrolled in the program and an exit form when the child leaves the program. The latter is important and can provide a sense of how many children are leaving, where they are going, and why (dissatisfaction with services? family relocated?).
- asking school principals or others to provide an annual profile of the students enrolled. An understanding of the students' family income and other characteristics will ensure that the program keeps up with the needs of students and may also contribute to outcome findings.
- asking program administrators to complete a mid-year and/or end-of-year staff report that would document and explain any staffing changes.
- asking program administrators and staff to include a mid-year and year-end report on program activities. Additionally, in parent education or other similar activities, participants may be asked to sign in (this will provide an opportunity to document how many participated) as well as to evaluate their satisfaction with the activities, which would provide qualitative data and also feedback about the success of the efforts and their relevance to participants.
- asking program administrators and staff to keep a log of other aspects of the program; the log would provide a systematic procedure for collecting information on the number of families or children referred for additional services, on collaborations with other agencies and organizations, and on staff development opportunities.

## A Word About Quality

We have discussed the issue of high-quality services in detail in Chapter 3, but it is worth repeating here. High-quality services are essential if we are to see positive, long-term benefits (Haskins 1989). Although the need for quality is fairly well-known in the area of child care services for preschool children (Barnett 1995; Frede 1995), it is less well-known but also true of other service components as well. One of the tasks in both the implementation process and in the evaluation is to monitor the quality of services. This monitoring may be accomplished by identifying indicators associated with the high quality of specific programs and following these in practice. For example, home visitation programs often require a minimum number of visits per family during the year to be effective, and certain procedures carried out during the home visits may be associated with a greater degree of success than other practices. Deviating from or otherwise adapting the program may dilute its effectiveness. For services such as child care, high quality means smaller classes and appropriate staff:child ratios, as well as curricula that are of interest to children (Frede 1995). For these services there are instruments that can be used to assess the quality of the environment (Harms and Clifford 1980), and they should be used routinely to ensure the provision of good quality services.

## Using the Evaluation

As we stated at the outset, the topics included in program evaluation are extensive, so our focus in this chapter has been to provide educators only with a broad understanding of some of the issues and an appreciation of their role in the evaluation. Depending on the availability of both financial and other resources, educators may limit the scope of the evaluation but should include evaluation activities as ongoing aspects of the planning, implementation, and operation of the program. The purpose and eventual use of the evaluation may be internal (for purposes of program improvement) or external (to seek continued support and funding). Using the evaluation for these purposes entails not only collecting the information but also analyzing it and preparing a report, preferably at the end of each year of the program's operation. The report should be concise, but nonetheless it should include not only the findings of the evaluation, but also a comprehensive description of the program or programs included, the rationale underlying the decision to implement the programs, the purposes of the evaluation and the methods used to collect and analyze the data, what the findings indicate, and what follow-up plans and recommendations for further actions are being made.

The evaluation reports will provide a historical accounting of the programs being implemented and a description of how the program has evolved over time. It should not be conceived of as a report that sits on a shelf but as a report that is useful for new staff orientation and for program improvement efforts. Perhaps even more important, the report can be disseminated to help other schools implement similar programs and, as Cook (1997) notes, to serve as concrete documentation of what works, when, and for whom.

# 8    What's Ahead

THE SCHOOL OF THE 21ST CENTURY is based on our belief that high-quality, affordable child care must be institutionalized and available to every child who needs out-of-home care. Our ability as a nation to compete economically with other nations, as well as to ensure our well-being, depends in great part upon the degree to which American children achieve their potential. In this book we discussed, among other options, the School of the 21st Century as a viable strategy for enabling us to use an existing system, the school, to better support children and families, beginning at the birth of the child.

21C is also a strategy that complements other reform initiatives that schools may want to implement, depending on their needs and resources; some schools, besides providing child care and support services, may have a large number of children who are unable to read by the fourth grade. In such schools, the School of the 21st Century may be implemented with programs such as Reading Recovery or Success for All, which provide teachers with training on how to better help children with basic academic skills. The School of the 21st Century also can work successfully with initiatives that focus on site-based management or other efforts related to school restructuring. Several CoZi community schools, which combine the School of the 21st Century and the School Development Program (Stern and Finn-Stevenson 1997), have been implemented, providing evidence that 21C can be implemented in combination with other approaches to school reform.

The 600 schools that have implemented the School of the 21st Century program thus far represent only a small fraction of the program's potential. The fact that these schools—in a variety of different communities and with varied resources—have not only implemented the program but also, in many cases, expanded upon and institutionalized it within their districts points to the feasibility of the approach. But the development of the program thus far, although impressive, is only the first step. Still ahead is the wider dissemination of the School of the 21st Century and its availability in many more schools.

## Strategies for National Dissemination

Slavin, Dolan, and Madden note that although the numerous reform initiatives that have been developed in recent years indicate a potential for fundamental changes in education, it is not certain that this potential will be realized: "[Some] changes will take place," they note, "but will these changes make a difference in the school success of a large number of children?" (Slavin, Dolan, and Madden 1994, 1). To realize the full potential of reform, a national infrastructure for professional development needs to be in place, and at this point such an infrastructure does not exist. Although Slavin's remarks are based on a national dissemination analysis of the Success for All and other similar reform efforts, they are applicable to the School of the 21st Century and reflect the lessons we have learned in the course of helping schools implement the program.

### Establishing Networks

We noted in Chapter 6 that in developing the School of the 21st Century we have taken a service-oriented approach that includes the provision of technical assistance and training to schools at the local and regional levels. We also have established a national center that operates a network of 21C schools. This bottom-up and top-down approach is critical, since any program needs to have both vision and direction from the top and coherence at the ground level, so that those who are actually implementing the program and delivering services can achieve success. McDonald (1996) underscores the importance of reform efforts that focus on the local school level, noting that before any national program can be scaled-up, it needs to scale down and be "brought into the closest possible contact with actual children [and teachers]" (248). Fullan (1994) notes that any school reform effort, if it is to be fully and effectively implemented on a wide scale, must find strategies that can combine both a top-down and bottom-up approach to the program's development, and he suggests that one such strategy is networking.[1]

Indeed, the opportunity available to educators in 21C schools to join the 21C National Network has been one of the reasons they have been able to successfully implement, sustain, and expand the program in their districts. Educators who join the network are able not only to share ideas and learn from one another but also to contribute to as well as benefit from the social support inherent in an effective network. Other program developers also have found that social support is essential when schools implement programs, often making the difference between success and failure in implementation: "An isolated school out on the frontier of innovation can sometimes hang on for a few years, but lasting change is far more likely when schools work together as part of a network ... [and] share a common vision and language" (Slavin, Dolan, and Madden 1994, 26).

Other educational practitioners and researchers write about the importance of networking as a strategy for creating systemic change. Honing (1994) notes that networks need to be purposeful and structured and must be developed to support a vision for change. Although informal attempts to get together and network often occur, Honing emphasizes that if networks are to be used as a strategy for widespread implementation of a program, they should be well-managed and organized. Within this context, he describes networking as "a large scale attempt to link significant numbers of schools through support networks organized around powerful visions or themes for improvement. This approach [is] designed to extend reform to schools [that are] willing to change but [that are] stymied without some organized assistance" (794).

Fullan also notes that networks, either within one school district or encompassing a larger number of schools, should be purposeful and organized, adding further that they should include:

1. Regular, systematic staff development sessions for different levels of individuals in the school (e.g., program coordinators, teachers, principals, central office personnel). This multi-level approach to staff development is essential, given variations in responsibility.
2. Several different ways of sharing ideas (conferences, meetings, newsletters, and websites are some of our examples in the 21C network).
3. Integration with school-wide and district-wide priorities that include, in part, the leadership of the principal and collective action by the teachers. (We note, too, that successful 21C schools are those that integrate the program within the school so that it is perceived as every bit as important as and related to the academic programs.)
4. Commitment to regularly assessing the program's progress and recognizing that the program must be continually refined and improved upon.

These features of an effective network demonstrate that such an effort goes beyond facilitating social support among participants; also critical to the effectiveness of the network is the fostering of a deep and ongoing commitment to the program, as reflected in its integration within the school and in opportunities for staff development. The latter is an important function of the network, according to Fullan (1994), since program implementation entails bringing about change in the school and "change requires external facilitation to support internal capacity building" (422).

## Expanding the 21C Network

The 21C National Network currently in place, as described in Chapter 6, is operated out of the 21C National Center and includes various activities, such as:

- national and regional training conferences
- the development of multimedia informational and training tools and their dissemination through various mechanisms
- different levels of membership affiliation to reflect the change in status as schools progress from planning and initial implementation of the program to full implementation and eligibility to apply to become National Demonstration Sites
- peer training, wherein experienced 21C educators provide training to as well as mentor and assist newcomers
- National Demonstration Sites around the country to showcase the program and provide implementation assistance

**Facilitating the Development of an Affiliate Network.**  Building upon the success we have experienced with the National Network, our plan now is to strengthen the National Network as well as facilitate the development of state, regional, and local 21C affiliate networks. This development would mean that besides belonging to the National Network, educators implementing 21C also would establish local networks and thus serve a greater number of staff. The activities of the affiliates would be similar to those of the National Network but would address the specific needs of the members and include both formal and informal meetings among participants. The state and regional affiliate networks, for example, might include among their members principals and 21C program coordinators and/or central office staff, as well as representation from other agencies working in collaboration with the schools. At the local level, several small school districts in the same vicinity might form a network whose participants include teachers and program staff as well as staff from collaborating community-based organizations and agencies. Or, a large district with multiple schools implementing the program may opt to have its own network, thereby providing opportunities for the staff to think collectively about their goals and objectives, to get to know one another on a personal as well as professional level, and to establish mechanisms for mutual assistance.

**Linkages to Affiliate Networks.**  The number of affiliate networks, as well as their function, would increase over time as more schools implement 21C. Eventually, each affiliate network would provide not only regularly scheduled meetings but also regularly scheduled workshops that would complement the National 21C conference by addressing local training and information dissemination needs. This long-term strategy of national and affiliate networks is feasible, as demonstrated by the National Association for the Education of Young Children (NAEYC). NAEYC, as a national membership organization, provides overall direction to the field of early childhood education, publishes materials, and hosts an annual conference. Its affiliate associations for the education of young children exist at the local, regional, and state levels throughout the country, and these, too, function as membership organizations.

The 21C National Center would operate the 21C National Network and would also facilitate and provide assistance to the affiliate networks and serve as their link to current research in child development and innovations in program implementation and evaluation. The National Center also would conduct relevant research and evaluation, provide policy guidelines, promote the concept of schools' role in the provision of child care and family support services, and produce and disseminate both practical and conceptual publications relevant to the approach. Although the affiliate networks would address some of the needs of educators in 21C schools, the existence of a national center is an essential aspect of promoting the program as well as sustaining it at the local level. As Slavin, Dolan, and Madden (1994) note: "To survive the inevitable changes of superintendents, principals, teachers, and district policies, school staffs need to feel that there is a valued and important group beyond the confines of their district that cares about and supports what they are doing" (30).

**Training the Trainers.** Another critical role for the 21C National Center is ensuring quality of services at the local level. This function requires widespread training opportunities for potential trainers and frequent site visits, which become problematic as the number of 21C schools increases. We have tried without much success to broker the provision of training and technical assistance to other organizations in different parts of the country and found that the quality of technical assistance and training was compromised. Although our failure here may have been due to the fact that we tried the approach before we established the National Center, which would have served in an oversight capacity, negative experiences with brokering training functions are noted by other program developers as well (Slavin, Dolan, and Madden 1994; Joyner 1995).

In another approach to provide training to an increasing number of schools, we employed part-time regional staff located in different states and thus closer to the schools needing assistance (S. H. Miller 1994). However, the regional staff felt isolated and needed to come to the national headquarters at Yale frequently for briefing and training, which proved to be expensive. Thus we have opted for employing full-time implementation associates at Yale, each of whom is responsible for providing training, site visits, and consultation to a certain number of schools. We also have made use of our peer trainers, as we discussed in more detail in Chapters 5 and 6.

In expanding our capacity to provide training and assistance to more schools, we plan to use parts of the two approaches discussed above; that is, we will hire and train implementation associates at the National Center, and although some of them will operate from the National Center, others, with several years' experience in implementing 21C as well as providing training, will operate from regional training locations that are tied to 21C National Demonstration Sites. Examples of potential trainers include the retired principals and superintendents in some of our 21C National Demonstration Sites and program directors in several of our other established sites who may be ready for a career change; these people have implementation know-how; they have previously provided implementation assistance to educators as part of the peer training we have established; they are members of the 21C National Faculty and, as such, provide training at the national 21C conferences; and, finally, they can either travel to a newcoming 21C school to provide assistance, or they can arrange for training to be provided at the 21C National Demonstration Site with which they were affiliated. Since some of the staff at 21C schools have nearly ten years of experience with the program, the pool of potential associates is quite large and with time will increase even more. Although such associates have a great deal of experience, they would still participate in "training the trainers" events to be developed and hosted by the 21C National Center.

The 21C National Center and Network, as well as the affiliate networks, would operate on the basis of membership fees and contractual agreements for the provision of training and technical assistance to schools and state-level agencies. Although in this way the networks would become self-supporting eventually, an initial investment to build up our capacity would be essential, as we noted in Chapter 6.

## Changing Our Conception of the School

### Structural Changes

Networks associated with programs support implementation efforts and are important for both the short-term success of reform initiatives and in the long term, to ensure widespread implementation. However, networks focus essentially on program implementation rather than on the school building and the actual working conditions in the school. Programs such as the School of the 21st Century significantly expand upon the traditional mission of the school and radically alter the use of the school, so changes in school structure are needed if program implementation is to be facilitated broadly.

**Changing How Schools Function.** The term "school restructuring" refers to various strategies related to changing how schools function. Often, the term is used to refer to a specific reform initiative, but the term also is used more broadly to encompass various activities. Mitchell (1990) describes some such restructuring activities, noting that these may focus on:

- changing the working conditions of the teaching staff through changes in roles and responsibilities
- changing the management structure of the school so that, among other things, teachers have more discretion over curriculum and instructional decisions
- changing instructional strategies to better address the learning needs of students
- changing how schools go about enrollment (for example, school choice, magnet schools)
- changing staff development and in-service teacher training to include broader opportunities for teachers to undertake training
- changing the nature and coordination of student support services to better support the needs of students, especially those at risk for educational failure

The latter example would include efforts such as the School of the 21st Century that provide nonacademic support services to all children and parents who may need such services. Since 21C schools bring about extensive changes—which often include not only opening the doors to children at a younger age and the provision of nonacademic support services such as child care but also the other changes described above, such as site-based management and changes in staff roles and responsibilities—the opposite also occurs. That is, a school may implement site-based management or another similar initiative and decide later on that it also needs to provide nonacademic support services such as the School of the 21st Century to students and families (Mitchell 1990; McDonald 1996).

**Changing the Physical Design of the School Building.** Besides restructuring activities and the overall function of the school, it is often essential to redesign the physical building. Consider just a few aspects of a program such as 21C—providing nonacademic support services; reaching out to and involving parents; serving children from birth on; using the school the whole day, year-round; you can see that the changes created in the school are substantial. If we are to institutionalize the program and ensure its implementation in schools across the country, it is also essential that we adopt strategies for changing how we conceptualize the use of school buildings.

Donahoe (1993) contends that changes in the physical structure of the school are essential since schools cannot continue to function in the traditional way. He focuses not only on the need to redesign the school building but also on the time changes required by society's need for longer school days and the use of the building year-round. Schools of the 21st Century already are making essential changes in the use of the school building. However, to facilitate widespread implementation, new schools should be constructed to include provisions that will facilitate the extension of the school day and school year and broaden the use of the building with the new mission of the school in mind. In other words, schools should be designed to:

- accommodate the needs of infants and toddlers as well as of older students
- enable parents as well as others in the community to use the school building
- encourage the provision of services before and after the academic programs

Such design and policy changes would facilitate implementation of the program and eliminate some of the challenges to implementation we discussed in Chapter 5. This idea is not radical nor without precedent; in Ontario, Canada, for example, a law required any new school building to include space for before- and after-school programs, making it substantially easier for educators to provide such services. This is also an opportune time to institute such changes. Not only are increasing numbers of schools expanding upon the traditional mission of the school and coming to see the school building as a service center for the entire community (Blank 1998), but many of the nation's schools are in such a dilapidated state that radical renovations or the building of entirely new structures are issues confronting many communities. Johnston (1998) notes that although some communities decide to demolish old school buildings and build new structures, many states, Connecticut and Maryland among them, have chosen to provide financial assistance to enable some school districts to renovate old school buildings, making them not only safer but also more applicable to various new uses. Whatever the approach, the opportunity is present to conceptualize the use of the school building in keeping with current societal needs.

## Changes in Culture and Climate of the School

The above-noted changes in school buildings and school activities and programs need to be accompanied by changes in the culture of schools. Fullan (1993, 1994) refers to this as "reculturing," which he defines as the process of developing new values, beliefs, norms, and conceptions. He notes that existing school cultures are antithetical to the kinds of activities included in many reform initiatives. Fullan claims further that although the attempt has been made to create necessary changes through site-based management and other school restructuring initiatives, these changes have affected only certain school practices and not the overall school culture—how teachers and other staff think, and how they regard their role and the mission of the school (Fullan 1993). Sarason (1971) has long emphasized the importance of changing the culture of the school, noting that the failure to institute changes in relationships and to address other school culture issues thwart reform efforts. McDonald (1996) regards the lack of cultural change as a deep-seated barrier to all school reform initiatives. Peterson, McCarthey, and Elmore (1996), in their analysis of several school restructuring efforts, found that although changes in student grouping patterns and time allocation, or initiatives such as team teaching, did take place as a result of the restructuring efforts, there were no changes in how teachers taught. Thus Peterson, McCarthey, and Elmore note that "while school structures can provide opportunities for learning new practices, the structures, by themselves, do not cause the learning to occur" (119). Admittedly, some educators do change in the course of a schools' adoption of reform initiatives, but what is needed now is "to move to scale by enabling the majority of teachers and schools to operate in these [new] ways and thereby create a critical mass of new norms necessary to sustain a culture of systemic reform" (Fullan 1994, 422).

**Teacher Preparation Programs.** We have found that in many 21C schools positive changes occur after several years of the program's implementation, when all, or at least the majority of, teachers in the school embrace the 21C concept and see the potential benefits of providing early care and support services to students and families. However, leadership and staff changes present challenges and the need for continual orientation and training. Some of the problems we have encountered have been related to resistance to change on the part of some teachers, as well as the lack of preparedness on the part of new teachers hired to work in the schools. Often, teachers lack an understanding of the new roles of schools and of the importance of nonacademic support services and, for a time at least, either inhibit or thwart change (Fullan 1993, 1994). Although ongoing staff development sessions can address this issue, other, more effective approaches need to be explored and instituted.

One way to achieve systemic changes in the school culture is to change the way prospective teachers are trained. Higher education institutions in general have been criticized concerning their approach to preparing students and have been asked to reexamine their approach (Dinham 1994). Although various disciplines are criticized in this regard, particular problems are noted among teacher preparation programs (Sarason, Davidson, and Blatt 1986). Shartrand et al. (1997) analyzed teacher preparation programs and teacher certification requirements from fifty-one state departments of education (including the District of Columbia) to determine if and to what extent these programs and requirements include such areas of study as parent involvement and early childhood. They found that in the majority of states, such areas of study are not included in teacher certification requirements and, further, that most of the teacher preparation programs did not provide prospective teachers with the opportunity to study about child development, early childhood, parent involvement, and other similar topics. With regard to family involvement in particular, they note that "serious discrepancy [exists] between pre-service teacher training and the types of family involvement activities that teachers [are] increasingly being expected to perform in schools" (1).

**Difficulties Faced by Teacher Preparation Programs.**   Fullan (1993) also documents failures in teacher preparation programs, noting that "society has failed teachers in two senses of the word. It gives teachers failing grades for not producing better results. At the same time, it does not help improve the conditions that would make success possible" (104). In a chapter he titled "Teacher Education: Society's Missed Opportunity," Fullan (1993) linked failure to adopt successful reform initiatives on a wide scale to inadequacies in the way teachers are trained; Sarason, Davidson, and Blatt (1986) and Goodlad (1990) make a similar point.

The failures on the part of higher education institutions to provide appropriate teacher training and relevant courses affect not only prospective teachers but also practicing teachers. They often have no opportunities to enhance their knowledge and acquire skills that would facilitate their working in schools that attempt to address children's and families' nonacademic needs. Hence there is a need to establish not only changes in teacher preparation programs but also close linkages and collaborative relationships between teacher preparation programs in higher education and school systems (see Box 8.1). This linkage would enable teachers to learn about and accept change and would lay the foundation for what Fullan (1993) refers to as "continuous learning" and refinement of knowledge and skills.

Researchers have identified the knowledge and skills required to link child care and education and to enable teachers to work more effectively with families and to address students' needs, as well as to become team players in a school that implements programs such as 21C. Such knowledge areas and skills include an understanding of how children learn and of the environmental factors that impact children's ability to succeed academically, of the relationship between children's early experiences and their later ability to profit from instruction, of the families' role in children's ed-

BOX 8.1   University-School Collaborations

Overall, teacher preparation programs in higher education institutions around the country fail to prepare teachers to work in schools that respond to the needs of students and families. However, there are a few examples of university-school collaborations that contribute to the development and effectiveness of schools engaged in the provision of early care and family support services (Harkavy 1992). Among the 21C school network, there are two such examples. In Saint Joseph, Missouri, the public school district is implementing the program, working closely with the higher education institutions nearby to ensure not only effective implementation and evaluation of the program but also that teachers in training have internship opportunities in the School of the 21st Century and that practicing teachers have opportunities for further education to enhance their understanding of issues related to early care and family support.

In an example of community college and corporate collaboration in Buffalo, New York, an inner city school in Buffalo and a building that once housed a church have been transformed to include not only computer-based and summer tutoring programs for elementary and secondary school students but also after-school and other services associated with the School of the 21st Century (Massey, Evans, and Harriman 1992). The effort, which includes components of but is broader than most 21C schools (Halpern 1992), began with the incorporation of a parent organization (Parents for Quality Education, Inc.) and the assistance of the Erie County Bar Association's Volunteer Lawyers Program, as well as of various foundations and corporations and Houghton College. To its initial efforts, the team worked to add early care and family support. In addition to assisting in the implementation of the various services and activities, the college used the site to train teachers and early childhood and family day care providers (Ballard, Cosby, and Massey 1992).

ucation and how to effectively communicate and work with parents (Adelman and Taylor 1998). Shartrand and her colleagues (1997) surveyed sixty teacher education programs and found that only nine offered courses in such areas as family involvement in school. They also identified challenges teacher preparation programs face when they attempt to change course work to include new areas of study. The challenges include:

- the lack of a system to support research and model development to facilitate needed changes in teacher preparation programs
- the lack of resources to implement needed changes
- negative attitudes frequently held by faculty members, as well as some prospective teachers, who feel schools should focus on academics only

- state and federal mandates, as well as some of the policies of universities and colleges, which place many restrictions and requirements on teacher preparation programs, thus creating barriers to implementing needed changes

## Policy Implications

### Recommendations for Change

The discussion above illustrates the discrepancy that exists between educators' attempts to respond to the realities in the lives of students and families and the policies that would facilitate their ability to do so. It is clear that although commitment to the program on the part of educators and vision and leadership on the part of program developers are essential to successful school reform, they are, in and of themselves, insufficient. If schools implementing early care and support services are to realize their potential, and if quality implementation is to occur on a wide scale, we also need policy changes at various levels of government, as well as in higher education.

In the course of this chapter we have identified several recommendations for specific actions that would facilitate widespread implementation of school-based early care and family support initiatives. Included are recommendations

- to dedicate funds for and develop the infrastructure to support staff development opportunities at the local, regional, and national levels;
- to facilitate changes in the structure and culture of the school to better enable educators to implement early care and family support services; and
- to establish changes in how prospective teachers are trained and to make available opportunities for knowledge and skill enhancement for practicing teachers.

**Local and State Action.**   Besides these specific actions, we call for policy changes that would make the proposed actions a reality. Such policy changes need to undertaken at the local level especially. Some programs may be undertaken by the school building leadership or by the district as a whole without the explicit support of the school board. However, for reform programs to be institutionalized, accepted as an ongoing and important aspect of the school's mission, and made available to every student who needs them, school board support is essential. Such support can often mean the difference between a program implemented for a short period of

---

BOX 8.2   Key Role of School Board Members

"It is time for school boards to deal with the reality that, by themselves the best instructional reforms cannot produce desired results when large numbers of students are not performing well" (Center for Mental Health in Schools 1998).

---

time and then forgotten and one that becomes part of the very fabric of the school and is here to stay.

Several researchers underscore the importance of local action, noting how crucial such action is for successful long-term and widespread implementation of reform initiatives (Cunningham 1990; Fullan 1993, 1994; McDonald 1996). As we noted earlier, McDonald (1996) notes that in attempts to go to scale in implementing a program, one must first "scale down," focusing on actions at the local level. Fullan (1993) notes that widespread change occurs when enough people moving in the same direction coalesce: "A top-down structural change does not work. You can't mandate what happens because there are no shortcuts to changes in systems' 'cultures'" (143).

Changes in many schools are under way, and there are numerous examples of schools implementing the School of the 21st Century and related services that support family life, ultimately promoting students' ability to do well academically. However, there are also many examples of educators who are unable to implement such programs because of resistance among some members of the school administration or the board. If sufficient change is to occur to make a difference to large numbers of children, school board members as well as educators need to be convinced that the provision of early care and family support is indeed part of the mission of the school and should be seen as an investment rather than as a spending of funds that has no relevance to academic success.

Widespread local recognition of this idea and of the importance of expanding the traditional mission of the school can be facilitated by state legislative and administrative leadership. The provision of financial support to accommodate structural and cultural changes in the school as well as technical assistance is one of the state-level actions that would support school-based changes of sufficient scale to make a difference to large numbers of children. Also, as we noted earlier, state action with regard to teacher certification requirements would facilitate higher education's response to needed modifications in teacher preparation programs, thereby ensuring that teachers have the knowledge and understanding of the new missions of schools.

**National Leadership.**   National leadership can serve as a catalyst for change at the local and state levels. Such national leadership is imperative at the federal level, which can facilitate change by providing financial and other incentives to states and local school boards to take action in implementing nonacademic support programs for all children from birth on. Leadership on the part of the federal government is needed also to support research, development, and evaluation activities that will ensure that locally implemented programs and services adhere to quality of service principles and have a positive impact on children's development.

Equally important is national leadership on disseminating information about the importance of the early years in children's development and the implications this early period has for later success in school. The support of federal government in this regard is essential and may be accomplished by establishing an office specifically dedicated to promoting and overseeing schools' role in the provision of early care and family support services. Also important is the leadership of national professional associations and organizations. Such associations and organizations can disseminate information to their membership as well as endorse federal, state, and local action to support linking child care and education.

## *Learning from Other Countries*

The need for child care and family support services is not unique to the United States. In the Fourth Annual Conference on Women, held in Beijing in 1995, it was noted that although women in every part of the world hold responsibilities in politics, business, and other sectors, they face concerns regarding child care. In some countries, lack of adequate child care holds down women's wages by forcing them to take jobs that provide flexible hours or enable them to bring children to the workplace. In other countries, girls drop out of school to care for siblings while their mothers work. A glance at various countries' child care practices and policies reveals a great deal of contrast. Whereas mothers in countries such as China are forced to leave their children alone at home while they work in the fields, countries such as Sweden and France provide high-quality care to all children (Shellenbarger, Moffett, and Chen 1995; Kamerman 1998).

In Sweden, families are entitled to a one-year paid maternity or paternity leave so that at least one of the parents can spend the first year with the child. By paying for child care and requiring employers to allow the parent to work part-time until the child is age 12, policies continue to protect and assist families once the parent goes back to work. The Swedish pro-family policies are designed to enable women to work (hence 85 percent of all women are in the workforce) and to address gender equity issues in the workplace, although the latter issue has not been addressed adequately: Men still earn higher salaries and are more likely to be promoted than

women (Milbank 1995). Nevertheless, women in many countries are envi-
ous of the generous child care and maternity leave laws that Swedish
women enjoy.

The French child care system is of particular relevance to efforts in this
country to link child care and education. The system, described by Regenstein, Silow-Carroll, and Meyer (1995), includes the *ecole maternelle,* or
preschool, which provides publicly supported universal early care and education to children ages 2 to 5. The *ecole maternelle* links preschool to every
elementary school and has been available universally since 1975. Although
it includes elements of child care, its focus is broader and its primary purpose is to enhance children's development and prepare them for later
schooling. Participation is voluntary. Although increasing numbers of children are enrolled, funding limits enrollment of some 2-year-old children;
but virtually all 3-, 4-, and 5-year-old children are in the *ecole maternelle*
system, though some, especially younger than age 2, are in privately operated programs.

The cost per child for preschool education in France is about $2,500 a
year. National financing amounts to about 56 percent of the total funding
and is paid for primarily through a value-added tax. This tax covers the
full cost of teachers' and special education staff salaries. Municipal governments contribute about 34 percent of the cost, paid primarily through municipal taxes. These taxes pay for teacher aides' salaries as well as building
construction and maintenance. Parents pay approximately 10 percent of
the total cost for the wrap-around care they may need before or after the
operational hours of the *ecole maternelle* (Richardson and Marx 1989; Regenstein, Silow-Carroll, and Meyer 1995).

The *ecole maternelle* is an integral part of the public school system in
France, with the actual facilities located either in or next to the school. Services are provided six days a week from 7:30 A.M. to 6:00 P.M. For a large
part of the day, educational programming is provided, and the balance of
the time is for unstructured play activities and rest. On Wednesdays, there
is no educational programming as such, but working parents can pay for
having their children in school on that day. Since teachers are off, teacher
aides look after the children, ensuring continuity of care.

Of significance in the French system is the extensive effort put into providing assistance and training to teachers in the *ecole maternelle* and in
nursery schools for younger children, as well as the effort put into providing training to family day care providers who often look after younger children. At the *ecole maternelle,* teachers have the equivalent of a master's degree in early childhood and elementary education, and some of the teachers
are expected to carry out administrative tasks in addition to teaching and
caring for the children.

Also of significance is the fact that although the French system provides
universal access to preschool, there is still a special effort to reach out to

and address the needs of children at risk for educational failure. This effort is accomplished through Zones of Educational Priority, which focus on intervention strategies in communities with a high percentage of immigrants whose children have problems with language and other issues. Zones of Educational Priority provide, among other things, increased staff (which allows individual attention to the children), specialized personnel, longer hours of operation, efforts to involve parents as well as various health and social services. This effort, together with the focus on universal access to preschool, has meant improvements in the rates at which children pass first grade, an indication that the children are on a trajectory of educational success (Richardson and Marx 1989).

There are some issues that remain to be addressed in France: The use of public funds comes with constraints and means that, on average, classrooms contain twenty-seven children; teachers, although relatively well-paid, feel they are accorded a lesser position and status in the educational hierarchy.

Nevertheless, as this brief description demonstrates, France, without mandating enrollment in preschool, has made available universal access to preschool by creating a nationwide network of preschools that links early care to the public education system. A thriving private nursery school sector still exists in France, so parents do have a choice, but there is also a system of child care in public schools, ensuring that all children who need care can participate.

We are not advocating instituting a similar system here; the focus of our proposal for the School of the 21st Century is for the program to be funded primarily through parental fees on a sliding scale calibrated to family income. Nevertheless, there are some lessons for us in the French example. Drawing on the work of Regenstein, Silow-Carroll, and Meyer (1995), we can see that it is not necessary to make preschool compulsory in order to make preschool enrollment nearly universal, nor do we have to preempt the private child care sector in order to link child care and education; programs in public schools can coexist with private preschool programs, providing parents with choice.

Perhaps the most important lesson is that France is making an investment in its children; the citizens of France believe that early childhood programs translate into better outcomes in school performance. In France, where for many years the population was aging, children assume importance, for without children the French people recognize that they have no future. This pronatal focus on policy is unlikely to be supported in the United States, a point made by Kamerman (1998). However, as a society, we need to think about our nation's future and should regard financial and other support of child care and family support services as an investment in human capital. We have the know-how to address the needs of children and families, and we have numerous examples of successful programs. We need societal will to bring these to scale.

## Notes

1. Our work with the 21C Network confirms Fullan's findings, and, where relevant, we share some of our experiences in parentheses.

# References

Aber, L., Brooks-Gunn, J., and Maynard, R. 1995. The effects of welfare reform on teenage parents and their children. *The Future of Children* 5, no. 2: 53–71.

Abt, C. C. 1974. Social programs evaluation: Research allocation strategies for maximizing policy payoffs. In *The Evaluation of Social Programs,* edited by C. C. Abt, 41–53. Beverly Hills, Calif.: Sage.

Adams, G., and Poersch, N. 1997. Who cares? State commitment to child care and early education. *Young Children* 52, no. 4: 66–69.

Adelman, H., and Taylor, T. 1998. *Restructuring Boards of Education to Enhance Schools' Effectiveness in Addressing Barriers to Student Learning.* Los Angeles, Calif.: UCLA, School Mental Health Project.

Adelson, J. 1997. What we know about day care. *Commentary* 104, no. 5: 52–54.

Ainsworth, M., Blehar, M., Waters, E., and Wall, S. 1978. *Patterns of Attachment in the Strange Situation and at Home.* Hillsdale, N.J.: Lawrence Erlbaum.

Albee, G. W. 1986. Toward a just society: Lessons from observations on the primary prevention of psychopathology. *American Psychologist* 41: 891–898.

Albee, G. W., and Gullotta, T. P. 1997. *Primary Prevention Works.* Thousand Oaks, Calif.: Sage.

Albrecht, K., ed. 1991. *Quality Criteria for School-Age Child Care Programs: Revisions and Expansions of the Accreditation Criteria of the National Academy of Early Childhood Programs to Reflect School-Age Children and Youth.* Alexandria, Va.: Project Home Safe, American Home Economic Association.

Albrecht, K., and Plantz, M. 1993. *Tools for Schools: Contracting for School-Age Child Care.* Alexandria, Va.: Project Home Safe, American Home Economic Association.

Arvey, H. H., and Tijerina, A. 1995. The school of the future: Implementation issues in a school-community connection. In *School-Community Connections: Exploring Issues for Research and Practice,* edited by L. C. Rigsby, M. Reynolds, and M. Wang, 311–356. San Francisco: Jossey-Bass.

Assessing School-Age Quality (ASQ). 1995. *Assessing School Age Child Care.* Wellesley, Mass.: National Institute of Out-of-School Time.

Ballard, D., Cosby, D., and Massey, C. P. 1992. The convergence of two worlds. In *Universities and Community Schools,* edited by I. Harkavy, 22–28. Philadelphia: Pennsylvania Program for Public Service, University of Pennsylvania.

Barnett, W. S. 1985. *The Perry Preschool Program and Its Long-Term Effects: A Benefit-Cost Analysis.* Ypsilanti, Minn.: High/Scope.

_____. 1993a. Benefit-cost analysis of preschool education: Findings from a twenty-five-year follow-up. *American Journal of Orthopsychiatry* 63, no. 4: 400–508.

_____. 1993b. Economic evaluation of home visiting programs. *The Future of Children* 3, no. 1: 93–112.

_____. 1993c. New wine in old bottles: Increasing the coherence of early childhood care and education. *Early Childhood Research Quarterly* 8: 519–558.

_____. 1995. Long-term effects of early childhood programs on cognitive and school outcomes. *The Future of Children* 5, no. 13: 25–50.

Baumarind, D. 1990. Effective parenting during early transitions. In *Advances in Family Research*, edited by P. Coen and E. Hetherington, 39–59. Hillsdale, N.J.: Earlbaum.

Behrman, R., and Quinn, L. 1994. Children and divorce: Overview and analysis. *The Future of Children* 4, no. 1: 4–14.

Belsky, J. 1981. Early human experience: A family perspective. *Developmental Psychology* 17: 3–23.

_____. 1987. Infant day care: A cause for concern. *Zero to Three* 7, no. 3: 1–3.

_____. 1988. The effects of infant day care reconsidered. *Early Childhood Research Quarterly* 3: 235–272.

Berlau, J. 1998. Is the U.S. still a "Nation at Risk?" *Investors Business Daily*, August 31, 1.

Berrueta-Clement, J. R., Schweinhart, J. J., Barnett, W. S., Epstein, A. S., and Walker, D. P. 1984. *Changed Lives: The Effects of the Perry Preschool Program on Youths Through Age 19*. Ypsilanti, Minn.: High/Scope Press.

Betson, D. M., and Michael, R. T. 1997. Why so many children are poor. *The Future of Children* 7, no. 2: 25–39.

Blank, H. 1994. *Protecting Our Children: State and Federal Policies for Exempt Child Care Settings*. Washington, D.C.: Children's Defense Fund.

Blank, H., and Blum, B. 1997. A brief history of work expectations for welfare mothers. *The Future of Children* 7, no. 1: 28–38.

Blank, M. 1998. *Learning Together*. Washington, D.C.: Brookings Institute.

Blau, D., and Hotz, V. 1992. Special issues on child care: Introduction. *Journal of Human Resources* 27, no. 1: 1–99.

Bornstein, M. H., ed. 1995. *Handbook of Parenting*. Vol. 3, *Status and Social Conditions of Parenting*. Mahwah, N.J.: Lawrence Erlbaum.

Borquez, J. 1994. Unemployment and work interruption among African-American single mothers: Effects on parenting and adolescent socioemotional functioning. *Child Development* 65, no. 2: 562–589.

Bowlby, J. 1969. *Attachment and Loss*. Vol. 1, *Attachment*. New York: Basic Books.

_____. 1989. *Secure Attachments*. New York: Basic Books.

Boyer, E. 1992. Foreword to *Heart Start: The Emotional Foundations of School Readiness*, by Zero to Three/National Center for Clinical Infant Programs. Arlington, Va.: Zero to Three/National Center for Clinical Infant Programs.

Bradley, A. 1997. Schools take a fresh look at bolstering teachers. *Education Week*, June 25, 8.

Bradley, R., Caldwell, B., Rock, S., Barnard, K., and Gray, C. 1989. Home environments and cognitive development. *Developmental Psychology* 25: 217–235.

Brazelton, T. B. 1985. Stress and the family. *Infant Mental Health Journal* 9, no. 1: 65–71.

Bredenkamp, S. 1989. *Developmentally Appropriate Practice in Early Childhood Programs Serving Children from Birth Through Age 8*. Washington, D.C.: National Association for the Education of Young Children.

Bredenkamp, S., and Copple, C., eds. 1997. *Developmentally Appropriate Practice in Early Childhood Programs*. Rev. ed. Washington, D.C.: National Association for the Education of Young Children.

Bridgeman, A., and Phillips, D., eds. 1998. *New Findings on Poverty, Child Health, and Nutrition: Summary of a Research Briefing*. Washington, D.C.: National Academy Press.

Bronfenbrenner, U. 1979. *The Ecology of Human Development and Experiments by Nature and Design*. Cambridge, Mass.: Harvard University Press.

Brooks-Gunn, J., and Chase-Lansdale, D. L. 1995. Adolescent parenthood. In *Handbook of Parenting*. Vol. 3, edited by M. Bornstein, 113–150. Mahwah, N.J.: Lawrence Erlbaum.

Brooks-Gunn, J., and Duncan, C. 1997. The effects of poverty on children. *The Future of Children* 7, no. 2: 55–71.

Brown, J. L., Gershoff, S., and Cook, J. 1992. The politics of hunger: When science and ideology clash. *International Journal of Health and Sciences* 22, no. 2: 8–18.

Brown, L. 1998. New scientific evidence on cognitive development: Why nutrition comes up an ace. Address given at the School of the 21st Century Annual Conference, Yale University Bush Center in Child Development and Social Policy, New Haven, Conn., July 25.

The Bush Center in Child Development and Social Policy. 1995. *The Role of the Teacher in the School of the 21st Century*. New Haven, Conn.: The Bush Center in Child Development and Social Policy.

Cain, V., and Hofferth, S. 1989. Parental choice of self care for school age children. *Journal of Marriage and the Family* 51: 65–77.

Caldwell, B. 1985. What is quality child care? In *What Is Quality Child Care?* edited by B. Caldwell and A. Hilliard, 1–16. Washington, D.C.: National Association for the Education of Young Children.

Carnegie Corporation of New York. 1994. *Starting Points: Meeting the Needs of Our Youngest Children*. New York: Carnegie Corporation of New York.

———. 1996. *Years of Promise*. New York: Carnegie Corporation of New York.

Center for Mental Health in Schools. 1998. *Restructuring Boards of Education to Enhance Schools' Effectiveness in Addressing Barriers to Student Learning*. Los Angeles, Calif.: Center for Mental Health in Schools, University of California–Los Angeles.

Center for the Future of Children. 1992. Analysis. *The Future of Children* 2, no. 1: 6–18.

Center on Hunger, Poverty, and Nutrition Policy. 1995. *The Link Between Nutrition and Cognitive Development in Children*. Medford, Mass.: Tufts University School of Nutrition.

Chaskin, R., and Richman, H. 1992. Concerns about school-linked services: Institution-based versus community-based models. *The Future of Children* 2, no. 1: 107–117.

Child Care Action Campaign. 1988. *Child Care: The Bottom Line*. New York: Child Care Action Campaign.

_____. 1993. *Linking Child Care and Education.* New York: Child Care Action Campaign.

Children's Aid Society. 1995. *Building a Community School.* New York: Children's Aid Society.

Children's Defense Fund (CDF). 1994. *First Steps, Promising Future: State and Pre-Kindergarten Initiatives in the Early 1990s.* Washington, D.C.: Children's Defense Fund.

_____. 1998. *The State of America's Children Yearbook 1998.* Washington, D.C.: Children's Defense Fund.

Chira, S. 1986. A mother's place: Taking the debate about working mothers beyond guilt and blame. In *Family and Work: Bridging the Gap,* edited by S. Coontz, 39–51. Cambridge, Mass.: Ballinger Publishing Co.

_____. 1991. Social work goes to school—A special report. *New York Times,* May 15, A1.

Cicchetti, M., and Cummings, M., eds. 1990. *Attachment in Infancy and the Preschool Years: Theory, Research, and Intervention.* Chicago: University of Chicago Press.

Clarke-Stewart, K. A. 1982. *Day Care.* Cambridge, Mass.: Harvard University Press.

_____. 1989. Infant day care: Maligned or malignant? *American Psychologist* 44, no. 2: 266–273.

Clarke-Stewart, K. A., Allhusen, V. D., and Clements, D. C. 1995. Nonparental caregiving. In *Handbook of Parenting.* Vol. 3, *Status and Social Conditions of Parenting,* edited by M. Bornstein, 151–176. Mahwak, N.J.: Lawrence Erlbaum.

Clarke-Stewart, K. A., and Fein, G. 1983. Early childhood program. In *Handbook of Child Psychology,* edited by P. H. Mussen, 917–1000. New York: Wiley.

Cochran, M., and Niego, S. 1995. Parenting and social networks. In *Handbook of Parenting.* Vol. 3, *Status and Social Conditions of Parenting,* edited by M. Bornstein, 393–418. Mahwak, N.J.: Lawrence Erlbaum.

Cohen, A. 1996. A brief history of federal financing for child care in the United States. *Future of Children* 6, no. 2: 26–40.

Coleman, J. S. 1987. Families and schools. *Educational Researcher* 16: 28–32.

Coltoff, P. 1998. *Community Schools: Education Reform and Partnership with Our Nation's Social Service Agencies.* Washington, D.C.: Child Welfare League of America.

Comer, J. P., Haynes, N. M., Joyner, E. T., and Ben-Avie, M. 1996. *Rallying the Whole Village: The Comer Process for Reforming Education.* New York: Teachers College Press.

Committee for Economic Development (CED). 1991. *An Unfinished Agenda: New Vision for Child Development and Education.* New York: Committee for Economic Development.

_____. 1993. *Why Child Care Matters.* New York: Committee for Economic Development.

_____. 1994. *Putting Learning First: Governing and Managing the Schools of High Achievement.* New York: Committee for Economic Development.

Cook, J., and Brown, L. 1994. *Two Americas: Comparisons of U.S. Child Poverty in Rural, Inner City, and Suburban Areas.* Medford, Mass.: Tufts University School of Nutrition.

Cook, T. 1997. Lessons learned in evaluation over the past twenty-five years. In *Evaluation for the 21st Century*, edited by E. Chelimsky and W. Shadish, 30–32. Thousand Oaks, Calif.: Sage.

Coontz, S. 1986. The way we really are: Coming to terms with America's changing family. In *Family and Work: Bridging the Gap*, edited by S. Coontz, 1–9. Cambridge, Mass.: Ballinger Publishing Co.

Corcoran, M., and Chaundry, M. 1997. The dynamics of childhood poverty. *The Future of Children* 7, no. 2: 40–54.

Crnic, K., and Lamberty, G. 1994. Reconsidering school readiness: Conceptual and applied perspectives. *Early Education and Development* 5, no. 2: 91–105.

Cunningham, L. 1990. Reconstituting local government for well-being and education. In *Educational Leadership and the Changing Contexts in Families, Communities, and Schools*, edited by L. Cunningham and B. Mitchell, 135–154. Chicago: National Society for the Study of Education.

Davis, W. E. 1994. Putting learning first. *Education Week*, December 7, 18–21.

Deemer, E., Desimone, L., and Finn-Stevenson, M. 1998. School-based child care: How and why it works. *Principal* 77, no. 3: 43–46.

Desimone, L., Finn-Stevenson, M., and Henrich, C. 1999. *Whole-School Reform in a Low-Income African-American Community: The Effects of the CoZi Model on Teachers, Parents, and Students*. New Haven, Conn.: The Bush Center in Child Development and Social Policy.

Dinham, S. H. 1994. Challenge and vision for professional schools in higher education. *Educational Researcher* 23, no. 8: 33–34.

Donahoe, T. 1993. Finding the way: Structure, time, and culture in school improvement. *Phi Delta Kappan*, December, 301–310.

Drazen, S., and Haust, M. 1994. *Increasing Children's Readiness for School by a Parental Education Program*. Binghamton, N.Y.: Community Resource Center.

Dryfoos, J. 1994. *Full Service Schools: A Revolution in Health and Social Services for Children, Youth, and Families*. San Francisco: Jossey-Bass.

———. 1998. *A Look at Community Schools in 1998*. New York: Fordham University, National Center for Schools and Communities.

Dumas, L. S., and Frassler, D. G. 1997. *Help Me, I'm Sad: Recognizing, Treating, and Preventing Childhood Depression*. New York: Viking.

Duncan, G., and Brooks-Gunn, J., eds. 1997. *Consequences of Growing Up Poor*. New York: Russell Sage Foundation.

Dunn, L., and Kontos, S. 1997. What have we learned about developmentally appropriate practice? *Young Children* 52, no. 5: 4–38.

Ebb, E. 1994. *Child Care Tradeoff: States Make Painful Choices*. Washington, D.C.: Children's Defense Fund.

Economic Policy Council. 1986. *Family Income in America*. Washington, D.C.: Family Policy Institute.

Elias, M. 1997. Reinterpreting dissemination of prevention programs as widespread implementation with effectiveness and fidelity. In *Establishing Preventive Services*, edited by R. Weissberg, T. Gullotta, R. Hampton, B. Ryan, and G. Adams, 283–289. Thousand Oaks, Calif.: Sage.

Elias, M., Gager, P., and Leon, S. 1998. Spreading a warm blanket of prevention over all children: Guidelines for selecting substance abuse and related prevention curriculum for use in the school. *Journal of Primary Prevention* 19: 239–260.

Elkind, D. 1987. *Miseducation: Preschoolers at Risk*. New York: Alfred E. Knopf.

_____. 1988. Educating the very young: A call for clear thinking. *NEA Today* 6, no. 6: 22–27.

_____. 1991. Early childhood education in the postmodern era. In *Perspectives on Early Childhood Education*, edited by D. Elkind, 3–17. Washington, D.C.: National Education Association.

Entwisle, D., and Alexander, K. L. 1990. Beginning school math competence. *Child Development* 61: 454–471.

Epstein, J. 1992. School and family partnerships. In *Encyclopedia of Educational Research*. 6th ed., edited by M. Alkin, 314–364. New York: MacMillan.

Epstein, J., and Lee, S. 1995. National patterns of school and family connections in the middle grades. In *The School-Family Connection*, edited by B. Ryan, G. Adams, T. Gullotta, R. Weissberg, and R. Hampton, 108–154. Thousand Oaks, Calif.: Sage.

Epstein, W. M. 1997. Social science, child welfare, and family preservation: A failure of rationality in public policy. *Children and Youth Services Review* 19: 41–60.

Farran, D., and Shonkoff, J. P. 1994. Developmental disabilities and the concept of school readiness. *Early Education and Development* 5, no. 2: 141–151.

Farran, D. C., Silveri, B., and Culp, C. 1991. Public schools and the disadvantaged. *New Directions for Child Development* 53: 65–73.

Farrow, F., and Joe, T. 1992. Financing school-linked, integrated services. *The Future of Children* 2, no. 1: 56–67.

Fight Crime/Invest in Kids. 1997. *After School Crime or After School Programs: Report to the U.S. Attorney General*. Washington, D.C.: Fight Crime/Invest in Kids.

Finn-Stevenson, M. 1992. *Iowa's Innovative Program for At-Risk Elementary School Students: Final Results of the First Phase of the Evaluation*. Des Moines, Iowa: Department of Education.

Finn-Stevenson, M., and Desimone, L. 1998. Linking child care and support services with the school: Pilot evaluation of the School of the 21st Century. Paper presented at the American Sociological Association, San Francisco, Calif., April 17.

Finn-Stevenson, M., Desimone, L., and Chung, A. 1998. Linking child care and support services with the school: Pilot evaluation of the School of the 21st Century. *Children and Youth Services Review* 20, no. 3: 177–205.

Finn-Stevenson, M., Emmel, B., and Barbuto, J. 1988. *Issues of Parental Leave: Its Practice, Availability, and Future Feasibility in the State of Connecticut. Report to the Connecticut Task Force to Study Work and Family Roles*. New Haven, Conn.: The Senate, State of Connecticut.

Finn-Stevenson, M., and Gillette, S. 1996. *The Iowa Innovative Early Elementary Program Serving Students at Risk in Kindergarten Through Third Grade. Evaluation Report. Phase IV: Summary of Findings 1990–1996*. Des Moines: Iowa Department of Education.

Finn-Stevenson, M., Gillette, S., and Brown, M. 1997. *The Iowa Innovative Early Elementary Program Serving Students at Risk in Kindergarten Through Third Grade. Evaluation Report. Phase V: Summary of Findings 1990–1997*. Des Moines: Iowa Department of Education.

Finn-Stevenson, M., and Stern, B. 1996. CoZi: Linking early childhood and family support services. *Principal* 75, no. 5: 6–10.

Finn-Stevenson, M., and Trzcinski, E. 1989. *Parental Leave in Connecticut: A Feasibility Study of 2000 Corporate Policies*. Study conducted for the Connecticut legislature.

Finn-Stevenson, M., Ward, B., Young, A., and Raver, C. 1990. *Process Evaluation on the School of the 21st Century*. New Haven, Conn.: Yale University, The Bush Center in Child Development and Social Policy.

Finn-Stevenson, M., and Ward, P. 1990. Outreach to family day care: A national volunteer initiative. *Zero to Three* 10, no. 3: 18–21.

Fiske, E. 1992. *Smart Schools, Smart Kids*. New York: Simon and Schuster.

Frede, E. 1995. The role of program quality in producing early childhood program benefits. *The Future of Children* 5, no. 3: 115–132.

Friedman, D. 1987. *Family Supportive Policies: The Corporate Decision-Making Process*. New York: Conference Board.

Fromberg, D. 1989. Kindergarten—Current circumstances affecting curriculum. In *Teachers College Record*. New York: Teacher's College of Columbia University.

Fullan, M. G. 1992. *Successful School Improvement: The Implementation Perspective and Beyond*. Philadelphia: Open University.

_____. 1993. *Change Forces: Probing the Depths of Education Reform*. New York: Falmer.

_____. 1994. Coordinated top-down and bottom-up strategies for educational reform. In *The Governance of Curriculum,* edited by S. Fuhrman and R. Elmore, 186–202. Alexandria, Va.: Association for Supervision and Curriculum Development.

_____. 1996. Turning systemic thinking on its head. *Phi Delta Kappan,* February, 420–423.

Furstenberg, F. 1994. History and current status of divorce in the United States. *The Future of Children* 4, no. 1: 29–43.

Furstenberg, F., Hughes, M., and Brooks-Gunn, J. 1992. The next generation: Children of teenage mothers. In *Early Parenthood,* edited by M. Rosensheim and M. Testa, 113–135. New Brunswick, N.J.: Rutgers University Press.

Galambos, N., and Garbarino, J. 1985. Adjustment of unsupervised children in a rural setting. *Journal of Genetic Psychology* 146, no. 2: 227–231.

Galinsky, E., Howes, C., Kontos, S., and Shinn, M. B. 1994. *The Study of Children in Family Child Care and Relative Care*. New York: Families and Work Institute.

Gamble, T. J., and Zigler, E. 1986. Effects of infant day care: Another look at the evidence. *American Journal of Orthopsychiatry* 56: 26–42.

Garbarino, J., and Sherman, D. 1980. High-risk neighborhoods and high-risk families: The human-ecology of child maltreatment. *Child Development* 51, no. 1: 188–198.

Gardner, S. L. 1992. Key issues in developing school-linked, integrated services. *Future of Children* 2: 85–94.

Garmezy, M. 1985. Stress resistant children: The search for protective factors. In *Recent Research in Developmental Psychopathology,* edited by J. E. Stevenson, 14–29. Oxford: Pergamon.

Geiger, K. 1994. Putting learning first. *Education Week,* September 12, 19.

General Accounting Office. 1994. *Elementary School Children: Many Change Schools Frequently, Hurting Their Education*. Washington, D.C.: General Accounting Office.

Gilliam, W., Ripple, C., Zigler, E., and Leiter, V. In press. The comprehensive child development program: What went wrong? *Early Childhood Research Quarterly.*

Ginter, M. A. 1981. *An Exploratory Study of the "Latchkey Child": Children Who Care for Themselves.* New Haven, Conn.: Yale University.

Goffin, S. 1992. Early childhood education in the public schools: The necessity for building relationships. *Early Education and Development* 3, no. 2: 83–85.

Gold, S. D., and Ellwood, D. 1995. *Spending and Revenue for Children's Programs.* Washington, D.C.: The Finance Project.

Goldberg, L. 1996. Commentary on funding child care proposals. *The Future of Children* 2, no. 2: 138–139.

Gomby, D., and Larson, C. 1992. Evaluation of school-linked services. *The Future of Children* 2, no. 1: 68–84.

Goodlad, J. 1990. Studying the education of educators: From conception to findings. *Phi Delta Kappan,* June, 698–701.

Gore, S. 1980. Stress buffering functions of social supports: An appraisal and clarification of research models. In *Stressful Life Events: Their Nature and Effects,* edited by B. S. Dohrenwend and B. P. Dohrenwend, 65–80. New York: John Wiley.

Gormley, W. T. 1995. *Everybody's Children: Child Care As a Public Problem.* Washington, D.C.: Brookings Institute.

Gottfried, A. E., Gottfried, A., and Bathurst, K. 1995. Maternal and dual-earner employment status and parenting. In *Handbook of Parenting.* Vol. 2, *Biology and Ecology of Parenting,* edited by M. Bornstein, 139–160. Mahwah, N.J.: Lawrence Erlbaum.

Goyette-Ewing, M. 1992. Children's after-school arrangements: A study of supervision and development. Ph.D. Diss., Dept. of Psychology, Yale University.

Grady, M. K. 1995. A case for assessing intermediate outcomes. In *School-Community Connections: Exploring Issues for Research and Practice,* edited by L. C. Rigsby, M. Reynolds, and M. Wang, 143–148. San Francisco: Jossey-Bass.

Green, B. L., and MacAllister, C. 1998. Theory-based participatory evaluation: A powerful tool for evaluating family support programs. *Zero to Three* 18, no. 4: 30–36.

Greenberg, M., and Savner, S. 1996. *A Brief Summary of Key Provisions of the Temporary Assistance for Needy Families Block Grant of the Personal Responsibility and Work Opportunity Reconciliation Act of 1996.* Washington, D.C.: Center for Law and Social Policy.

Gullotta, T. P. 1997. Operationalizing Albee's incidence formula. In *Primary Prevention Works,* edited by G. W. Albee and T. P. Gullotta, 3–22. Thousand Oaks, Calif.: Sage.

Gunnar, M. 1996. *Quality Care and the Buffering of Stress Physiology: Its Potential in Protecting the Developing Human Brain.* Minneapolis: University of Minnesota, Institute of Child Development.

Halpern, R. 1995. *Rebuilding the Inner City: A History of Neighborhood Initiatives to Address Poverty in the United States.* New York: Columbia University Press.

Halpern, S. C. 1992. University-community projects: Reflection on lessons learned. In *Universities and Community Schools,* edited by I. Harkavy, 44–48. Philadelphia: Pennsylvania Program for Public Service, University of Pennsylvania.

Hamburg, D. 1994. Foreword to *Starting Points Meeting the Needs of Our Youngest Children.* New York: Carnegie Corporation of New York.

Harkavy, I., ed. 1992. *Universities and Community Schools*. Philadelphia: Pennsylvania Program for Public Service, University of Pennsylvania.

Harms, T., and Clifford, R. M. 1980. *Early Childhood Environment Rating Scale*. New York: Teachers College Press.

Haskins, R. 1989. Beyond metaphor: The efficacy of early childhood education. *American Psychologist* 44, no. 2: 274–282.

Hauser-Cram, P. 1991. *Early Education in the Public Schools: Lessons from a Comprehensive Birth-to-Kindergarten Program*. San Francisco: Jossey-Bass.

Hausman, B. 1990. *Innovative Models to Guide Family Support and Education Policy in the 1990s: Analysis of Four Pioneering States*, edited by H. Weiss, 24–40. Cambridge, Mass.: Harvard Family Research Project.

Hausman, B., and Weiss, H. 1988. *Missouri Case Study Report*. Cambridge, Mass.: Harvard Family Research Project.

Hayes, C. D., Palmer, J. L., and Zaslow, M. J., eds. 1990. *Who Cares for America's Children? Child Care Policy for the 1990s*. Washington, D.C.: National Academy Press.

Helburn, S., ed. 1995. *Cost Quality and Child Outcomes in Child Care Centers: Technical Report*. Denver: Center for Research in Economic and Social Policy, University of Colorado.

Helburn, S., and Howes, C. 1996. Child care cost and quality. *The Future of Children* 6, no. 2: 62–82.

Herman, J., Morris, L., and Fitz-Gibbon, C. 1998. *Evaluators' Handbook*. Thousand Oakes, Calif.: Sage.

Hernandez, D. J. 1993. *American Children: Resources from Family, Government, and the Economy*. New York: Russel Sage Foundation.

_____. 1997. Poverty trends. In *Consequences of Growing Up Poor*, edited by G. Duncan and J. Brooks-Gunn, 18–34. New York: Russell Sage Foundation.

Hetherington, E. 1989. Coping with family transitions: Winners, losers, and survivors. *Child Development* 60: 1–14.

Hetherington, E. M., and Stanley-Hagan, M. 1995. Parenting in divorced and remarried families. In *Handbook of Parenting*. Vol. 3, *Status and Social Conditions of Parenting*, edited by M. Bornstein, 233–254. Mahwah, N.J.: Lawrence Erlbaum.

Hewlett, S. A. 1986. *A Lesser Life*. New York: Warner Books.

_____. 1992. *When the Bough Breaks: The Cost of Neglecting Our Children*. New York: Aldyne DeGrueter.

Hewlett, S. A., and West, C. 1998. The war against parents: What we can do for American beleaguered moms and dads. In *Family and Work: Bridging the Gap*, edited by S. Coontz, 79–91. Cambridge, Mass.: Ballinger Publishing Co.

Hickey, N. W. 1990. County shares youth problems but not solutions: Pilot program seeks to clear way for children to receive health, educational, and social services. *Los Angeles Times,* January 15, 7.

Hickey, N. W., Lockwood, J., Payzant, T. W., Wenrich, J. W. 1990. *New Beginnings: A Feasibility Study of Integrated Services for Children and Families—Final Report*. San Diego, Calif.: County of San Diego, Office of Chief Administrative Officer.

Hirsch, E. D. 1996. *The Schools We Need and Why We Don't Have Them*. New York: Doubleday.

Hirsh-Pasek, K. 1991. Pressure or challenge in preschool? In *Academic Instruction in Early Childhood*, edited by L. Rescola, 1–13. New York: Basic Books.

Hofferth, S. 1991. *National Child Care Survey*. Washington, D.C.: Urban Institute.

_____. 1996. Child care in the United States today. *The Future of Children* 6, no. 2: 41–61.

Hofferth, S., and Chaplin, D. 1994. *Caring for Young Children While Their Parents Work: Public Policies and Private Strategies.* Washington, D.C.: Urban Institute.

Hofferth, S., and Wissoker, D. 1992. Price, quality, and income in child care choices. *Journal of Human Resources* 27, no. 1: 70–111.

Hoffman, L. W. 1986. Work, family, and the child. In *Psychology and Work: Productivity, Change, and Employment,* edited by M. S. Pallak and R. O. Perloff, 33–47. Washington, D.C.: American Psychological Association Press.

_____. 1989. Effects of maternal employment on the two-parent families. *American Psychologist* 44, no. 2: 283–292.

Hollister, R. B., and Hill, J. 1995. Problems in the evaluation of community-wide initiatives. In *New Approaches to Evaluating Community Initiatives: Concepts, Methods, and Contexts,* edited by J. P. Connell, A. C. Kubisch, L. B. Schorr, and C. H. Weiss, 127–172. Washington, D.C.: Aspen Institute.

Holloway, S. D., Reichhart-Erickson, M. 1988. The relationship of day care quality to children's free-play behavior and social problem-solving skills. *Early Childhood Research Quarterly* 3: 39–53.

Holtzman, W., ed. 1992. *School of the Future.* Austin, Tex.: American Psychological Association and Hogg Foundation for Mental Health.

Honing, B. 1994. How can Horace best be helped? *Phi Delta Kappan,* June, 794–799.

Howes, C. 1987. Quality indicator in infant and toddler child care: The Los Angeles study. In *Quality in Child Care: What Does the Research Tell Us?* edited by D. Phillips, 81–88. Washington, D.C.: National Association for the Education of Young Children.

_____. 1988. Peer interaction of young children. Monographs of the *Society for Research in Child Development* 53: 217–247.

_____. 1989. Infant child care. *Young Children* 44, no. 6: 24–28.

_____. 1990. Can the age of entry into child care and the quality of child care predict adjustment in kindergarten? *Developmental Psychology* 26, no. 2: 292–303.

Howes, C., and Hamilton, C. 1993. The changing experience of child care. *Early Childhood Research Quarterly* 8: 15–32.

Howes, C., and Olenick, M. 1986. Family and child care influences on toddler compliance. *Child Development* 57: 202–216.

Howes, C., Olenick, M., and Der-Kiureghian, T. 1987. After school child care in an elementary school: Social development and continuity and complementarity of programs. *Elementary School Journal* 88, no. 2: 93–103.

Howes, C., Phillips, D., and Whitebook, M. 1992. Thresholds of quality: Implications for social development of children in center-based care. *Child Development* 63: 449–460.

Howes, C., Rodning, C., Galluzzo, D., and Myers, L. 1988. Attachment and child care: Relations with mother and caregiver. *Early Childhood Research Quarterly* 3: 403–416.

Howes, C., and Smith, E. 1995. Relations among child care quality, teacher behavior, children play, emotional security, and cognitive activity in children. *Early Childhood Research Quarterly* 10, no. 4: 381–404.

Huberman, M. 1992. Critical introduction to *Successful School Improvement,* edited by M. Fullan, 1–20. Philadelphia, Pa.: Open University Press.

Hughes, F. P. 1991. *Children, Play, and Development.* Boston, Mass.: Allyn and Bacon.

Huston, S. C., Garcia-Coll, C., and McLoyd, V. C., eds. 1994. *Child Development* 65, no. 2: Special issue on children in poverty.

Institute of Medicine. 1989. *Research on Children and Adolescents with Mental, Behavioral, and Developmental Disorders.* Washington, D.C.: National Academy Press.

Iscoe, L. 1995. *The Project Coordinators: A Key to the School of the Future.* Austin, Tex.: Hogg Foundation.

Jehl, J., and Kirst, M. 1992. Getting ready to provide school-liked services: What schools must do. *The Future of Children* 2, no. 1: 95–106.

Johnson, L., LaMontagne, M., Elgas, P., and Bauer, A. 1998. *Early Childhood Education: Blending Theory, Blending Practice.* Baltimore, Md.: Brooks.

Johnston, R. C. 1998. Administrators joining preservationists to save schools. *Education Week* 18, no. 6: 6, 19.

Joyner, E. 1995. Personal communication with M. Finn-Stevenson regarding School Development Program (SDP).

Kagan, L., Goffin, S., Golub, S., and Pritchard, E. 1995. *Toward Systemic Reform and Service Integration for Young Children and Their Families.* Falls Church, Va.: National Center for Service Integration.

Kagan, S. L., and Cohen, N., eds. 1997. *Funding and Financing Early Care and Education.* New Haven, Conn.: The Bush Center in Child Development and Social Policy.

Kahn, A., and Kamerman, S. 1992. *Integrating Services Integration: An Overview of Initiatives, Issues, and Possibilities.* New York: National Center for Children in Poverty.

Kamerman, S. B. 1998. Does global retrenchment and restructuring doom the children's cause? Paper presented at the University Lecture, Columbia University, November 30.

Kamerman, S. B., and Kahn, A. J. 1995. *Starting Right: How America Neglects Its Youngest Children and What We Can Do About It.* New York: Oxford University Press.

Karweit, N. L. 1989. Effective preschool programs for students at risk. In *Effective Programs for Students at Risk,* edited by R. E. Slavin, L. Karweit, and N. A. Madden, 75–102. Boston, Mass.: Allyn and Bacon.

Kirst, M. 1991. Improving children's services. *Phi Delta Kappan,* August, 615–618.

_____. 1992. Supporting school-linked children's services. In *Rethinking School Finance.* Vol. 17, edited by A. R. Odden, 298–321. San Francisco: Jossey-Bass.

_____. 1994. Equity for children: Linking education and children's services. *Educational Policy* 8, no. 4: 583–590.

Kirst, M., and Kelly, C. 1995. Collaboration to improve education and children. In *School-Community Connections: Exploring Issues for Research and Practice,* edited by L. C. Rigsby, M. Reynolds, and M. Wang, 21–44. San Francisco: Jossey-Bass.

Kisker, E., Hofferth, S., Phillips, D., and Farquar, E. 1990. *A Profile of Child Care Settings.* Washington, D.C.: Urban Institute.

Kisker, E., and Ross, C. 1997. Arranging child care. *The Future of Children* 7, no. 1: 99–109.

Klass, C. S. 1996. *Home Visiting: Promoting Healthy Parent and Child Development*. Baltimore, Md.: Brooks.

Klerman, L. 1991. *Alive and Well? Health Care for Children in America*. New York: National Center for Children in Poverty.

Knitzer, J. 1993. Children's mental health policy: Challenging the future. *Journal of Emotional and Behavioral Disorders* 1, no. 1: 8–16.

Kontos, S., and Fein, R. 1987. Child care quality, compliance with regulations, and children's development. In *Quality in Child Care: What Does the Research Tell Us?* edited by D. A. Phillips, 57–80. Washington, D.C.: National Association for the Education of Young Children.

Kurdek, L., and Blisk, D. 1983. Dimensions and correlates of mothers' divorce experiences. *Journal of Divorce* 6, no. 40: 1–24.

Ladd, G. W., and Price, J. M. 1987. Predicting children's social and school adjustment following the transition from preschool to kindergarten. *Child Development* 58(October): 1168–1189.

Lally, J., Torres, Y., and Phelps, P. 1994. Caring for infants and toddlers in groups. *Zero to Three* 14, no. 5: 1–8.

Lamb, M. 1998. Nonparental caregiving. In *Child Psychology*. Vol. 1, *Child Psychology in Practice*, edited by I. Sigel and K. A. Renninger, 73–134. New York: John Wiley.

Lande, J. S., Scarr, S., and Gunzenhauser, N. 1989. *Caring for Children: Challenge to America*. Hillsdale, N.J.: Lawrence Erlbaum.

Larner, M., Terman, D., and Behrman, R. 1997. Welfare to work: Analysis and recommendations. *The Future of Children* 7, no. 1: 4–19.

Larson, C., Gomby, D., and Behrman, R. 1992. School linked services: Analysis. *The Future of Children* 2, no. 1: 6–18.

Larson, J. 1992. The evaluation of Family Resource Centers. *The Future of Children* 2, no. 1: appendix.

Layzer, J., and St. Pierre, R. 1996. *Early Childhood Programs: Adding a Two-Generation Perspective*. Cambridge, Mass.: Abt Associates.

Levy, J., and Shepardson, W. 1992. Look at current school-linked service. *The Future of Children* 2, no. 1: 44–55.

Lewit, E. 1992. Child indicators. *The Future of Children* 2, no. 1: 127–130.

Lewit, E., Terman, L., and Berman, R. 1997. Children and poverty: Analysis and recommendation. *The Future of Children* 7, no. 2: 4–24.

Long, L., and Long, T. 1984. *The Handbook for Latchkey Children and Their Parents*. New York: Arbor House.

Lopez, M., and Hochberg, M. 1993. *Paths to Readiness*. Philadelphia, Pa.: Pew Charitable Trusts.

Lubker, M. 1995. Schools' involvement in Medicaid. *Newsletter of the School of the 21st Century and Family Resource Centers* 2: 5. New Haven, Conn.: Yale University, The Bush Center in Child Development and Social Policy.

Luthar, S., Doernberger, C., and Zigler, E. 1993. Resilience is not a unidimensional construct: Insights from a prospective study of inner-city adolescents. *Development and Psychopathology* 5: 703–717.

Maccoby, E. E., and Mnookin, R. H., eds. 1992. *Dividing the Child: Social and Legal Dilemmas of Custody*. Cambridge, Mass.: Harvard University Press.

Maeroff, G. 1998. *Altered Destinies*. New York: St. Martin's.

Mason, M. A., Skolnick, A., and Skolnick, S. 1998. *All Our Families: New Policies for a New Century*. New York: Oxford University Press.

Massey, C., Evans, V., and Harriman, G. 1992. Together for the children. In *Universities and Community Schools*, edited by I. Harkavy, 29–33. Philadelphia: Pennsylvania Program for Public Service, University of Pennsylvania.

McCabe, J. 1995. A program evaluation: Does the Center Project effectively reduce parental stress? Ph.D. Diss., University of Colorado at Denver.

McCall, R., Green, B., Strauss, M., and Groark, C. 1997. Issues in community-based research and program evaluation. In *Handbook of Child Psychology*, edited by P. H. Mussen, 955–997. New York: Wiley.

McCartney, K. 1984. The effects of a quality day care environment upon children's language development. *Developmental Psychology* 20, no. 2: 244–260.

McCartney, K., Scarr, S., Phillips, D., Grajek, S., and Schwarz, J. 1982. Environmental differences among day care centers and their effects on children. In *Day Care: Scientific and Social Policy Issues*, edited by E. Zigler and E. Gordon, 59–71. Boston, Mass.: Auburn House.

Mccoby, E. E., Kahn, A. J., and Everett, B. A. 1992. *Dividing the Child: Social and Legal Dilemmas of Custody*. Cambridge, Mass.: Harvard University Press.

McDonald, J. P. 1996. *Redesigning Schools: Lessons for the 21st Century*. San Francisco: Jossey-Bass.

McLeod, J., and Shanahan, M. 1993. Poverty, parenting, and children's mental health. *Sociological Review* 58, no. 3: 351–366.

McLoyd, V. 1990. The impact of economic hardship on black families and children: Psychological distress, parenting, and socioemotional development. *Child Development* 61, no. 2: 311–346.

———. 1998. Children in poverty: Development, public policy, and practice. In *Handbook of Child Psychology*, edited by I. E. Sigel and K. A. Renninger, 135–210. New York: Wiley.

McLoyd, V., Jayarantne, T., Ceballo, R., and Borquez, J. 1994. Unemployment and work interruptions: Effects on parenting. *Child Development* 65, no. 2: 562–589.

Meyers, A., Sampson, A., Weitzman, M., Rogers, B., and Kayne, H. 1989. School breakfast and school performance. *American Journal of Diseases in Children* 143: 1234–1239.

Milbank, D. 1995. Laws help Mom but hurt her career. *Wall Street Journal*, August 25, B1–B6.

Miller, B. M. 1994. Out of school time: Effects on learning in the primary grades. Paper prepared for the Carnegie Task Force on Learning in the Primary Grades, New York.

Miller, S. H. 1994. *Planning for Growth: Strategic Options*. New Haven, Conn.: Yale University, The Bush Center in Child Development and Social Policy.

Miringoff, M. 1993. *The Index of Social Health*. New York: United Nations Children's Fund.

Mitchell, A. 1988. *The Public Schools' Early Childhood Studies: The District Survey*. New York: Bank Street College of Education.

Mitchell, A., and Dichter, H. 1993. *Financing Child Care in the United States.* Cambridge, Mass.: Harvard Family Research Project.

Mitchell, B. 1990. Children, youth, and restructured schools. In *Educational Leadership and Changing Contexts in Families, Communities, and Schools,* edited by L. Cunningham and B. Mitchell, 19–51. Chicago: National Association for the Study of Education.

Moen, P., and Dempster, M. C. 1987. Employed parent: Roles strain, work time, and preferences for working less. *Journal of Marriage and Family* 49: 579.

Moore, E., and Phillips, C. 1989. Early schooling: Is one solution right for all children? *Theory into Practice* 28, no. 1: 58–63.

Morrill, W. 1992. Overview of service delivery to children. *The Future of Children* 2, no. 1: 32–43.

National Association of Elementary School Principals. 1986. One parent families and their children: The school's most significant minority. *Principal* 60: 31–37.

_____. 1993. *Standards for Quality School Age Child Care.* Alexandria, Va.: National Association of Elementary School Principals.

National Association of State Boards of Education. 1988. *Right from the Start.* Alexandria, Va.: National Association of School Boards of Education.

National Black Child Development Institute (NBCDI). 1988. *Safeguards: Guidelines for Establishing Child Development Programs for 4-Year-Olds in Public Schools.* Washington, D.C.: National Black Child Development Institute.

National Center for Children in Poverty. 1996. *One in Four: America's Youngest Poor.* New York: National Center for Children in Poverty.

National Center for Clinical Infant Programs (NCCIP). 1987. *Charting Changes in Infants, Families, and Services.* Washington, D.C.: National Center for Clinical Infant Programs.

National Commission on Excellence in Education. 1983. *A Nation at Risk: The Imperative for Educational Reform.* Washington, D.C.: U.S. Department of Education.

National Educational Goals Panel. 1995. *Building a Nation of Learners.* Washington, D.C.: National Education Goals Panel.

National Education Association (NEA). 1990. *Early Childhood Education in the Public School.* Washington, D.C.: National Education Association.

National Education Summit. 1996. Policy statement, March. URL: www.summit96.ibm.com.

National Institute of Child Health and Human Development (NICHD). 1997. Mother-child interaction and cognitive outcomes associated with early child care. Paper presented at the Poster Symposium, biennial meeting of the Society for Research in Child Development, Montreal, April 17.

Nelson, R. 1982. The politics of federal day care regulation. In *Day Care: Scientific and Social Policy Issues,* edited by E. Zigler and E. Gordon, 276–306. Boston, Mass.: Auburn House.

Neugebauer, R. 1991. Pre-kindergarten in the public schools: Status report 1. *Child Care and Information Exchange* 82: 5–13.

_____. 1996. How's business? Status report 9 on non-profit child care. *Child Care and Information Exchange* 87: 60–66.

Olds, D., Henderson, C. R., Cole, R., Eckenrode, J., Kitzman, H., Luckey, D., Pettit, L., Sidora, K., Morris, P., and Powers, J. 1998. Long-term effects of nurse home visitation on children's criminal and antisocial behavior—15 year follow-up of a randomized controlled trial. *Journal of the American Medical Association* 280, no. 14: 1238–1244.

Olson, L. 1997. Annenberg challenge proves to be just that. *Education Week,* July 25, 1, 30–32.

Orenstein, P. 1994. Children are alone. *New York Times,* sec. 6, 18.

Owen, M. T., and Mulvihill, B. A. 1994. Benefits of parent education and support program in the first three years. *Family Relations,* April, 206–212.

Packard, V. 1983. *Our Endangered Children: Growing Up in a Changing World.* Boston: Little Brown.

Parents As Teachers. 1995. *A Select Review of Past and Current Evaluations of the Parents As Teachers Program.* St. Louis, Mo.: Parents As Teachers.

Payzant, T. W. 1992. New beginnings in San Diego: Developing a strategy for inter-agency collaboration. *Phi Delta Kappan,* February, 139–146.

Peshkin, A. 1995. The complex world of an embedded institution: Schools and their constituent publics. In *School-Community Connections: Exploring Issues for Research and Practice,* edited by L. C. Rigsby, M. Reynolds, and M. Wang, 229–258. San Francisco: Jossey-Bass.

Peterson, P. L., McCarthey, S. J., and Elmore, R. 1996. Learning from school re-structuring. *American Educational Research Journal* 33, no. 1: 119–154.

Pfannenstiel, J. C. 1989. *New Parents As Teachers Project: A Follow-Up Investigation.* Jefferson City: Missouri Department of Elementary and Secondary Education.

Pfannenstiel, J., Lambson, T., and Yarnell, Y. 1991. *Second Wave Study of the Parents As Teachers Program.* Overland Park, Kans.: Research and Training Associates.

Pfannenstiel, J., and Seltzer, D. 1985. *Evaluation Report: New Parents As Teachers Project.* Overland, Kans.: Research and Training Associates.

Phillips, A., ed. 1996. *Playing for Keeps.* Washington, D.C.: National Association for the Education of Young Children.

Phillips, D. 1987. *Predictors of Quality Child Care.* Washington, D.C.: National Association for the Education of Young Children.

———. 1988. Quality in child care: Definitions. Paper presented at the Symposium on Dimensions of Quality in Programs for Children, A. L. Mailman Family Foundation, White Plains, N.Y., June 6.

Phillips, D., Howes, C., Whitebook, M. 1992. Teacher characteristics and effective teaching in child care: Findings from the national child care staffing study. *Child Youth Care Forum* 21, no. 6: 399–414.

Phillips, D., McCartney, K., Scarr, S., and Howes, C. 1987. Selective review of infant day care research: A cause for concern. *Zero to Three* 1, no. 3: 18–21.

Phillips, D., Mekar, D., Scarr, S., McCartney, K., and Abbott-Shinn, M. 1998. *Paths to Quality Child Care: Structural and Contextual Influences.* Charlottesville, Va.: University of Virginia Press.

Plomin, R., and Daniels, D. 1987. Why are children in the same family different from one another? *Behavioral and Brain Sciences* 10: 1–16.

Plomin, R., DeFries, J., and Fulker, D. W. 1988. *Nature and Nurture During Infancy and Early Childhood.* New York: Cambridge University Press.

Posner, J., and Vandell, D. 1991. *An Ecological Analysis of the Effects of After School Care.* Madison: University of Wisconsin.

Posner, J. K., and Vandell, D. L. 1994. Low-income children in after-school care: Are there beneficial effects of after-school programs? *Child Development* 65, no. 2: 440–456.

Powell, D. 1991. Parents and programs: Early childhood as a pioneer in parent involvement and support. In *The Care and Education of America's Young Children: Yearbook of the National Society for the Study of Education,* edited by S. Kagan. Chicago: National Society for the Study of Education.

Powell, D. R. 1989. *Families and Early Childhood Programs.* Washington, D.C.: National Association for the Education of Young Children.

_____. 1991. How schools support families: Critical policy tensions. *Elementary School Journal* 91, no. 3: 307–319.

Regenstein, M., Silow-Carroll, S., and Meyer, J. 1995. *Early Childhood Education: Models for Expanding Access.* Washington, D.C.: The Economic and Social Research Institute.

Reischauer, R. 1987. *An Analysis of the U.S. Job Market.* Washington, D.C.: Congressional Budget Office.

Reissman, F. 1986. Support groups as preventive intervention. In *A Decade of Press in Primary Prevention,* edited by M. Kessler and S. E. Golston, 14–21. Hanover, N.H.: University Press of New England.

Rich, D. 1985. *The Forgotten Factor in School Success: The Family.* Washington, D.C.: Home-School Institute.

Richardson, G., and Marx, E. 1989. *A Welcome for Every Child: How France Achieves Quality in Child Care—Practical Ideas for the United States.* New York: The French-American Foundation.

Richardson, J. L., Dwyer, K., McGuigan, K., Hansen, W. B., Dent, C., Johnson, C. A., Sussman, S. Y., Brannon, B., and Flay, B. 1989. Substance use among eighth-grade students who take care of themselves after school. *Pediatrics* 84, no. 3: 556–560.

Rigsby, L. C., Reynolds, M., and Wang, M., eds. 1995. *School-Community Connections: Exploring Issues for Research and Practice.* San Francisco: Jossey-Bass.

Riley, D., Steinberg, J., Todd, C., Junge, S., and McClain, I. 1994. *Preventing Problem Behavior and Raising Academic Performance in the Nation's Youth: The Impacts of 64 School Age Child Care Programs in 15 States.* Madison: University of Wisconsin.

Ripple, C., Gilliam, W., Chanana, N., and Zigler, E. In review. Should Head Start be devolved to the states? Evidence from state-funded preschool initiatives. *American Psychologist.*

Robison, E. 1993. *An Interim Evaluative Report Concerning a Collaboration Between the Children's Aid Society, New York Board of Education, Community School District 6, and the I.S. 218 Salome Urea De, Henriguez School.* New York: Children's Aid Society.

Rodman, H., Pratto, D. J., and Nelson, R. S. 1985. Child care arrangements and children's functioning: A comparison of self-care and adult-care children. *Developmental Psychology* 21: 413–418.

Rossi, P. H. 1998. Evaluating community development programs: Prospects and problems. In *Community Development Programs,* edited by R. Ferguson and W. Dickens, 69–75. Washington, D.C.: Brookings Institute.

Rubenstein, J., and Howes, C. 1979. Caregiving stability and day care. *Developmental Psychology* 16: 31–37.

———. 1983. Social-emotional development of toddlers in day care: The role of individual differences. *Developmental Psychology* 16: 31–37.

Rubenstein, J., Howes, C., and Boyle, M. 1981. A two year follow-up of infants in community-based day care. *Journal of Child Psychology and Psychiatry* 8: 1–11.

Ruopp, R., Travers, J., Galantz, F., and Coelen, C. 1979. *Children at the Center: Final Report of the National Day Care Study.* Vol. 1. Cambridge, Mass.: Abt Books.

Rust, O. F. 1989. Early childhood in public education: Managing change in a changing field. *Teachers College Record* 90, no. 3: 452.

Rutter, M. 1979. Protective factors in children's responses to stress. In *Primary Prevention of Psychopathology,* edited by W. Kent and J. Rolf, 130–139. Hanover, N.H.: University Press of New England.

———. 1980. *Changing Youth in a Changing Society.* Cambridge, Mass.: Harvard University Press.

———. 1996. Psychopathology of research: Prospects and priorities. *Journal of Autism and Developmental Disorders* 26, no. 2: 257–275.

Sameroff, A. J., and Chandler, M. J. 1975. Reproductive risk and the continuum of caretaking casualty. In *Review of Child Development Research,* edited by F. D. Horwitz, 399–420. Chicago: University of Chicago Press.

Sameroff, A. et al. 1987. Intelligence quotient scores of 4-year-old children: Social-environmental risk factors. *Pediatrics* 79, no. 3: 343–350.

Sarason, S. 1971. *The Culture of the School and the Problem of Change.* Boston: Allyn Bacon.

———. 1995. *Parental Involvement and the Political Principal.* San Francisco: Jossey-Bass.

Sarason, S., Davidson, K., and Blatt, B. 1986. *The Preparation of Teachers: An Unstudied Problem in Education.* Cambridge, Mass.: Brookline Books.

Scarr, S., and McCartney, K. 1983. How people make their own environments: A theory of genotype-environment effects. *Child Development* 54: 424–535.

Scarr-Salapatek, S. 1975. Genetics and the development of intelligence. In *Review of Child Development Research,* edited by F. Horowitz, 311–341. Chicago: University of Chicago Press.

School-Age Child Care Project. 1996. *Fact Sheet on School Age Children.* Wellesley, Mass.: Center for Research on Women, Wellesley College.

Schorr, L. 1997. *Common Purpose: Strengthening Families and Neighborhoods to Rebuild America.* New York: Anchor Books.

Schorr, L., and Schorr, D. 1988. *Within Our Reach: Breaking the Cycle of Disadvantage.* New York: Doubleday.

Schorr, L., and Weiss, C. 1995. *New Approaches to Evaluation Community Initiatives: Concepts, Methods, and Contexts.* Washington, D.C.: Aspen.

Schultz, T. 1996. Commentary on funding child care proposals. *The Future of Children* 2, no. 2: 139–141.

Schweinhart, L. J., Barne, H. V., and Weikart, D. P. 1993. *Significant Benefits: The High/Scope Perry Preschool Study Through Age 27.* Ypsilanti, Minn.: High/Scope Press.

Scott-Jones, D. 1995. Parent-child interactions and school achievement. In *The Family School Connection,* edited by B. Ryan, G. Adams, T. Gullotta, and R. Weissberg, 75–107. Thousand Oaks, Calif.: Sage.

Seitz, V., and Apfel, N. H. 1999. Effective interventions for adolescent mothers. *Clinical Psychology: Science and Practice* 6: 50–66.

Seligson, M., and Fink, D. 1989. *No Time to Waste: An Action Agenda for School Age Child Care.* Wellesley, Mass.: School Age Child Care Project.

Seligson, M., and Marx, F. 1988. *The Public School Early Childhood Study: The State Survey.* New York: Bank Street College of Education.

Shartrand, A., Weiss, A., Kreider, H., and Lopez, M. 1997. *New Skills for New Schools: Preparing Teachers in Family Involvement.* Cambridge, Mass.: Harvard Family Research Project.

Shellenbarger, S., Moffett, M., and Chen, K. 1995. Around the world, women are united by child care woes. *Wall Street Journal,* August 25, 1:5.

Shore, R. 1997. *Rethinking the Brain: New Insights into Early Development.* New York: Families and Work Institute.

Shuster, S., Finn-Stevenson, M., and Ward, P. 1990. *The Hard Questions in Family Day Care: National Issues and Exemplary Programs.* New York: National Council of Jewish Women.

Sigel, I. 1991. Preschool education: For whom and why? *New Directions for Early Childhood* 53: 83–91.

Singer, J., and Singer, D. 1979. The value of imagination. In *Play and Learning,* edited by B. Sutton-Smith, 195–218. New York: Gardner.

Skolnick, A. 1998. Families in transition. In *All Our Families: New Policies for a Changing World,* edited by M. A. Mason, A. Skolnik, and S. Skolnick, 1–19. New York: Oxford.

Slavin, R., Dolan, L., and Madden, N. 1994. *Scaling-Up: Lessons Learned in the Dissemination of Success for All.* Baltimore, Md.: Johns Hopkins University, Center for Research on the Education of Students Placed at Risk.

Small, J. 1996. *Collaborative, Community-Based Research on Adolescents: Using Research for Community Change.* New York: Cambridge University Press.

Smith, S. 1991. Two-generation program model: A new intervention strategy. *Social Policy Report* 5, no. 1: 190–199.

Steinberg, L. 1986. Latchkey children and susceptibility to peer preschool. *Developmental Psychology* 22: 433–439.

Stern, B. M., and Finn-Stevenson, M. 1997. The Comer/Zigler Initiative: Combining the School of the 21st Century with the School Development Program. In *Child by Child, School by School: Strengthening Our Communities Through Educational Change,* edited by School Development Program National Staff and J. Comer, 39–45. New York: Teachers College Press.

Stern, D. 1988. *The Interpersonal World of the Infant.* 2d ed. New York: Basic Books.

Stevenson, H. 1983. *Making the Grade: School Achievement in Japan, Taiwan, and the United States.* Stanford, Calif.: Center for Advanced Study in Behavioral Sciences, Stanford University.

Stevenson, H., Stigler, J., Lee, S., Lucker, G., Kitamura, S., and Itsu, C. 1985. Cognitive performance and academic achievement of Japanese, Chinese, and American children. *Child Development* 56: 718–734.

Stipek, D. J. 1992. *Self-Evaluation in Young Children.* Chicago: University of Chicago Press.

Stipek, D., Feiler, R., Daniels, D., and Milburn, S. 1995. Effects of different instructional approaches on young children's achievement and motivation. *Child Development* 66: 209–223.

Stipek, D., Rosenblatt, L., and DiRocco, L. 1994. Making parents your allies. *Young Children,* March: 4–9.

Stoney, L., and Greenberg, M. 1996. The financing of child care: Current and emerging trends. *The Future of Children* 6, no. 2: 83–102.

Szanton, E. 1992. *Head Start: The Emotional Foundations of School Readiness.* Washington, D.C.: National Center for Clinical Infant Programs.

Thatcher, R., Lyons, G., Rumsey, J., and Krasnegor, N., eds. 1997. *Developmental Neuroimaging: Mapping the Development of Brain and Behavior.* San Diego, Calif.: Academic Press.

Tirozzi, G. 1996. Early childhood education and school-linked services: Fundamental components of school reform. *Commentaries* 2: 1. Washington, D.C.: National Association of State Board of Education.

Todd, C., Albrecht, K., and Coleman, M. 1990. School age child care: A continuum of options. *Journal of Home Economics* 10: 46–52.

Tuma, J. M. 1989. Mental health services for children. *American Psychologist* 44: 188–199.

Uchitelle, L. 1994. Moonlighting plus: Three-job families on the rise. *New York Times,* August 16, 1, 3A.

University of California Cooperative Extension. 1993. *Preventing Problem Behaviors and Raising Academic Performance in California Children: The Impact of School-Age Child Care Programs.* University of California Cooperative Extension.

U.S. Department of Education. 1990. *National Assessment of Educational Progress.* Washington, D.C.: Government Printing Office.

U.S. Department of Labor. 1997. *Laborforce Participation of Women with Children Under Age 6.* Washington, D.C.: Bureau of Labor Statistics.

U.S. Department of Labor-Women's Bureau. 1993. *Handbook on Women Workers: Trends and Issues.* Washington, D.C.: U.S. Department of Labor.

U.S. General Accounting Office. 1995. *Early Childhood Centers: Services to Prepare Children for Schools Often Limited.* Washington, D.C.: U.S. General Accounting Office.

U.S. House Committee on Ways and Means. 1996. *Overview of Entitlement Programs: 1996 Green Book.* Washington, D.C.: U.S. Government Printing Office.

Valente, E., and Dodge, K. 1997. Evaluation of prevention programs. In *Establishing Preventive Services,* edited by R. Weissberg, T. Gullotta, R. Hampton, B. Ryan, and G. Adams, 183–218. Thousand Oaks, Calif.: Sage.

Valentine, J., and Stark, N. 1979. Parent involvement. In *Head Start: The Legacy of the War on Poverty,* edited by E. Zigler and J. Valentine, 133–141. New York: Free Press.

Vandell, D., and Corsaniti, M. 1990. Variation in early child care: Do they predict subsequent emotional and cognitive differences? *Early Childhood Research Quarterly* 5: 555–572.

Vandell, D., Hendersen, K., and Wilson, K. 1988. A longitudinal study of children with varying day care experiences. *Child Development* 59: 1286–1292.

Vandell, D., and Powers, C. 1983. Day care quality and children's free play activities. *American Journal of Orthopsychiatry* 53: 493–500.

Venner, S. 1997. *Realities and Choices: Helping States Enhance Family Economic Security*. Medford, Mass.: Center on Hunger, Poverty, and Nutrition Policy.

Wagstaff, L., and Gallagher, K. 1990. Schools, families, and communities. In *Educational Leadership and Changing Contexts in Families, Communities, and Schools*, edited by L. Cunningham and B. Mitchell, 91–117. Chicago: National Society for the Study of Education.

Walberg, H. J. 1984. Families as partners in educational productivity. *Kappan* 65: 397–400.

Walberg, H. J., and Greenberg, R. C. 1998. The Diogenes factor: Why it is hard to get an unbiased view of programs like Success for All. *Education Week*, April 8, 36.

Wallerstein, J., and Corbin, S. 1996. The child and the vicissitudes of divorce. In *Child and Adolescent Psychiatry: A Comprehensive Textbook*. 2d ed., edited by M. Lewis, 1118–1126. Baltimore, Md.: Williams and Witkins.

Ward, P., Shuster, C., and Finn-Stevenson, M. 1992. *Family Day Care: Issues and Concerns. Proceedings of a National Roundtable Discussion*. New Haven, Conn.: The Bush Center in Child Development and Social Policy.

Weikart, D., and Schweinhart, L. J. 1997. High/Scope Perry Preschool Program. In *Primary Prevention Works*, edited by G. Albee and T. Gullotta, 146–166. Thousand Oaks, Calif.: Sage.

Weiss, C. H. 1995. Nothing as practical as good theory: Exploring theory-based evaluation for comprehensive community initiatives for children and families. In *New Approaches to Evaluating Community Initiatives: Concepts, Methods, and Contexts*, edited by J. P. Connell, A. C. Kubisch, L. B. Schorr, and C. H. Weiss, 33–50. Washington, D.C.: Aspen Institute.

Weiss, H. 1989. State family support and education programs: Lessons from sixteen pioneers. *American Journal of Orthopsychiatry* 59: 32–48.

Weissberg, R., Kuster, C. B., and Gullotta, T. 1997. Prevention services from optimistic promise to widespread, effective practice. In *Establishing Preventive Services*, edited by R. Weissberg, T. Gullotta, R. Hampton, B. Ryan, and G. Adams, 1–26. Thousand Oaks, Calif.: Sage.

Werner, E., and Smith, R. 1992. *Overcoming the Odds: High Risk Children from Birth to Adulthood*. Ithaca: Cornell University Press.

Whitebook, M. D., Phillips, D., and Howes, C. 1990. *Who Cares? Child Care Teachers and the Quality of Care in America. Executive Summary, National Child Care Staffing Study*. Oakland, Calif.: Child Care Employee Project.

Whittaker, J., and Garbarino, J. 1983. *Social Support Networks: Informal Helping in the Human Services*. New York: Aldine.

William T. Grant Foundation. 1988. *The Forgotten Half: Non-College Youth in America*. New York: Commission on Work, Family, and Citizenship.

Winter, M., and McDonald, D. 1997. Parents as teachers: Investing in good beginnings for children. In *Primary Prevention Works*, edited by G. Albee and T. Gullotta, 119–126. Thousand Oaks, Calif.: Sage.

Yale Bush Center in Child Development and Social Policy. 1992. *The School of the 21st Century: Guidelines for Implementation*. New Haven, Conn.: Yale University, The Bush Center in Child Development and Social Policy.

Yoshikawa, H. 1995. Long-term effects of early childhood programs on social outcomes and delinquency. *The Future of Children* 5, no. 3: 51–75.

Young, K. T., Marsland, K. W., and Zigler, E. 1997. The regulatory status of center-based infant and toddler child care. *American Journal of Orthopsychiatry* 67, no. 4: 535–544.

Zigler, E. 1987. A solution to the nation's child care problem: The School of the 21st Century. Paper presented at the Bush Center Policy Luncheon, Yale University, September 23.

Zigler, E., and Finn, M. 1981. From problem to solution: Changing policy as it affects children and families. *Young Children* 36: 31–59.

Zigler, E., and Finn-Stevenson, M. 1994. Schools' role in the provision of support services for children and families: A critical aspect of program equity. *Educational Policy* 8: 591–606.

Zigler, E., and Finn-Stevenson, M. 1995. The child care crisis: Implications for the growth and development of the nation's children. *Journal of Social Issues* 51, no. 3: 215–232.

Zigler, E., and Finn-Stevenson, M. 1996. Funding child care and public education. *The Future of Children* 6, no. 2: 104–121.

Zigler, E., Finn-Stevenson, M., and Stern, B. 1997. Supporting children and families in the schools: The School of the 21st Century. *American Journal of Orthopsychiatry* 67: 396–407.

Zigler, E., and Frank, M., eds. 1988. *The Parental Leave Crisis: Toward a National Policy.* New Haven, Conn.: Yale University Press.

Zigler, E., and Gordon, E. 1982. *Day Care: Scientific and Social Policy Issues.* Boston, Mass.: Auburn House.

Zigler, E., Hopper, P., and Hall, N. 1993. Infant mental health and social policy. In *Handbook of Infant Mental Health,* edited by C. H. Zeanah, 480–493. New York: Guilford.

Zigler, E., and Lang, M. 1991. *Child Care Choices.* New York: Free Press.

Zigler, E., and Muenchow, S. 1992. *Head Start: The Inside Story of America's Most Successful Educational Experiment.* New York: Basic Books.

Zigler, E., and Turner, P. 1982. Parents and day care workers: A failed partnership? In *Day Care: Scientific and Social Policy Issues,* edited by E. Zigler and E. Gordon, 113–119. Boston, Mass.: Auburn House.

Zigler, E., and Valentine, J. 1979. *Head Start: The Legacy of the War on Poverty.* New York: Free Press.

# Index